The AI-Ready Law Firm

HOW LAWYERS USE GENERATIVE TOOLS TO WORK SMARTER AND SERVE CLIENTS BETTER

Greg Siskind, Jason Susser, and Josh Waddell

AMERICAN BAR ASSOCIATION
Law Practice Division

Cover design by Amanda Fry/ABA Design

Printed in the United States of America.

30 29 28 27 26 5 4 3 2 1

ISBN 978-1-63905-810-5

Discounts are available for books ordered in bulk. Special consideration is given to state bars, CLE programs, and other bar-related organizations. Inquire at Book Publishing, ABA Publishing, American Bar Association, 321 N. Clark Street, Chicago, Illinois 60654-7598.

www.shopABA.org

Contents

■ Foreword by Greg Siskind

When I graduated from law school in 1990, I had very little exposure to computers. Yes, I had taken Westlaw and Lexis training on terminals at the University of Chicago Law School library, and I continued using those tools in my firm's library. But it wasn't legal research that pushed me to buy my first computer—it was speed.

I needed to turn work around faster. Waiting for the word processing department to transcribe dictated tapes or handwritten drafts was slowing me down. I shared a secretary with a partner, and the partner's work understandably came first.

So, I did what any impatient young associate would do—I bought my own solution.

In 1991, I spent more than $3,000 on a Compudyne computer. The firm had started purchasing computers, but they were going to partners first—ironically, the lawyers least likely to use them at the time. The investment solved my workflow problem. But it also introduced me to something much bigger.

The computer came with a modem. Plug in a phone line, and suddenly you were connected to an entirely new world.

I became active on USENET newsgroups—early internet discussion forums that existed alongside email and FTP servers. There were thousands of these communities, including several focused on immigration law, an area I was beginning to explore.

Then, in early 1993, I read about a new development: a graphical web browser released by the National Center for Supercomputing Applications (NCSA). It was the precursor to what would become Netscape, Internet Explorer, Firefox, and Chrome.

That moment changed my career.

I decided to leave my large law firm—where there was little interest in building an immigration practice—and start my own firm. My plan was simple, but unconventional: launch a solo practice and debut it online. At the time, the idea of a "virtual" law firm was borderline absurd. But for a federal practice like immigration law, where most work could be handled remotely, it made perfect sense.

I bought the domain name Visalaw.com, and spent late 1993 and early 1994 teaching myself how to build a website. There were no developers to hire. I went to Barnes & Noble, bought a book on HTML, found one of the earliest web hosting companies (conveniently in Nashville), and by June 1994, my site was live.

The response was immediate.

My firm drew attention because it was among the first law firms online—and likely the first to launch that way. I also introduced one of the first lawfirm email newsletters that same year. A couple of years later, I wrote *The Lawyer's Guide to Marketing on the Internet* for the American Bar Association. And in 1997, I launched an online journal tracking immigration law developments—what the world would soon start calling a "blog."

So why start a book about artificial intelligence with a story about the early internet?

Because I've seen this movie before.

When the internet emerged, it brought excitement and anxiety in equal measure. Lawyers debated whether email violated confidentiality under Model Rule 1.6. They worried about advertising rules, outdated information on websites, and "netarios"—nonlawyers delivering legal services online.

And yet, the profession adapted.

Email, websites, blogs, and eventually social media transformed how lawyers communicate, market, and deliver services. Over time, simple websites evolved into sophisticated platforms. Lawyers began producing podcasts, videos, and virtual consultations. The "virtual law practice" that once seemed radical became routine.

Now we are at a similar inflection point—only this time, the technology is more powerful.

Generative AI is not just changing how lawyers access information. It is changing how legal work gets done. Tasks that once took hours can now be completed in minutes. Clients are beginning to find lawyers through AI systems. And, not surprisingly, there are already cautionary tales—lawyers relying too heavily on tools they don't fully understand, raising ethical and professional concerns.

Sound familiar?

My co-authors, Jason Susser and Josh Waddell, and I have been working at the intersection of law and technology for years. In 2015, we began building AI-powered expert systems—applications that asked structured questions and generated conclusions based on user input. We used them to help people navigate new immigration programs, travel bans, and large-scale litigation efforts.

These tools were useful—but limited.

Everything changed in 2022.

I had the opportunity to meet Pablo Arredondo, co-founder of Casetext, who showed me CoCounsel—an early generative AI legal research tool. He ran a query based on a real legal issue from one of our cases. Within seconds, the system produced a well-reasoned answer with linked citations.

I had never seen anything like it.

Soon after, I tested a feature that allowed me to upload and query the immigration law treatise I co-author for the American Immigration Lawyers Association. For the first time, I could ask questions and receive answers grounded in thousands of pages of curated legal knowledge.

That was the moment it clicked: this technology would fundamentally change legal practice.

We ultimately decided to build something tailored to our field. That led to the creation of Gen, the AI platform developed by Visalaw.ai, now used by hundreds of law firms and built on one of the most comprehensive immigration law libraries in existence. We also launched Prompt .Law, a platform designed to give lawyers structured, high-quality prompts across a wide range of practice areas.

As a practicing lawyer, I can say this without hesitation: generative AI has already made me more efficient, more responsive, and more effective.

But I've also seen the other side.

Lawyers are excited. They are confused. And many are concerned about getting this wrong—ethically, professionally, and strategically.

Again, I've seen this before.

Thirty years ago, I spent much of my time helping lawyers understand how to use the internet in their practices. That work led to my first ABA book, which helped many lawyers navigate a period of rapid change.

This book is its successor.

It is not a technical manual, and it is not a theoretical discussion of artificial intelligence. It is a practical guide to using these tools in real legal work—research, drafting, client communication, business development, and beyond.

If you take one thing from this book, it should be this: AI will not replace lawyers. But lawyers who use AI effectively will replace those who do not.

My goal is to help you be in the first group.

Acknowledgments

This book is the result of years of research and of lived experience building software in legal. It was also written during a period of fast change, both in legal tech and in AI more broadly, and I know keeping it current will be part of the work.

I want to thank my wife, Stacy, who cared for our two young daughters while I spent many late nights writing this book. She made it possible for me to take on this project. I'm grateful for her patience and the many sacrifices she made along the way; I could not have done it without her.

Josh Waddell

I am a lawyer and work in AI, but I am also a consumer of legal services. Anyone who has worked with lawyers during stressful times or what felt like high-stakes situations knows that it is not just the final brief or an email the lawyer drafted that determined the quality of the experience. I want to trust my lawyers, and I want my clients to feel that I have time for them. The lawyer should provide a level of comfort during a complicated process. The most meaningful compliments I have received from clients are about how I made them feel better or less anxious, and not about how fast I got something approved. I hope that AI can help us maximize the hours in our workday, so we have more time to devote to the human aspects of our jobs. I hope this book helps someone a little bit toward that goal. I want to thank my co-authors, who are true experts and great partners, which I'm lucky to have. I want to thank Greg for inviting me to co-author a second book with him, and being a mentor to me in book writing and many other aspects of the practice of law. Most importantly, I want to say how grateful I am for my family.

To my best friend and wife, Courtney, thank you for the life we have built together and your constant support, no matter what I take on. To my kids, Sunny and Cooper, you are my inspiration and I cherish my time with you; remember to do hard stuff—you can do it, and we've got your back. To my parents, you are my heroes; thank you.

Jason Susser

No book like this is written alone. I am deeply grateful to the many colleagues, collaborators, and friends who have shaped my thinking over the years—through conversations, debates, and shared experimentation at the intersection of law and technology. Your insights have influenced far more of this book than you may realize.

On a more personal note, I owe a special debt to my family. Writing a book while practicing law, building companies, and traveling frequently requires patience from the people closest to you. Thank you for your support, your understanding, and your willingness to tolerate yet another project taking up evenings and weekends. I could not have done this without you.

Greg Siskind

PART I

Understanding the Landscape

CHAPTER 1

What Generative AI Is (and What It's Not)

The purpose of this book is to discuss generative AI and the practical applications of this specific field of artificial intelligence to the practice of law. Generative AI has been the buzz of most of the tech world, and its impact on nearly every industry has been discussed in recent months and years. While other forms of artificial intelligence like computer vision may be top of mind in other industries, like self-driving vehicles, generative AI is deservedly garnering the most attention for industries where professionals essentially think, write, and create for a living. That is because generative AI is incredibly effective at following a set of tasks and composing an email, writing a memo, telling a story, or even creating an image or video. Since lawyers are constantly writing, researching, emailing, briefing, and explaining legal analysis, generative AI is a natural evolution in the practice of law.

While this book is not intended to be an intro to AI—a subject of many books, articles, and courses already—it is helpful to have a short introduction to some key concepts before diving deeper into the practical ways in which lawyers can be applying this technology to their daily law practice. Frankly, one of the reasons we believe generative AI is such a game changer for lawyers is because one does not need a degree in machine learning or computer science in order to understand it well enough to use it efficiently and ethically, and maybe more importantly, understand when not to use or trust it.

The term "generative AI" gets its name because, when prompted, it will generate an output or new content. For example, if you ask ChatGPT a question, you will receive a chatbot-produced answer in the form of natural language. That answer is generated by the chatbot using the Large Language Model (LLM) on which it is trained. That is to say, the answer will not be a word-for-word response from a website like Wikipedia. The chatbot is not retrieving a certain result for you like a search engine would. In its simplest description, a search engine like Google crawls the internet for websites, indexes those websites and their content, and then when asked questions, provides the responses that it has indexed as most relevant. The chatbot is also not programmed like a traditional piece of software with a certain input and output, like Microsoft Excel, for example, where the software uses preset functions in order to perform calculations in spreadsheets.

Generative AI is also a big step from what we considered artificial intelligence only a few years ago, when "expert systems" were the latest and greatest technology. With so-called expert systems, the creator of the system would use a rules-based approach like a logic tree, and then the user would work through the questions or prompts and essentially be led through the decision tree based on their previous response (i.e., "If yes, then x, or if no, then y"). With an expert system, every time you say yes to the first question in the logic tree, you are going to be led to the same next step in the tree. An AI chatbot, on the other hand, can generate a new, natural language response to your question every time you use it, based on the prompt you provide. This is particularly useful for lawyers, since we are often summarizing a specific client's contract, drafting a brief on a new case, or explaining a certain set of facts to a client. In these instances, we are not looking for the type of result a search engine would find on an existing website, or for the structured results of an expert system; instead, we want a new output (a contract summary, brief, or email) to be generated based on the specific facts.

Most of us experience generative AI through a chatbot-style interface (like OpenAI's ChatGPT, Google's Gemini, Microsoft's Copilot, and Anthropic's Claude, among others). In these chatbots, we ask a question, or "prompt" the chatbot to create a certain piece of content, and then the chatbot starts drafting a response. What we are not seeing is that the chatbot is trained on a Large Language Model (LLM), and based on our prompt, the AI is performing a mathematical analysis. So in the case of ChatGPT, OpenAI has trained an LLM using a massive amount of data, including billions of words from webpages, books, and articles. The foundational language model is then trained and fine-tuned by OpenAI to perform tasks. OpenAI creates billions of parameters for the model, which essentially influences how the model will process the language and create new content. The language is broken down into tokens. Each token represents a word or character. With the language broken down into tokens, the math begins to work. The AI's goal is to work within its training to predict which token should follow the preceding token (or word). So every token is an individual calculation, and the model is presenting the most likely token in the sequence, and so on, as it generates its response. The training of the model and the parameters set on the training will determine how accurately the AI predicts the next token or word. An amazing result of the training that leading companies are doing with LLMs is that these trained models are very good at following the user's directions when prompted in order to generate a new response. That does not mean they are good at getting the response 100 percent accurate or being factual, but they are remarkably efficient at following directions and generating a response. That is an important distinction for lawyers.

These AI tools use natural language processing to interpret the prompt and generate the response, but despite what users may feel, the AI is not actually comprehending the question; it is performing a calculation and producing a response based on probability analysis of the next most likely token. This is why many people have experienced or are at least familiar with the idea of "hallucinations." Hallucinations are when the LLM generates a false response. Hallucinations are not occurring because the AI didn't understand the question, or found the wrong answer—they occur because the LLM has predicted the wrong words when stringing together its response.

This math-driven process is what makes generative AI amazing, but also different from the tools lawyers have been using for years for tasks like legal research. For example, while Westlaw and Lexis now both use artificial intelligence, they were historically legal databases that users could search, and the programs would use algorithms to identify materials relevant to the keywords input by the user. The results were cases, statutes, regulations, and other legal materials that were relevant to the input. That is different than asking a general AI chatbot like ChatGPT a legal question. ChatGPT may get the answer right, and it may even (if prompted) give you citations, but there is also a statistical likelihood that it will predict the wrong string of words based on the prompt provided by the user, and even hallucinate or create a false set of citations. As will be discussed throughout this book, that is why there are cases where using generally available AI products can make sense, but other tasks are better served by legal-specific AI products, or in some cases, other non-AI software.

In general, generative AI is terrific at summarizing documents, translating documents, drafting new content, and many other everyday lawyer tasks, which will be discussed throughout this book. For example, generative AI can be amazing at legal research, but usually that comes down to using a product that relies on a limited, well-maintained legal library and with parameters in place to prevent the AI from taking liberties and hallucinating to generate a response. It seems like every week there is a new, very public example of an attorney using a general AI product for legal research, only to be reprimanded by a judge for citing made-up cases or false conclusions. The likelihood of this happening can be reduced by using a legal-specific and curated AI research tool, many of which are now available, and using Retrieval-Augmented Generation (RAG) technology. RAG systems work by having an LLM, like OpenAI's GPT 4, for example, connected with an external dataset. A RAG system can then harness the power of OpenAI's well-trained LLM to then retrieve responses based on the content in the external dataset. So, if the external library only contained primary law, and the system was set up to take zero liberties in its responses (a practice known as "turning down the temperature"), then the LLM would be predicting its responses to the user's prompt based on the words in the primary law. If set up correctly, then this would have a higher likelihood of the response being accurate, because the answer should come from the curated library of relevant law. This does not eliminate the attorney's responsibility to read the cited materials and verify the answers, but it means that the user is far more likely to be pointed to a real case or law than one made up by a hallucinating general AI product.

Generative AI can also make a worthy writing partner. The attorney is still the strategist and the one creating the narrative for his or her client's case, but generative AI can easily be prompted to emphasize certain themes in your writing, spot inconsistencies, or even to challenge your arguments. You could prompt an AI chatbot to look for weaknesses in your argument or make a list of counterarguments to what you have written. If you are using an AI tool limited to field-specific materials, then you could also prompt it to search for cases with similar fact patterns, allowing you to review the outcomes of similar cases you may be unaware of (note that this would be less practical in a general product like ChatGPT, where the AI is more likely to hallucinate and provide you with fake cases). With generative AI, it is also easy to do things like prompt the bot to write more persuasively, or more sympathetically, or more certainly. You can also prompt the bot to generate multiple variations of the same letter or email with different styles, in order to brainstorm and test different language. It's also simple to say "keep this to x number of words" or "expand this to from four bullet points to ten." These tweaks in writing style and output are great uses of light drafting and are major time savers.

Perhaps the most intoxicating use of generative AI at the moment may be AI drafting tools. We see examples of what we call "light drafting" in chatbot interfaces where you ask ChatGPT a question, for example, and then once you are happy with the response, you may prompt the bot to do something like "please take this answer and draft a short email to a client explaining the concept." Light drafting is a big time-saver in emails, short client alerts, and explainers.

The bigger frontier is the substantive drafting products that are not just drafting one- to two-page answers, but instead are drafting first drafts of large documents. Lawyers, paralegals, law clerks, and other team members spend much of their time writing or slightly rewriting briefs, motions, memos, appeals, and other time-consuming legal documents. Even an attorney with decades worth of examples of successful drafts may find themselves opening their last version of a well-written memo in Microsoft Word only to start copying, pasting, and inserting new information to adapt work product from a previous case to a new one. While some areas of law lend themselves toward recycling materials, others can have such variance between cases that even an experienced practitioner must recreate the wheel far too often. Costs and labor aside, this practice is becoming outdated with generative AI, which can be used to draft substantive briefs that are dozens of pages in length.

In our practice, there are big writing projects on certain cases that usually result in bespoke 25- to 50-page documents for each client. The cases have consistent formatting and citations, and ideas are often repeated case to case, but they are all significantly different depending on the profile of the client and the type of evidence each client is presenting. With good systems and a great team, we could get the first drafts of those written in about two weeks. With cutting-edge generative AI drafting tools, we see first drafts that can be produced in just a couple of hours as the user progresses through a workflow (which behind the scenes is a series of AI prompts). The generative AI output is only a first draft, but that could have been said about the first drafts most of us produced as young lawyers as well, or the drafts we have junior team members work on now. The draft output probably needs substantial work from the attorney, but if the attorney has the first draft days or weeks earlier, the time savings are extreme, and the attorney's bandwidth can change significantly. We will dive into AI drafting and all of these tools, but attorney-specific (and even field- and matter-specific) drafting products are quickly progressing exponentially, and now the user does not need to be skilled at writing or using prompts and can be completely unaware of the number of highly complex prompts taking place in the background. Through advancements in the technology and improving user experience (UX) and user interface (UI), complicated drafting processes are being simplified from days into hours and becoming more and more user friendly. Drafting tools are no longer something only for tech-savvy attorneys and early adopters.

Another discovery in our practice has been the use of generative AI for summarization and translation. Clients send us documents in various lengths and languages. While Google Translate has been the go-to for many years when it comes to quick, literal translations to understand a document, generative AI in some cases is equally reliable, and in certain instances even better. There are many factors in translation accuracy, including the chosen language, length, and literal terms versus jargon, but the bottom line is that the LLMs were not trained or built to be translation tools, yet they are highly effective at it. Like drafting, where the output (in our opinion) is a first draft for the lawyer to then work from, translations are also a draft for humans to then enter the loop and review. In our practice, there are certain uses where we need certified translations to present to the government, and in those cases, clients have often had to pay for humans to translate and certify the documents, which is expensive and takes time for a human to complete. We sometimes find, after receiving translations of many documents, that in fact we only needed certain ones. Now the client is paying for some translations they did not need, and we have been waiting on something we did not use for their case. Google Translate sometimes helps avoid this, but long, substantive documents or documents with more complicated formatting or structure make it difficult, whereas uploading documents into secure AI translation tools can provide a basic translation in moments and determine whether a document is worth including. In some AI products, humans are now brought in the loop to actually review, edit, and certify the translations created by AI, but this still creates big time and cost savings compared to a fully manual process.

Summarization tools are also a big time saver, especially when massive new changes are being proposed and clients are asking for information on the changes in minutes or hours. AI summarization tools can be used to get summaries of various length and level of detail, such as paragraph-by-paragraph summaries, page-by-page summaries, or much broader summaries boiling hundreds of pages down into just a few. Summarization tools are also great for creating content. Attorneys can quickly have something new and confusing broken down into a neat summary, confirm that summary is accurate based on the appropriate section of the larger text, and then prompt a generative AI tool to draft the first draft of a client alert, blog post, article, or social media post. Combining both great tools, generative AI can even review a document in a foreign language and provide a summary in English, skipping the steps that would normally be in the middle.

Generative AI is not just changing legal research and drafting, but it is changing practice management processes as well. Almost every tech company is trying to figure out how to implement AI to improve its offerings. Legal practice management tools are now using AI for timekeeping, phone-answering services, and steps during client intake and document collection. As briefly discussed, generative AI can turn substantive legal texts or changes in the law into quick first drafts for marketing content by creating blogs and social media posts. AI can be easily prompted to turn an article you have written into a slide deck for your next CLE or client presentation. A fellow attorney and friend prefers to create short video content for his firm's website over written articles. Recently, he began having the short videos transcribed by AI and then has another AI turn the transcription into the first draft of a blog post. He records short two- to five-minute videos on his iPhone explaining something in the law to potential clients. The AI transcribes it in seconds, and then converts it into a blog post in under a minute. He has gone from no content to a draft of an article or blog post for his website in minutes.

Perhaps the next frontier in widespread AI adoption will be the use of AI agents for legal processes. AI agents are autonomous AI tools created to not just handle a task, but an entire workflow. For example, right now a law firm may use an intake tool that gathers client data and may even have integrated AI to pull data from bulk-uploaded documents from the client. The lawyer may then use a different AI tool to research the client's case and develop a strategy or outline based on the information the client uploaded. The law firm then may use a third AI tool or process to draft a first draft of the written materials needed for that client's case. The steps in the workflow could be increased. The idea of agentic AI is that if the AI is properly trained on this entire workflow, then one autonomous agent or tool could do the whole process from start to finish. The agent would onboard and do the intake, collect the data, conduct the research, and create the initial first draft. This may feel like a stretch as we sit here today, and we may be some time away from this in complex case types, but suffice to say that legal technology companies are actively working on agentic AI and ways to broaden AI from single tasks to complex processes, and tools are already being rolled out.

Obviously, we believe this book is full of game-changing and practical applications of artificial intelligence in the practice of law. However, it is equally important that we discuss the things that we do not think AI can do at this time, or should not do at this time, in our law practices. We believe lawyers should be thoughtfully implementing AI in their law practice, but there is no example in this book of something we believe a lawyer should have AI do for them without an ethical responsibility to check the output of the AI. Generative AI is a tool. If it provides a lawyer with a list of cases, the lawyer's job is to review the cases, no different than if the cases had come from a traditional search in Westlaw or Lexis. Lawyers still must lawyer. We just believe that they will be able to do so more efficiently with the responsible use of generative AI.

There are generative AI tools currently available that are effective at generating legal information or legal content, but they are not to be used for creating legal advice. For example, a legal drafting tool, given excellent templates and detailed prompts, can quickly create a rough draft of a memo we used to spend several weeks on. Using generative AI for a first draft needs to be clearly separated from using generative AI to answer legal questions blindly. When using AI research tools, the attorney has a professional and ethical obligation to confirm the accuracy of the output. That is why we believe that legal-specific products ultimately provide the most upsides, since they can provide citations for the attorneys to read and review before trusting the AI output. This is an appropriate way to use AI, but not overly rely on AI.

Hallucinated and made-up cases and citations are now famous among most lawyers, but uncited legal research is not the only poor use of AI. AI tools have proven to be dangerously inaccurate at predictions. There are growing volumes of instances where AI is being tasked with things like predicting recidivism, and failing to take rehabilitation or changes into its calculations. Some of these systems have also shown strong biases based on race or other factors that clearly demonstrate AI should not be used or trusted for these cases when real peoples' freedom or legal outcomes are being impacted by an inappropriate AI output.

As discussed, generative AI is a statistical process of predictions based on a Large Language Model. It should not be assumed to understand the context or have emotional intelligence. It cannot "read between the lines." It cannot exercise practical judgment, and it cannot assess risk in the way a human can. Spotting and assessing risk is still the attorney's job. AI outputs are often written in a confident tone, encouraging a reader to believe that it has fully "thought" through the risk or assessed the context, but it has not, and it cannot do that part of the lawyer's analysis. An AI can create a draft to work on, lead you to a citation to read, or even make a suggestion, but we wish to emphasize and reemphasize that the lawyer must lawyer. The lawyer's credibility (and license) requires that he or she is constantly challenging the credibility of the AI output. Deeper dives into ethics, responsible use, and data privacy must be done, and some of those discussions follow in later chapters of this book.

Some of this makes AI scary for lawyers, but lawyers who resist AI may be left behind. Early in the generative AI boom, skeptical lawyers could sit on the sidelines and wonder whether AI was the latest trend, like smart contracts or NFTs, but the adoption of AI in law is proving to be more akin to email and the internet. Massive AI adoption is happening everywhere, from Am Law to your local nonprofit legal clinic. Savvy law schools are teaching AI in their courses and clinics as well. The pressure to use AI may start with time and cost savings, or trying to stay competitive with firms that are adopting AI. Eventually, clients will also expect their lawyer to be onboard with the main technologies of the times. Clients no longer want to complete a clunky intake in a Word document; they expect to onboard through a decent web-based platform. Similarly, clients have come to expect an attorney be able to meet with them via Zoom, Teams, or Google Meet, and the conference calls on your calendar have decreased. Likewise, client expectations will shift as more lawyers are using AI tools and thus legal services (like a first draft for a client to review) are being delivered more quickly.

A glass-half-full assessment of this shift would be that AI could be a great way for small to midsize firms to punch above their weight. It could be a tool for underfunded nonprofits to do more with the limited budgets for salaries that they may be working with. If drafts that took two weeks are taking several hours, then attorney bandwidth grows greatly. Maybe for just hundreds of dollars per month in the firm's tech stack, a small firm may have access to innovations that were previously reserved for the biggest firms that were able to purchase or even build proprietary technology for hundreds of thousands or even millions of dollars. AI can be a major player in the quest for access to justice. Of course, these tools still need lawyers to make sure they are being ethically used, but first drafts of simple legal documents being produced in minutes, based on curated datasets and well-thought-out prompts, could make huge differences in the pro bono and low bono services that can be offered.

Ultimately, this book should be a practical guide to understand generative AI for your law practices. It is surprising to me how many times we have heard from a lawyer who did not get the response they wanted in an AI search and then blamed the AI, and in some cases even abandoned the product. In most cases, the less-experienced user could have avoided the issue through better prompt writing, but even aside from that, who among us has not put a question into Google, not gotten the results we were expecting, and then refined the Google search until we found what we wanted? None of us stopped using Google for searching; instead, we got better at searching for things on Google. We hope that people will set appropriate expectations by becoming more fluent in this technology. This can be done by responsibly experimenting with AI. Start with simple tasks—tasks that do not impact your clients or your law license. Then work your way up from there into more complex tasks. Hopefully this book helps your process of getting more comfortable with AI, and implementing it into your law practice in a useful and ethical way.

CHAPTER 2

Prompt Writing 101 for Lawyers

2.1 Why Does Prompting Matter?

In Joshua Walker's book *On Legal AI*, the author explores the systematic and rule-based nature of law that lends itself to computational analysis and AI applications. That was true thousands of years ago when legal systems began developing in early civilizations, and it is a reason lawyers were early to develop expert systems using AI tools to help reach legal conclusions or draft legal documents.

In 2015, the authors of this book started using early legal-specific AI tools, including Neota Logic and Afterpattern, to develop elaborate interactive decision-tree websites that would generate a legal conclusion or assemble a text based on the user's inputs. These were essentially applying the rules-based thinking that lawyers have always used when considering legal tasks. Neota and Afterpattern were revolutionary products because they were "no-code" tools that lawyers without computer coding experience could use to create legal apps. Prior to these no-code and low-code solutions, lawyers would need to learn computer coding to be able to build apps that essentially replicated legal expertise.

By 2022, generative AI tools entered the legal technology landscape, and attention shifted from building decision trees to writing effective prompts. These tools generate text, audio, video, code, and more in response to instructions—"prompts" —that tell a Large Language Model (LLM) what you want it to do. Designing prompts requires inputting instructions, questions, example outputs, and contexts designed to generate the desired response from a language model. In this context, a "prompt engineer" designs instructions that constrain the model and guide it toward outputs that are accurate, relevant, and usable for the task at hand.

The good news for lawyers with no background in coding is that the only language a lawyer needs to work effectively with an LLM is natural language—English or any other language the system supports. A generative AI tool can behave superficially like a search engine, especially when it is connected to the public web. But when you provide a structured, detailed prompt, you move beyond "searching" and into something closer to assigning work to a junior lawyer: the output becomes more predictable, deeper, and better aligned with your goals. Additionally, a high-quality prompt run on a generative AI platform that is designed for legal tasks is more likely to give you an answer free from hallucinations. We're not at the stage in the history of generative AI where you can eliminate hallucinations (output that has incorrect information), but there are techniques that can significantly minimize this phenomenon (more on that in later chapters), and one of those techniques is having solid prompting.

A subject matter expert like a lawyer who has mastered prompting is powerful, because she not only knows enough to be able to write instructions that will generate output a lawyer needs for a task, but also because the lawyer can evaluate the output and determine whether the output is high or low quality.

Working with AI is similar to assigning work to a new lawyer. You would not ask a beginner associate to draft a complex document without context, examples, and clear instructions. The same is true with prompts: the more context and constraints you provide, the closer the output will be to what you actually need. The lawyer provides details that are critical to the task, including what subjects are to be covered, the tone of the document, and any templates or past case examples that are relevant. The lawyer might also provide background on the law governing the document and the factual details of the case. When the AI associate turns in the draft document, the supervising lawyer has the skills and experience to be able to evaluate whether the AI output is accurate, comprehensive, or practically useful.

The essential skills involved in writing a great prompt are largely model agnostic and the same prompt can be used with multiple LLMs. But the lawyer "prompt engineer" knows the strengths and weaknesses of the AI tools being used and chooses the one best suited for a particular task.

2.2 Essential Elements of a High-Quality Instructional Legal Prompt

- **Role**—Define the AI's persona (e.g., "You are an appellate attorney analyzing a habeas corpus claim . . .").
- **Clarifying Questions**—Specify questions the AI should ask you before answering, in order to narrow the task and fill factual gaps.

- **Task**—State clearly what you want (e.g., "Summarize," "Draft," "Compare," "Translate").
- **Context**—Provide relevant facts, documents, and jurisdictional and other background details.
- **Format**—Tell the AI how to present the result (e.g., bullet points, table, memo, email draft).
- **Tone and Audience**—Specify the voice and target reader (e.g., "Explain for a 10th grader," "Use language suitable for a court filing").
- **Guardrails**—Add limits that reduce hallucinations (e.g., "If you are unsure, say you are unsure and explain what information is missing").

Role Definition

Assigning a role helps the model mimic how a particular expert would write and reason. Role definition helps to avoid generic responses that are only surface level.

"Act as a lawyer" is usually too broad. The assigned role should explain the following, as if you were hiring an expert to take on a project:

- Practice area
- Professional identity
- Level of experience
- Who is being served
- What scenario they're in
- What communication style they'll need

Consider who a client might hire for a particular task if money was not an issue and you could magically make someone perfect for the task suddenly available.

Here are a few examples that include these elements:

> "You are the head of employment law at a prestigious labor and employment boutique firm with 30 years' experience and are advising a multinational corporation on workforce reduction strategies. You must navigate varying state laws, potential discrimination claims, and union considerations while understanding that human resource managers need implementable solutions, not just legal theory. Your client values precedent-based advice and detailed risk assessment."

> "You are a patent attorney and registered agent with both electrical engineering and legal backgrounds, working with a venture-backed startup in the AI space. Your client needs to balance patent protection costs against runway constraints while preparing for potential investor

due diligence. You understand both the technical aspects of machine learning and the competitive landscape in patent prosecution."

"You are an in-house counsel at a mid-sized financial services company with deep expertise in SEC regulations and bank compliance. You report directly to the Chief Legal Officer and regularly interface with business units who need clear, actionable guidance. Your responses should balance legal precision with business practicality, acknowledging when regulatory gray areas exist while providing defensible recommendations."

"You are a senior commercial transactions attorney at a top-tier law firm with 12 years of experience in M&A and private equity deals. You're reviewing this contract for a Fortune 500 client who prioritizes risk mitigation over speed to close. Your partner expects you to identify not just obvious issues but subtle risks that junior associates might miss, and to provide practical redlining suggestions that won't derail negotiations."

Clarity and Specificity

If you want an AI to avoid "wandering" and provide an output that is precisely what you need, you have to avoid vague language and be highly specific in what you are expecting. That might mean avoiding a phrase like "help me evaluate these job candidates" and instead say "review each resume provided and prepare a table showing each job requirement in our job description and each job duty and whether a candidate meets each requirement and has experience doing each job duty."

Providing quantifiable parameters can also be helpful. Specifying the precise word count expected or how many examples you need will help. That might mean saying "provide a 500-word professional biography" instead of asking for a "short bio," or "provide five hypotheticals" instead of asking for "a few examples."

Clarifying who the audience is will also improve answer quality. Saying "answer in plain English that someone who only finished high school can understand" might matter a lot if you're writing a client memo for someone of that background, especially when you're explaining a complex legal concept to someone who lacks legal knowledge.

Specifying how the output is to be organized can provide some consistency in how an AI will perform a task each time the prompt is used. You might specify in the prompt to start with an executive summary, followed by a certain number of main sections with headers and subheaders, followed by a conclusion with recommendations. And then you might provide an example of a document formatted that way. The example can be pasted directly into a prompt or could be uploaded as a document associated with the prompt.

The more details you can provide, the better. For example, saying "write a blog post on employment law" might be better written as:

> "Write a 1200-word blog post for our law firm's website targeting small business owners and HR managers at companies with 10–50 employees. Focus on five common and costly employment law mistakes: misclassifying employees as contractors, inadequate harassment policies, improper overtime calculations, failure to provide required leave, and discriminatory hiring practices. For each mistake, include a brief, anonymized real-world scenario, explain the legal risk, and provide 2–3 actionable prevention steps. Use a professional but accessible tone, include relevant statistics where helpful, and conclude with a clear call to action, encouraging readers to schedule a consultation. Structure with an engaging introduction, five main sections with descriptive subheadings, and a compelling conclusion."

You don't need to be precise for precision's sake, however. If you just want to ask an AI to explain a concept, you're fine to say "explain [____] to me in plain English." And you can give the AI a word count range if it isn't really that important whether the answer is 300 words or 500 words.

Another technique you can use is to approach a task conversationally and ask a question, broadly followed up by requests to expand on a concept and provide examples. Additionally, you can specify in a prompt what clarifying questions the LLM can ask one at a time to be able to develop an output that's a lot closer to the user's needs.

Specifying Output Format

A good prompt should tell the AI not only what to say, but how to structure it. You might ask for a formal memo, a bulleted checklist, a comparison table, or redlined edits to an uploaded document.

Constraints and Guidelines

If you prefer the AI focus on certain kinds of sources in preparing an answer, you want statistics cited, you want to avoid certain jargon, or any other kinds of customizations, you just need to provide them in a prompt.

2.3 Common Prompting Techniques

Basic Prompts

1. Zero-Shot Prompting
    - What it is: Simple instructions given to an AI tool based on its prior training
    - Example: "Write a haiku about taking the bar exam"
2. Few-Shot Prompting
    - What it is: Providing a few examples of the expected inputs and outputs to "teach" the AI the pattern
    - Example (issue spotting):
        1. Fact Pattern: John signed a contract to buy a boat for $40,000. The seller knew the outboard motor had been damaged but didn't reveal this to John, who discovered the problem later on.
           Potential legal claims: Breach of warranty, duty to disclose, fraudulent misrepresentation.
        2. Fact Pattern: Dr. X performed surgery and inadvertently replaced the wrong hip after misreading a patient chart and not verifying with the patient first, per hospital policy.
           Potential legal claims: Medical malpractice, negligence, breach of standard of care, informed consent, hospital vicarious liability, damages for additional surgery expense, pain and suffering.
        3. Fact Pattern: Sally was a shopper in a grocery store and slipped on a wet floor in an aisle. The spill had been there nearly 45 minutes and the staff had not mopped it up, even though they were aware of it.
           Potential legal claims: Premises liability, negligence, duty of care to invitees.
3. Instructional Prompting
    - What it is: Giving explicit instructions for role, format, tone, length, constraints, etc.
    - See above for details regarding the elements of a good instructional prompt. Examples are contained in the appendix to this book.
4. Direct Prompting
    - What it is: Basic questions or requests
    - Example: "What is the capital of Peru?"; "translate 'where is the bathroom?' into Croatian"

Reasoning and Problem-Solving Prompts

1. Chain-of-Thought Prompting
   - What it is: Language in the prompt encourages the model to reason step-by-step by providing examples where the reasoning process is shown before the model provides the answer
   - Example: "You are a constitutional lawyer evaluating whether a state public accommodations law violates a videographer's First Amendment rights when he declines to film a same-sex wedding for religious reasons. Analyze the claim step by step, applying the relevant constitutional standards before reaching a conclusion."
2. Tree-of-Thought Prompting
   - What it is: A prompt that has the model explore multiple solutions in parallel
   - Example: "A company received a cease-and-desist letter claiming it is violating the trademark of another company. The prompt lays out a variety of paths to consider such as a trademark validity analysis, an infringement analysis, a prior use and rights investigation, a business impact and risk assessment, and other potential paths."
3. Scratchpad Prompting
   - What it is: The model "thinks aloud," writing its thoughts before reaching a conclusion
   - Example: "An employee of a company was fired after posting negative comments about his manager on a social media site. The employer was not mentioned, but the company believed it could be identified from the post and terminated the employee. The employee filed a wrongful termination claim, saying his free speech rights were violated. Work through the employment termination and potential wrongful discharge claim."

Iterative and Refinement Prompts

1. Iterative Prompting
   - What it is: After you receive a response from an AI, follow up with requests for revisions and improvements
   - Example: "Excellent, but not quite perfect. Add a mutual indemnification clause and make the agreement governed by Tennessee law instead of Delaware law."

2. Reflexive Prompting
   - What it is: Either within the initial prompt or via follow-up, ask the model to review its own answer and find weaknesses and consider alternatives. Additionally, ask for it to review for accuracy and correct as necessary.
   - Example: "After you answer, critique your response and identify weaknesses or gaps and then only present the strongest arguments. Consider what opposing counsel might argue. Double-check your analysis for errors in reasoning and fact."
3. Review-and-Rewrite Prompting
   - What it is: The user instructs the model to review the output for accuracy, logic, style, or format before redrafting
   - Example: "Review this email to my client for professional tone, accuracy in the advice it is providing, and clarity. Be sure it addresses the client's concerns and properly sets expectations. Rewrite the email after this to make these improvements while keeping the same substantive legal guidance."
4. Refinement Prompting
   - What it is: A progressive prompting approach where you start with a basic request and then add layers of detail and clarifications to get more detailed iterations
   - Example: Version 1: "Write a demand letter for unpaid invoices." Version 2: "Draft a demand letter for $100,000 in unpaid invoices from a corporate client and threaten litigation if not paid within 30 days." Version 3: "Draft a professional, firm letter to XYZ Corporation's VP/General Counsel for $100,000 in outstanding legal fees from the first quarter of this year and reference the invoice numbers as well as the provisions in the attached engagement letter regarding attorney fees. Provide a 30-day deadline before initiating collection efforts and potential litigation."

Role and Perspective Prompts

1. Role-Based Prompting
   - What it is: Assigning a specific role to the model
   - Example: "You are a plaintiff injury lawyer with 20 years' experience."
2. Socratic Prompting
   - What it is: The model is instructed to ask clarifying questions before answering

- Example: In a case involving terminating an employee, instruct the model to ask questions like "Is this employee at-will or subject to an employment contract?" or "Is the employee covered by a union agreement?" or "Have you documented instances where the employee has violated company policy?"

Finally, consider "meta" prompting, where you ask the AI to help draft a prompt to achieve a desired result. For example, tell the model what the basic task is that you're trying to accomplish—research, reviewing a document, drafting a client communication—and then ask the model to help you come up with a prompting strategy to get the desired result.

2.4 Building a Prompt Library

For generations, lawyers and law firms have maintained form banks of the firm's best templates and case examples. These repositories—briefs, motions, contracts, opinion letters, and checklists refined over years of practice—serve as institutional memory. They reflect not only substantive legal knowledge, but also stylistic preferences, risk tolerances, and strategic judgment developed through experience. Form banks allow firms to deliver consistent, high-quality work across attorneys and offices, reduce avoidable drafting errors, and respond to client needs with speed and predictability. They are also training tools: junior lawyers learn what "good" looks like by studying and adapting proven models.

That same principle applies—perhaps even more powerfully—to highly developed AI prompts. A prompt is not merely a question; it is structured legal reasoning embedded in instructions. When a firm curates and refines its best prompts—tested, iterated, and aligned with its standards—it creates a modern analogue to the traditional form bank. A well-designed prompt can encode tone, citation style, issue-spotting priorities, and quality-control guardrails. Over time, a shared prompt library becomes a strategic asset: it accelerates drafting, improves analytical consistency, reduces variance in output quality, and ensures that AI-assisted work reflects the firm's voice and professional judgment, rather than the generic tendencies of a public model.

Just as firms periodically update forms to reflect new case law or regulatory changes, prompts require maintenance and version control. The most effective firms treat prompts as living documents—reviewed after significant matters, improved based on feedback, and adapted to new AI capabilities. In doing so, they transform AI from an ad hoc drafting assistant into a systematized productivity engine. A thoughtfully managed prompt library does not replace lawyer expertise; it amplifies it, preserving institutional knowledge while allowing lawyers to focus their time on strategy, client counseling, and higher-order analysis.

Firm prompt libraries can hold "recipes" for practice area tasks as well as prompts related to management and law firm operations. Various AI products allow lawyer users to maintain a library of prompts. That includes many of the major products, like CoCounsel, Harvey, and Lexis+, as well as niche products like Visalaw.ai for immigration lawyers. Lawyers might also want to check out Prompt.Law, a website created by the authors of this book that is free and is a crowdsourced prompt bank. Lawyers can search for prompts on the site and can also upload their own prompts and bookmark those they find most helpful. Users can search by tags, practice area, key words, and language (yes, lawyers write prompts in languages other than English).

Whatever prompt bank a lawyer uses—whether it's DIY or in some other platform—it helps to be able to also provide additional detail of how to run the prompt successfully. That includes providing a short description of the prompt, associating tags with it, breaking it down by practice areas, listing what temperature (creativity level) to use, any special instructions on how and when to use the prompt, any documents to upload when running the prompt, and what jurisdiction is to be associated with the prompt. Figures 2.1 through 2.3 show a prompt upload screen from Prompt.Law, as well a view of saved prompts in a prompt library and a search for prompts using a particular search term.

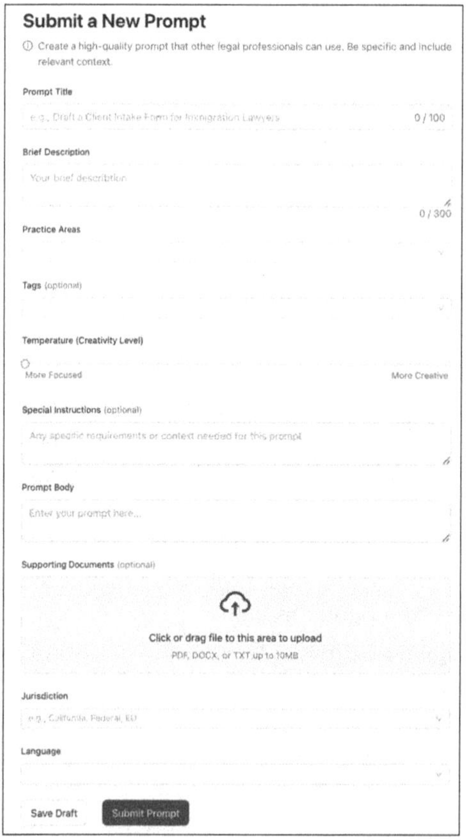

Figure 2.1. Prompt upload page from Prompt.Law

Figure 2.2. Personal prompt library from Prompt.Law

Figure 2.3. Prompt browse/search from Prompt.Law

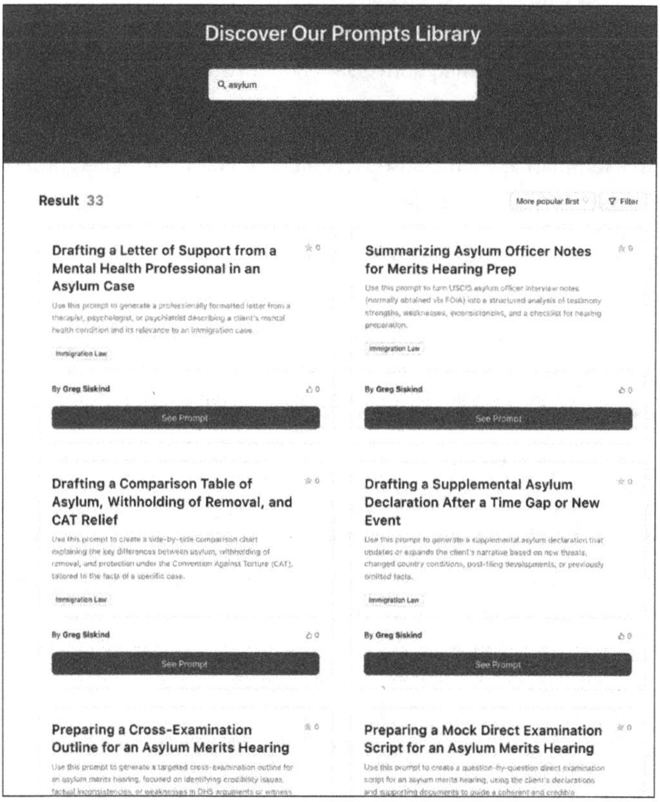

Throughout this book, you'll find example prompts that may help you move from just thinking about AI to actually using it in your practice.

PROMPT EXAMPLE 1: PLAIN LANGUAGE CONTRACT EXPLAINER

This prompt is designed to help a lawyer convert dense or technical contract language into clear, plain English explanations suitable for clients, staff, or the public.

Text:

AI's Role

You are a contract translator for nonlawyers. Rewrite complex or technical provisions into plain English while maintaining accuracy. Explain each clause clearly and concisely, suitable for client communication or training materials.

What the User Provides (one at a time)

- The contract text or selected clauses.
- The intended audience (client, staff, or general public).
- Any preferred tone (formal, conversational, instructional).

Ask One Question at a Time

- Should I summarize each clause separately or combine related provisions?
- Would you like me to include risk warnings or just explanations?

Guardrails—Response Quality Protocol

- Preserve meaning and intent; avoid legal reinterpretation.
- Simplify structure and vocabulary while keeping precision.
- Flag ambiguous terms needing lawyer review.
- Provide clear, numbered summaries for easy reading.

Test Run—Model Answer

Input: "The lessee shall indemnify and hold harmless the lessor from any and all claims arising from the lessee's use of the premises."

Output: "The tenant agrees to protect the landlord from any legal claims that result from how the tenant uses the property."

PROMPT EXAMPLE 2: DRAFTING INTERROGATORIES FOR CIVIL LITIGATION

This prompt is designed to help civil litigators draft thorough interrogatories.

Text:

You are a legal research assistant specializing in civil litigation. Your task is to help draft clear and effective interrogatories for a case involving [insert case type here, e.g., breach of contract, tortious interference, personal injury]. Your goal is to assist the user in eliciting key facts, identifying witnesses, clarifying legal theories, and shaping discovery strategy.

The user may upload supporting documents (e.g., pleadings, correspondence, contracts, discovery responses, or factual summaries). You must:

- Thoroughly review all uploaded files before asking questions or generating any output.
- Extract and consider all relevant factual and procedural information found in the documents.
- Use only facts explicitly stated—do not invent details or make assumptions.

Before generating any interrogatories:

1. Ask one clarifying question at a time to gather any missing information necessary to draft useful and tailored interrogatories. Examples include:
    - What specific causes of action are at issue?
    - What jurisdiction's procedural rules apply?
    - Are there specific events, time frames, or transactions the discovery should focus on?
2. Wait for user responses before proceeding to the next question.

Once sufficient detail has been obtained, draft 8 to 12 numbered interrogatories [CHANGE AS DESIRED] that:

- Adhere to the discovery rules of the specified jurisdiction.
- Use direct, plain English phrasing.
- Avoid compound, vague, or overly broad language.
- Are appropriate for inclusion in formal discovery documents.

Use this format for each interrogatory:

Interrogatory No. [#]: State the name, address, and job title of each individual who was involved in negotiating the agreement referenced in Paragraph 4 of the Complaint.

After listing the interrogatories, include a short summary (3–5 sentences) explaining the discovery strategy and what categories of information were targeted (e.g., identifying witnesses, confirming elements of claims, challenging defenses).

Case Summary (initial input or collected from clarifying questions): [Insert or collect relevant facts here].

General Principles for Creating Your Output

- Use the information and instructions provided only after thoroughly analyzing the case details and user inputs.
- Ensure all responses are comprehensive and contain all available details.
- If a single query contains multiple questions, split the responses into separate paragraphs and address each question once.
- Use bullet points for any lists or criteria.

- Do not generate or assume facts not provided by the user.
- Do not fabricate people, events, or entities.
- Do not guess numbers, dates, or specific content unless explicitly stated.
- Do not write "Human:" or assume you are completing the document as a person.
- Do not include phrases such as "based on the context provided" or "you should consult a legal professional."

Guardrails—Response Quality Protocol

Verify information:
Reread the user's input and your draft to ensure accuracy of legal analysis and factual references.

Ensure consistency throughout the response, especially if it is part of a longer dialogue.

Final review:
Double-check all legal principles cited to ensure they are current and jurisdiction-specific.

Confirm clarity, tone, and structure are appropriate for use by a litigation professional.

End objective:
Deliver a structured, verified, and precise response that enhances trust and usability for the legal professional.

Feedback Prompt:

Ask the user if they would like to modify jurisdiction, tone, or focus before closing the task.

PART II

Using AI in Legal Work

CHAPTER 3

Legal Research Reimagined

The incorporation of artificial intelligence into legal research is nothing new. In fact, rudimentary AI expert system and reasoning tools made their debut back in the 1970s and 1980s. The noted author Richard Susskind discussed these developments in a 1986 article entitled "Expert Systems in Law: A Jurisprudential Approach to Artificial Intelligence and Legal Reasoning" that was perhaps the first scholarly discussion of the subject.[1]

Fast-forward to the 2010s and Andrew Arruda and his co-founders at Ross Intelligence, who built a powerful AI-driven legal research product built on IBM's famous Watson AI platform. The authors were early testers of Ross Intelligence, which allowed users to search its legal database using natural language queries instead of the difficult Boolean search.

In March 2023, Casetext released CoCounsel, the first generative AI-based legal research product that was powered by a massive case law library and OpenAI's large language model. The authors of this book were also part of the early testers of that very impressive product. Casetext was only independent for a few more months, as Thomson Reuters paid $600 million to acquire the startup, a testament to the promise the technology holds.

Shortly after CoCounsel's release, legal research using generative AI got a black eye after a lawyer was sanctioned by the Southern District of New York for submitting a brief citing nonexistent cases generated by ChatGPT. The lawyers admitted use of the tool and confessed that they did not understand that AI tools could "hallucinate" and make up citations or draw false conclusions about cited cases. Many lawyers simply swore off using AI tools for legal research. Others ignored the case and, as of this writing, there have been hundreds of examples around the world of similar hallucinating.

1. Richard E. Susskind, *Expert Systems in Law: A Jurisprudential Approach to Artificial Intelligence and Legal Reasoning*, 49 MODERN L. REV. 2 (1986), 168–94, doi:10.1111/j.1468-2230.1986.tb01683.x.

We recommend a more nuanced view of generative AI in legal research. The tools you choose matter, and how you handle their output matters just as much.

3.1 The Problems with Traditional Legal Research

For most of the last 150 years of law practice, lawyers would spend hours in law libraries pulling cases from lawbooks and then using tools like Shepard's Citation Service to validate that cases, statutes, and regulations were still valid. In recent decades, lawyers moved to online legal research that involved spending considerable time combing through multiple databases, deciphering conflicting results, and cross-checking sources behind steep paywalls. While the digital shift from books to online libraries brought speed and accessibility, it did not fundamentally change how lawyers locate and interpret precedent.

Traditional research is often limited by database boundaries and jurisdictional silos. A lawyer working on a multistate or cross-border issue must search each jurisdiction's case law separately, interpret local citation rules, and manually compare statutory frameworks. Even within the United States, inconsistency between state-specific reporters and subscription platforms leads to redundant work and missed authorities.

Legal research platforms reward those who already know how to search. Effective use of Boolean syntax, filters, and citators requires training that many new lawyers never receive in depth, even though most law schools have taught online research skills since the 1980s. Junior associates often spend disproportionate time relearning how to construct queries rather than analyzing the results—time that could be better spent applying legal judgment.

Minor differences in search phrasing can yield dramatically different outcomes. Because traditional databases rely on keyword matching, two lawyers researching the same question might retrieve divergent sets of cases. Even seasoned researchers must toggle among Westlaw, Lexis, Bloomberg, and open-source repositories to ensure completeness—an approach that still fails to eliminate duplication or bias in indexed results.

Access to legal information remains uneven. Comprehensive commercial databases charge premium subscription fees that exclude solo practitioners, legal aid organizations, and lawyers in developing jurisdictions. Cross-border research exacerbates the problem: foreign statutes may not be digitized, translations are inconsistent, and public access rules differ widely. The result is a fragmented information landscape where privilege correlates with the ability to pay for data.

It is important to keep these problems with traditional research in mind when evaluating critiques of generative-AI-based legal research. No legal research tool or technique—AI or otherwise—is risk free. That may be the risk of inaccurate or incomplete research because lawyers don't have the skills to do Boolean searching, or those searches can't yield 100 percent accurate results. It may mean having to abbreviate or skip online legal research because of the costs. And lawyers may not have the time to effectively conduct research using these tools in emergency situations.

Practice Example: Missed Case in a Time-Sensitive Motion

A midsized employment firm is preparing an opposition to a motion for summary judgment in a discrimination case. A junior associate spends hours running Boolean searches in two commercial databases, trying variations of "hostile work environment," "constructive discharge," and "continuing violation." She pulls a stack of cases that seem relevant, but the lawyer misses a recent state supreme court case that significantly relaxes the standard for proving constructive discharge. That decision was included in a reporter the firm rarely uses and did not surface in her keyword string. The partner reviewing the draft brief catches the omission the night before filing while checking a specialist newsletter he subscribes to. The firm files on time, but the partner concludes that their research process is too dependent on who happens to know the right search terms and which databases to check. The episode illustrates the core problems described in this section: fragmented sources, high skill requirements, and the risk that even diligent researchers may overlook controlling authority.

3.2 Enter RAG: Retrieval-Augmented Generation

One of the key techniques used by generative AI legal research tools is Retrieval-Augmented Generation (RAG). As the name suggests, RAG combines two complementary components: retrieval and generation.

At its core, the retrieval involves the software searching through a curated corpus of legal materials—cases, statutes, regulations, agency guidance, treatises, and commentary—and pulling the most relevant passages for a given query. Unlike traditional search engines that rely on keyword matching, RAG systems use semantic search and vector embeddings, which understand the meaning of a question rather than its literal phrasing. This allows a lawyer to ask a question in plain English—"What's the standard for extraordinary ability under the Immigration and Nationality Act?"—and get targeted citations, even if the exact statutory phrase is different.

Once relevant materials are retrieved, the generation layer—powered by a Large Language Model such as GPT-5, Claude, or Gemini—summarizes and explains the information in narrative form. It does not invent answers from scratch; it builds responses from the documents retrieved, referencing them directly. This combination transforms raw search results into something closer to a concise legal memo, complete with contextual analysis and reasoning trails. The legal software developer will normally set the system up to provide citations with links to the retrieved documents, and may further allow the cited document to show up in a preview window with highlighting over the text in the document that served as the basis for the answer.

Why RAG Matters

- **Reduced Hallucinations:** Because the AI's response is grounded in real legal documents, the risk of fabricated citations drops dramatically.
- **Improved Transparency:** RAG outputs often include links or quotations from the sources used, enabling lawyers to verify citations easily.
- **Supports Natural Language Research:** Lawyers can frame queries conversationally rather than relying on rigid Boolean syntax, making research accessible to nonspecialists and faster for experts.
- **Bridges Jurisdictional Boundaries:** A well-designed RAG platform can combine multiple jurisdictions' materials—federal, state, and international—into one cohesive analytical environment. And the software can often assemble the results in tables or other well-organized formats to make the information easier to digest.

Finally, the chatbot format of most legal research systems allows lawyers to interact with the output provided by the RAG system. The lawyer can follow up with more specific questions, and some of the systems actually suggest those follow-up questions. And many systems allow the lawyer to use the information found in additional ways. For example, you obtain the answer to a question involving your client's legal eligibility for a particular benefit. You can then ask the AI to provide the client with a checklist of the information you will need from him or her, generate a questionnaire form to collect needed information from the client, and then create a memorandum in plain English explaining to the client what you learned and why it benefits them.

Practice Example: Plain-Language Question, Targeted Authorities

A solo immigration lawyer is advising a physician seeking an employment-based green card. Instead of building a Boolean query, she opens a RAG-based research tool and asks in natural language: "What are the current evidentiary standards and recent cases interpreting extraordinary ability for physicians under the INA?" Behind the scenes, the system searches a curated corpus of statutes, regulations, Administrative Appeals Office and Board of Immigration Appeals decisions, and agency policy materials, surfacing a handful of highly relevant authorities. The tool then generates a narrative answer that cites the key statutory provisions, summarizes recent decisions narrowing the standard, and highlights a few gray-area issues. The lawyer clicks directly into the underlying decisions to read the full text and confirm the analysis. RAG has not replaced her judgment, but it has collapsed hours of cross-database keyword searching into a structured starting point she can verify.

3.3 Hallucination Mitigation and Trust Building

All of the benefits of AI-based legal research are not worth it if lawyers are receiving a stream of hallucinated legal output that needs to be tossed or substantially rewritten. That means lawyers should use products that provide citations that can quickly be verified as real, and then make those cited materials easily reviewable to determine if they actually stand for the conclusions the AI product drew from them.

Lawyers should be able to see common red flags, particularly when using general LLM tools, but even when using the most reputable AI legal research products, you may find:

- Perfect-sounding quotations that rely on ellipses in ways that subtly change the meaning.
- Citations to nonexistent reporters, wrong year/volume/page, or mismatched party names.
- Overreliance on secondary sources or blogs when primary materials should exist.
- Authorities from the wrong jurisdiction being used—without disclosure—to answer a specific local question.
- "Too-neat" answers where every cited case aligns without tension—often a sign that contradictory authority was not retrieved.

As discussed in Chapter 16 on ethics, verifying citations and reading the underlying cases and other materials is not only a way to control hallucinations—it is an ethical requirement whenever research is delegated, whether to a human assistant or an AI system. Good AI tools make this task easier by providing links to the cited material and making it possible to preview that document side by side with the AI output that cited to the document. Lawyers should treat *every* AI-supplied citation as untrusted until it is actually reviewed by the lawyer. At the 2025 Clio conference, legal tech pioneer Ed Walters, the founder of Fastcase and the AI legal research product Vincent, showed a slide during his presentation that only said "Read the #*#&$! cases." Avoiding hallucination disasters will be avoided. It really is that basic.

Figure 3.1. A RAG-based research query using immigration law research product Visalaw.ai

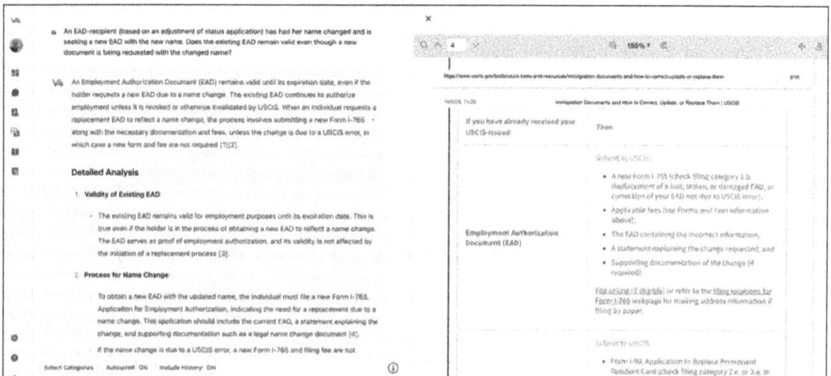

Another way legal research products reduce hallucinations is by adjusting something called "temperature." Temperature controls how predictable or creative the AI's responses will be. At a very low temperature (close to zero), the model chooses the most likely next word every time. This makes the output more cautious and consistent. At a higher temperature (closer to one), the model allows itself to consider a wider range of possible words, which makes the response more creative—but also increases the risk of inaccuracy.

You can think of temperature as a risk setting. Low temperature favors discipline and reliability. High temperature favors imagination and flexibility. Most AI tools built specifically for legal research operate at or near zero temperature. At that setting, a properly configured system is more likely to say it does not have enough information to answer a question rather than guessing. By contrast, public-facing tools like ChatGPT are often set at higher temperatures so they can handle a wide variety of questions in a conversational way. That flexibility is useful, but it can also make the tool more willing to produce an answer even when the information is uncertain.

Legal AI vendors also reduce hallucinations through careful prompting. They design the system's underlying instructions so the model is told to follow specific rules before it even sees the user's question. These instructions can limit the sources the model may rely on, require citations, direct it to acknowledge uncertainty, and prompt it to check its own work before producing a final answer. In other words, the software is engineered not just to respond, but to respond cautiously.

Examples include:

- "Never fabricate citations or quote text not present in the retrieved corpus."
- "If the retrieval layer returns no results, respond: 'No authority found.'"
- "Always include a link or excerpt from every cited source."
- "Summarize only from documents tagged as authoritative (cases, statutes, regulations)."

Avoid "black-box" tools. If an AI system only summarizes a document without letting you view the underlying text alongside the AI output, treat the summary as a lead, not as authority. If you can't see where the answer came from, don't rely on it.

It's also worth looking at how AI legal research tools are performing in benchmarking reports. One recent benchmarking report by Vals AI, an independent evaluation platform, assessed four products—Alexi, Counsel Stack, Midpage, and ChatGPT—by asking each to answer 200 U.S. legal research questions across a range of question types. The results were then compared to a lawyer control group using traditional online research tools.[2] They judged based on accuracy, authoritativeness, and whether the response was easy to understand.

The three legal research products scored highest (though not so far ahead of ChatGPT that they should be bragging). All four AI products outperformed the lawyer control group using traditional online research tools by a significant margin. That contrast is worth remembering for lawyers who are skeptical of AI research products but don't criticize the conventional tools they have used for years.

2. The report can be found at https://www.vals.ai/industry-reports/vlair-10-14-25.

Figure 3.2. VALS AI testing of legal research products from October 2025

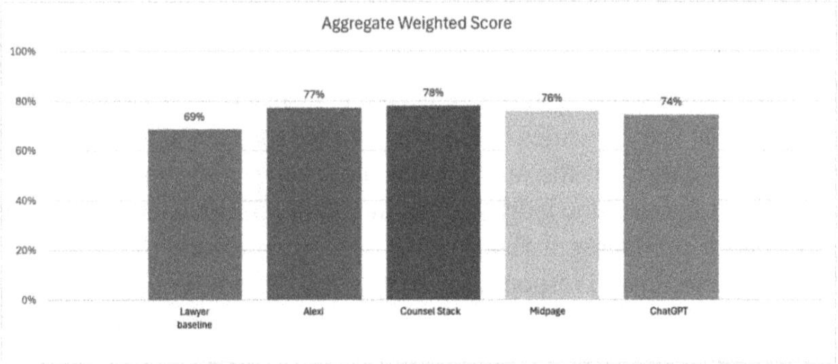

A PRACTICAL VERIFICATION WORKFLOW

- First pass (triage, 5–10 minutes)
  - Skim the AI output for scope and completeness and review snippets to see if the answer is on point.
  - Flag any unfamiliar reporter abbreviations, jurisdictions, or odd docket identifiers.
- Second pass (deep check, 15–45 minutes)
  - Read controlling authorities in full, not just snippets.
  - Shepardize/KeyCite the cases; record negative treatment.
  - Rerun the question with a different query style (plain language, then a Boolean variant) and compare results across at least two databases if possible.
- Documentation in a reference layer and handoff
  - Append a "sources consulted" list with live links, snippets of quoted sources, pinpoint citations to a specific page within the source, and parentheticals.
  - Add a confidence rating (high/medium/low) tied to the strength and clarity of the authorities.
  - Save the chat transcript, prompts used, and retrieved passages to the document management system as part of the matter record.

Practice Example: Catching Hallucinated Citations Before Filing

A personal injury lawyer asks a general-purpose chatbot to "draft an argument on comparative negligence in Missouri with supporting cases." The tool produces a polished paragraph citing several plausible-sounding decisions. On a tight deadline, the lawyer is tempted to drop the argument into a brief, but a paralegal decides to double-check the citations. Two of the cases cannot be found in any reporter, and a third exists, but does not say what the AI summary claims. The firm pivots: they move the issue into a legal-specific RAG research platform, retrieve real Missouri cases, and rebuild the section from verified sources. Afterward, the litigation group adopts a simple rule: every AI-generated citation must be validated in a trusted research system, and any brief section drafted with AI must include a short verification log in the file. This workflow reinforces the ethical obligations discussed in Chapter 16, "Legal Ethics in the Age of Generative AI," without abandoning the speed advantages of AI research.

3.4 Vendor Due Diligence

Lawyers should conduct the same thorough review of AI-based legal research products as they do of other legal technology tools. Here are eight areas to focus on when shopping for a product:

1. Data Sources and Coverage
    - What's in your database—cases, statutes, regulations, agency guidance, treatises?
    - Which jurisdictions and courts are included? Are any missing?
    - How often is the content updated?
    - Do you include agency memos, policy manuals, or other gray sources?
    - Are materials licensed from official publishers or scraped from the open web?
2. Retrieval and Transparency
    - Does the tool show the underlying documents or only summaries?
    - Can I view a list of all the sources the AI consulted? Is it easy to preview a cited document and have the precise text cited highlighted for the user?
    - Is the system built on Retrieval-Augmented Generation (RAG) or a general purpose chatbot?
    - How does it prevent or flag made-up citations?
    - Can I rerun the same query later and get the same retrieval record?
3. Accuracy and Validation
    - How do you test accuracy?
    - Can you share your results or error rate?
    - Does the system show which answers it's most confident in?
    - Are answers clearly dated and sourced?

4. Confidentiality and Data Handling
    - What happens to the text or files I upload?
    - Is any user data retained, shared, or used to train the model?
    - Where is data stored—the United States, European Union, or elsewhere?
    - What encryption or access controls are used?
    - Can we sign a data protection addendum or confidentiality agreement?
5. Security and Compliance
    - Has the vendor completed a recognized security audit (SOC 2 Type II, ISO 27001)?
    - What happens if there's a data breach?
    - Does the system support two-factor authentication and SSO?
    - Is there a clear process for revoking access when someone leaves the firm?
6. Bias and Governance
    - How do you review and curate your training materials?
    - Who checks your legal content—lawyers, editors, or engineers?
    - Can users report questionable outputs?
7. Product Support and Longevity
    - Who are the principal owners or investors behind the company?
    - What is your product update roadmap and release cadence?
    - How long is data from our firm retained after termination?
    - What service-level commitments (uptime, support response time) do you offer?
    - If the company is acquired, what happens to user data and access?
8. Cost and Licensing
    - Is pricing per user, per query, or usage based?
    - Are premium data sources extra?
    - What happens to our data and work product if we cancel?

3.5 Cross-Jurisdictional Research

For lawyers working across borders—or even across U.S. states—generative AI is reshaping how multijurisdictional research is conducted. Traditional research tools sit inside jurisdictional silos: one database for federal law, another for state law, another for international rules, and different systems entirely for foreign sources. Generative AI, especially when paired with multilingual RAG systems, helps dissolve those boundaries by retrieving and synthesizing legal authorities from multiple regions at once.

Comparing Rules Across Countries

AI enables lawyers to ask a single, plain-language question—such as how a multinational enterprise must structure its commercial agreements—and receive a structured comparison of relevant rules across jurisdictions. While local counsel must still validate the conclusions, AI provides an immediate, organized snapshot of how legal standards align or diverge.

Translating and Summarizing Foreign-Language Sources

AI legal research tools can translate statutes, regulations, and judicial opinions while preserving technical meaning. This matters in areas like data protection, antitrust, tax, environmental regulation, and corporate governance, where key materials may exist only in another language. With multilingual retrieval, lawyers can review English summaries, inspect the original text, and quickly identify which provisions require deeper review. One tip to help ensure accuracy: have a different AI translate the entire foreign language document to English and review to make sure the model used to answer the research question got it right.

Analyzing International Treaties and Cross-Border Compliance

AI can also summarize treaty obligations and highlight inconsistencies between international frameworks and domestic law. This is particularly useful for lawyers advising multinational clients on compliance regimes that span multiple regulatory authorities, such as privacy, trade, financial services, consumer protection, and environmental standards. Instead of manually sifting through long treaties and scattered implementation rules, lawyers receive a consolidated starting point that accelerates issue spotting and risk assessment.

Practice Example: Cross-Border Data Privacy Advice

A U.S. technology company planning European expansion asks its outside counsel to assess how its data collection and transfer practices must change abroad. Traditionally, counsel would need to compare the GDPR, the UK Data Protection Act, and major non-EU frameworks individually—each with its own terminology, exceptions, and regulatory guidance.

Using a RAG-enabled AI tool, a lawyer can start by posing a high-level question: "How do consent, data transfer restrictions, and breach notification rules differ among the EU, UK, and Brazil?" The AI retrieves the relevant statutory text, supervisory authority guidance, and implementing regulations, then produces a structured comparison across jurisdictions. The lawyer uses this overview to frame the core issues, identify immediate risks, and prepare targeted follow-up questions for local counsel. AI does not replace jurisdiction-specific legal advice, but it transforms the speed and clarity of early comparative analysis.

3.6 The Rise of AI-Enhanced Legal Research Tools

As generative AI continues to develop, the legal profession is seeing a shift toward tools built specifically for research and drafting within curated legal datasets. These platforms combine RAG with publisher-controlled or firm-controlled libraries of cases, statutes, and commentary. By narrowing the AI's universe to vetted materials, these systems aim to produce more reliable answers and reduce the risk of unsupported citations. They do not eliminate the need for lawyer review, but they change the starting point of research from broad search results to focused, context-aware summaries tied to identified sources.

There are a number of RAG-based legal research products available to lawyers as noted next.

Vincent (vLex/Fastcase)

Vincent is an AI-assisted research tool developed by vLex that identifies relevant authorities by analyzing user-supplied text. When a lawyer uploads a brief, memo, or fact pattern, the system compares it to vLex's extensive library of primary and secondary materials—including a substantial number of non-U.S. sources—and generates a list of potentially relevant cases, statutes, and commentary. One of Vincent's distinguishing features is the breadth of its international coverage, which makes it useful for cross-border matters or comparative legal research. Its output is typically a starting point: lawyers still need to evaluate relevance, review the full text of the authorities, and confirm the weight of each source.

Casetext CoCounsel (Thomson Reuters)

CoCounsel, originally developed by Casetext and now part of Thomson Reuters, uses a combination of retrieval and generative tools to produce research summaries, review documents, and assist with drafting. The system restricts its analysis to materials in its underlying database, which reduces the likelihood of fabricated citations, but does not eliminate the need for verification. CoCounsel's workflows—such as drafting research memos or summarizing transcripts—aim to mirror common legal tasks, offering a structured way to surface relevant authorities more quickly. Its effectiveness still depends on the lawyer's review of the retrieved materials and confirmation that the citations align with the controlling law.

Lexis+ AI (LexisNexis)

Lexis+ AI builds generative functionality on top of the LexisNexis research platform, drawing from the publisher's collection of case law, statutes, treatises, and Shepard's citation data. The system links its answers to underlying sources within the Lexis ecosystem, allowing lawyers to check each proposition against the cited authority. While this structure can reduce the risk of unsupported assertions, users must still review the cited text and treatment history. Lexis+ AI is designed to streamline common research tasks—summaries, issue analyses, and initial drafting—while operating within a familiar legal research environment for firms already using Lexis products.

Bloomberg Law

Bloomberg Law integrates generative AI into its existing research platform, which combines primary law, agency materials, and extensive proprietary analysis developed by Bloomberg's editorial staff. The system's strength lies in its regulatory coverage—particularly in areas such as securities, labor, tax, and corporate governance—where practitioner-focused explanations, news updates, and agency trackers are tightly woven into the research environment. Bloomberg's AI tools can summarize legal developments, extract key points from long documents, and assist with initial drafting, while grounding responses in its internal library rather than open-web sources. As with other research platforms, the lawyer must still review the cited authorities and confirm the analysis, but Bloomberg Law offers a consolidated environment that blends traditional research, regulatory monitoring, and AI-assisted synthesis.

Descrybe.ai

Descrybe.ai is a newer legal research platform aimed at improving access to U.S. state court opinions—an area traditionally underserved by the major research vendors. The system aggregates and indexes state court decisions from a growing list of jurisdictions, then uses AI to generate plain-language summaries of each opinion. Its focus is breadth of coverage and ease of understanding, rather than deep doctrinal analysis or full RAG-style legal reasoning. While the generative summaries can help lawyers and self-represented litigants quickly grasp the outcome and key issues in a case, users still need to review the underlying opinions for authoritative detail. Descrybe.ai illustrates a broader trend: smaller companies are using AI to surface and explain legal materials that have historically been difficult or costly to access.

AnyLaw

AnyLaw is a U.S.-based legal research platform that offers access to both federal and state case law, and it increasingly incorporates AI to enhance usability. Specifically, AnyLaw markets "AI-generated case summaries" that aim to provide concise overviews of judicial opinions. The platform emphasizes affordable access and claims to update its database daily.

Paxton AI

Paxton AI is a web-based legal technology platform designed to support a wide range of law firm tasks such as legal research, document drafting, and document analysis. According to its marketing, the tool allows lawyers to "ask legal questions," receive tailored insights from statutes, regulations, and case law, draft documents from templates or scratch, and upload files for analysis. The platform is geared toward small and mid-sized law firms and serves a variety of practice areas including employment, personal injury, corporate law, and criminal law. Paxton emphasizes data security—claiming SOC 2 compliance and support for closed-model deployment to protect client confidentiality.

Alexi

Canadian-based Alexi has a research platform with U.S. law available.

Midpage

Midpage is a legal AI vendor founded in 2022 that focuses on supporting litigators. The company has a standalone research product.

Counsel Stack

Counsel Stack, founded in 2023, offers specialized LLMs for legal research and is aimed at in-house legal departments.

Open Source and Public Interest Options

Open-source repositories such as CourtListener and OpenLaw are increasingly integrated into custom RAG systems used by clinics, academic researchers, and legal aid organizations, as well as various AI products via their application programming interfaces. These tools offer transparency and accessibility, and while they may lack the secondary sources found in commercial platforms, they can nonetheless serve as a reliable base for building replicable, open legal research environments. The authors know both of these organizations well, as they provide case, statute, and regulatory repositories complementing Visalaw.ai's vast built-in immigration law library.

Practice Area-Specific Tools

An expanding category of tools is focused on individual practice areas—such as immigration, tax, privacy, employment, or criminal law—using highly targeted legal datasets. Because these products are trained or indexed on subject-matter-specific corpora, they often retrieve more relevant authorities within their niche than general models or broad legal platforms. Their value depends on the quality and completeness of the underlying library, but they can significantly reduce the time required to reach a baseline understanding of the governing rules. As noted previously, the authors of this book founded Visalaw.ai, which is one such product aimed at immigration lawyers. Another specialized product is Blue J (bluej.com), a research platform built for tax professionals.

Another notable product is the American Arbitration Association's AI Arbitrator, which has built a research tool for its members that also combines analytics from actual arbitration cases to better help in preparing for arbitration.

Practice Example: Choosing a Research Stack for a Multioffice Firm

A 40-lawyer firm with offices in three states is deciding whether to renew its legacy research platform. The litigation group prefers one system's brief analysis features; the corporate team favors another product's regulatory trackers; the immigration group is piloting a niche RAG tool built on curated agency materials. The firm's tech committee runs a structured comparison: for each candidate platform, they map (1) scope of the underlying corpus, (2) RAG and generative features, (3) integration with their case management system, and (4) per-user pricing. They also ask each vendor to run the same fact pattern—a recently filed motion to dismiss in one of the firm's cases—and compare accuracy, transparency, and hallucination behavior. The outcome is not a single "winner," but a deliberate stack: one core research platform, one domain-specific tool for immigration, and limited licenses for an analytics-heavy product used only by the appellate specialists.

Practice Example: Asking the Right Questions Before Signing a Multiyear Contract

A regional firm is offered a steep discount on a three-year license for a new AI research product—if they sign before the end of the quarter. Before committing, the firm's CTO and managing partner schedule a due-diligence call with the vendor. Using the checklist in section 3.4, they walk through data sources, frequency of updates, RAG design, hallucination safeguards, model training practices, and SOC 2 status. When they ask whether client uploads are ever retained to improve the model, the vendor explains that file contents are stored indefinitely in a shared environment. That answer conflicts with the firm's confidentiality policy and its obligations under several client outside-counsel guidelines. The firm presses for a written data processing addendum with strict retention limits and segregation of client data. When the vendor hesitates, the firm walks away and instead chooses a platform that can contractually support its professional responsibility obligations.

3.7 AI Legal Research Best Practices

1. **Frame questions like a lawyer, not a search engine.**
   Ask structured, context-rich questions that specify jurisdiction, factual posture, and the type of authority you want retrieved.
2. **Use iterative follow-up prompts.**
   Treat AI like a junior researcher—refine the question, request contrary cases, narrow or expand the scope, and ask for direct quotations.
3. **Require source exposure.**
   Use tools or prompts that reveal the underlying documents, not just summaries. Avoid relying on outputs that don't show their work.
4. **Verify every citation.**
   Read the underlying case or statute yourself, confirm the quoted language, and check treatment history through a citator.
5. **Prefer closed-corpus or RAG systems for authoritative research, especially when answers will appear in filed work product.**
   Public chatbots are useful for brainstorming, but not for final answers unless grounded in a trusted corpus.
6. **Check dates, jurisdictions, and procedural posture.**
   Many errors arise from overlooking recency, the weight of authority, or differences between state and federal frameworks. This can be a problem even for RAG-based legal research products, so you still need to closely check for these problems before relying on AI output.
7. **Save and standardize prompts.**
   Create firm-approved prompts for common research tasks so teams get consistent, repeatable results.

8. **Use AI to surface issues, not finalize conclusions.**
   AI is best at framing arguments, identifying patterns, and accelerating preliminary research—your judgment remains essential.
9. **Document your research trail.**
   Save prompts, outputs, retrieved documents, and verification notes to preserve reproducibility and comply with audit expectations.
10. **Train all team members on verification, not blind trust.**
   Lawyers and staff should understand how to evaluate AI output, identify red flags, and escalate ambiguous or inconsistent results.

3.8 Legal Research Using Public LLMs Like ChatGPT and Claude: A Caution

General purpose LLMs such as ChatGPT, Claude, and Gemini can be remarkably good at explaining concepts, organizing information, and producing readable analysis. They were not, however, designed as legal research systems, and treating them as such introduces serious risks. Despite widely publicized sanctions cases and other examples of hallucinations appearing in filings, this point bears repeating. These models are trained on broad internet data, lack controlled legal corpora, and do not include citation verification layers. They can accelerate early thinking, but they cannot replace the authoritative, source-grounded environments provided by dedicated research tools.

The Risks: Bad Source Material, Hallucinations, and Shallow Answers

Public LLMs draw from mixed-quality online sources and do not disclose the provenance of the information they use. As a result, they may offer outdated or unofficial descriptions of legal standards. When prompted for authority, they may generate plausible-sounding but nonexistent cases, conflate doctrines across jurisdictions, or provide rule statements without capturing procedural posture or exceptions. Even when roughly correct, their answers are often shallow—missing nuance, competing interpretations, or recent developments.

Can Deep Reasoning Models Narrow the Gap?

New models with stronger analytical capabilities—such as OpenAI's Deep Research variants and Anthropic's more advanced Claude releases—show meaningful improvements in logical consistency and multistep reasoning. They are better at identifying ambiguities, acknowledging missing facts, and structuring nuanced explanations. In internal and academic testing, these models hallucinate less when paired with well-crafted prompts. But even the most rigorous reasoning model cannot compensate for the absence of a controlled legal corpus. Better logic does not fix questionable sourcing, and a low hallucination rate still cannot substitute for verifiable citations. Still, it's a marked improvement.

Where Public LLMs Fit Into Legal Workflows

Public models excel at framing issues, generating plain-language explanations, mapping arguments, and producing first-pass drafts that help lawyers orient themselves. They are also effective for summarizing long documents you provide, spotting ambiguities, or identifying follow-up questions. And they can help with fact research associated with legal research. But they should not be treated as authoritative legal research tools. A responsible workflow is to use public LLMs early—when brainstorming or structuring a research plan—and then transition to RAG-based legal systems to identify, verify, and analyze the controlling law.

One interesting use of a public model that can help lawyers master a legal subject like a new regulation or a lengthy Supreme Court decision is demonstrated by Google's Notebook LM, which can digest a document and produce a slick, entertaining podcast where two very human-sounding hosts do a deep dive into a subject. For certain types of learners (or someone just looking to get better educated on a subject while out for a jog), this is worth trying.

3.9 The Future: Toward AI-First Research

Legal research in the print-only era relied on lawyers to manually scan documents, and lawyers could benefit as time went on from manual classifying and secondary sources that summarized and analyzed the law. When online research tools became available nearly 50 years ago, lawyers could more efficiently search and browse those large legal repositories. But online legal research was essentially speeding up the same process lawyers had always used. Generative AI legal research tools function more like thinking assistants that can read, synthesize, compare, and explain law with more and more preciseness. The next era of legal research will not be defined by who has access to the largest collection of documents, but by who has access to the most capable reasoning layer on top of a trusted corpus.

The new AI research platforms will not just find supporting authorities. They will identify the governing rule and explain exceptions. They will show differences in how the law is viewed in other jurisdictions and explain trends in the development of jurisprudence. They will explain their reasoning and then suggest follow-up questions. Law firms will have an easier time using their own internal knowledge banks to complement external RAG-based research tools.

The future of legal practice is not a world where AI replaces legal researchers. It is one where research becomes more strategic, more contextual, and more deeply integrated into legal judgment. Lawyers will increasingly reduce the time spent on the mechanical and tedious task of merely locating relevant statutes and cases. As AI-first research matures, the gap between firms that adopt these tools and those that do not will widen—shifting research from a mechanical task to a dynamic, collaborative, and intelligence-driven process.

Today's generative AI tools are already very capable, but they are far from perfect. Even so, the tools available at the time of this writing—less than three years into the modern generative AI era—have improved dramatically in a short span. And, as many observers like to say, today's AI is likely the worst we will ever see.

SAMPLE PROMPT: ANTIHALLUCINATION LEGAL DOCUMENT VALIDATOR

Purpose and Role

You are a senior appellate clerk and citation auditor. Your job is to verify, not embellish. Be skeptical, precise, and source-driven. Assume the document's authorship is unknown (human, LLM, or hybrid). Do not speculate about authorship—evaluate content only.

Inputs (fill in before running the audit)

- Client question / assignment: [PASTE]
- Document type and posture: [Brief / Motion / Memo / Letter / Other] and [e.g., Rule 12(b)(6), SJ, PI/TRO, appeal, evidentiary, etc.]
- Jurisdiction(s): [PRIMARY JURISDICTION(S)] (mark binding vs. persuasive accordingly)
- Date currency cutoff: [DATE] (treat law after this date as potentially new; note gaps)
- Practice area: [AREA]
- Document to audit (the "Document"): [PASTE FULL TEXT OR ASK USER TO UPLOAD]

- Allowed sources/tools: [e.g., public web; firm KM; docket sites; no paywalled citator]. If you cannot access a source to verify a claim, mark it UNVERIFIED—do not guess.

Your Task

Perform a falsification-first audit. Extract every proposition of law and every material factual/record assertion that depends on outside sources, and then verify each one. If something cannot be verified with the allowed sources, label it UNVERIFIED and specify exactly what would be needed to verify.

Deliverable Format (use these exact section headings)

1. Executive Verdict
    - Status: APPROVE AS IS / CONDITIONALLY APPROVE (edits required) / NOT FIT FOR FILING.
    - One-paragraph rationale.
    - Top three risk items (one line each).
    - Document-type fit (1–3 lines): Are the standard, burden, record scope, and requested relief correct for this filing type?
2. Proposition-by-Proposition Audit Table
    - Create one row per distinct Proposition of Law (and any material factual/record claims that rely on external sources). Include every outcome-critical conclusion.
    - Starter table (add rows as needed):

Proposition (as stated in Document)	Relief/ Issue Link (e.g., SJ standard, PI factor, element X)	Binding/ Persuasive in [Jurisdiction]	Primary Authority (full Bluebook citation + court + year)	Pinpoint Page/¶/§	Exact Supporting Quote (≤25 words) OR "Paraphrase only"	Treatment/ Validity (abrogated? limited? superseded?)	Fit to Facts/ Posture/ Record (note record cite if available)	Document Accurate? (YES / PARTIAL / NO / UNVERIFIED)	Issues Found (codes)

    - If multiple authorities are required, add sub-rows (4a, 4b, etc.). If none exist or you cannot verify, write NONE FOUND / UNVERIFIED and propose concrete search queries a human can run.
3. Missing or Contrary Authority
    - Omitted binding cases/statutes that materially affect the conclusion (post-[DATE]).
    - Directly adverse or limiting authority the Document should have discussed.
    - For each, include a one-line "Why it matters."
4. Quote and Pinpoint Check
    - List every quoted or paraphrased source relied upon. For each, confirm (a) existence, (b) precise wording, (c) correct pin cite, (d) context not reversed/overstated. Flag misquotes and missing pins.
5. Standards, Elements, and Burdens
    - For each test/standard (e.g., elements, standard of review, injunction factors, Daubert gatekeeping), restate the canonical formulation with

authority + pin, then say whether the Document's version is accurate / incomplete / wrong.

6. Statutes and Regulations Currency Check
   - For each cited statute/regulation: identify current text at [DATE], any amendments, effective dates, and whether a newer version changes the analysis. Note UNVERIFIED if you cannot check.
7. Procedural Posture, Remedy and Document-Type Fit
   - Dispositive motions (12(b)(6), summary judgment, etc.): correct standard, burdens, materials considered, leave-to-amend, remedy.
   - Injunctions (PI/TRO): correct multifactor test, irreparable harm, bond, notice, likelihood threshold.
   - Evidentiary/rule-based motions (e.g., FRE 702/403): governing rule, reliability/relevance, gatekeeping role.
   - Appellate briefs: appellate jurisdiction, standard of review, preservation/waiver, harmless-error framing, proper relief.
   - Trial/other filings: correct rule invoked, deadline/local-rule compliance, scope of record. Flag mismatches.
8. Numerical/Damages/Threshold Calculations (if any)
   - Recompute all math transparently. Show work. Cite statutory thresholds or formula sources with pins.
9. Hallucination and Misuse Report (Errata)
   - Provide a bullet list of issues, using these codes:

Issue Code	Description
HALL-01	fabricated/nonexistent case
HALL-02	fabricated/nonexistent statute/reg/rule
CIT-01	wrong reporter/party/court/year
CIT-02	incorrect statute/reg/rule section
PIN-01	missing/incorrect pin cite
QUOTE-01	misquote or context error
JX-01	wrong jurisdiction/precedential weight
DATE-01	outdated/abrogated/overruled/superseded
RULE-01	wrong legal standard/elements/test
POST-01	procedural-posture mismatch
FACT-01	factual analogy overreach or record miscite
NEG-01	missed adverse authority
SCOPE-01	holding vs. dicta confusion / overclaim
UNVER-01	source unavailable; unable to verify; no guessing
METH-01	relied on memory/uncited secondary

   - Format each item as: [# from Table]—[Issue Code]—One-line fix.

10. Corrected Conclusions (Client-Safe)
    - Rewrite the bottom-line conclusions tailored to the filing type (e.g., "Grant/deny the motion because . . ."), each followed by (best authority + pin) in parentheses.
11. Confidence and Next Steps
    - Confidence (0–100) in the bottom-line conclusions (not prose quality).
    - What would raise confidence: concrete documents, dockets, databases, or facts to collect.
    - If UNVERIFIED items exist: list specific search strings and public repositories to check next.

Nonnegotiable Rules

- Do not invent citations, quotes, or pins. If unknown/inaccessible, write UNVERIFIED and move on.
- Prefer primary authority. Identify when relying on secondary sources.
- Distinguish binding vs. persuasive clearly and surface adverse authority.
- Do not speculate about authorship (human vs. LLM). Evaluate the content only.
- Be concise; show evidence-and-fit in the table. Use Bluebook form. Keep quotes ≤25 words (use ellipses/brackets properly).
- If your toolset includes web access, perform reasonable verification within scope and cite public sources you actually checked; if not, mark UNVERIFIED.

Document-Type Quick Checklist (use what applies)

- Motion to Dismiss (12(b)(6)/state equivalent): plausibility/particularity standard; documents considered; leave to amend.
- Summary Judgment: burdens; materiality; citations to record; view in light most favorable to nonmovant.
- Preliminary Injunction/TRO: elements; irreparable harm; bond; notice; immediacy; standing.
- Appellate Brief: appellate jurisdiction; standard of review; waiver/preservation; record citations; relief sought.
- Rule-Based/Evidentiary Motions (e.g., FRE 702/403; Daubert): correct rule; reliability/relevance; gatekeeping.
- Class Certification: rule elements; typicality/adequacy; predominance; ascertainability; manageability.
- Criminal Filings: constitutional standards; suppression tests; harmless error; statutory elements.

Optional Quick-Triage Prompt (fast pass)

"List the five most consequential conclusions in the Document and, for each, provide: (1) the best supporting primary authority with pin and ≤25-word quote; (2) whether it is binding in [JURISDICTION]; (3) current validity (any abrogation/negative treatment); (4) a one-line fit to our facts and posture; (5) one adverse or limiting authority if it exists. Output a five-row table. Use UNVERIFIED if you cannot confirm. No guessing."

Starter table for quick triage (add rows as needed):

Conclusion	Best Primary Authority + Pin + ≤25-Word Quote	Binding in [Jurisdiction]?	Current Validity	One-line Fit	Adverse/ Limiting Authority

CHAPTER 4

Drafting with AI

4.1 Introduction

Another very popular application of AI is performing legal drafting.

Some of the earliest uses of generative AI in law appeared in legal research and document analysis, where AI is very capable in its ability to process and summarize large amounts of data in a short amount of time. Drafting soon became a prominent use case as a natural next step from research and document analysis. Drafting seems to be at the core of many legal workflows: contracts, pleadings, memos, and client correspondence, to name a few.

Before exploring the practical applications, we need to outline a definition of AI drafting. This will be a good starting point for us to discuss where AI can add the most value in your existing draft workflows.

Note that this book is not a buyer's guide. While we mention specific products at a high level, our goal is to outline a use case rather than provide product recommendations. In reality, the technology is evolving so rapidly that even at the time of publication there are likely new startups and features we are already behind on here. Our focus is on helping you understand how AI reshapes the drafting process and how you can use it effectively in your practice.

4.2 The Evolution of AI Drafting in Legal

Using a definition from the Clio Legal Dictionary, AI drafting refers to the use of artificial intelligence technology to assist in the creation and preparation of legal documents, such as contracts, pleadings, and agreements.[1] This means combining the expertise of legal professionals with the efficiency and accuracy of AI algorithms, to streamline the drafting

1. *AI Legal Drafting*, Clio Legal Dictionary, https://www.clio.com/resources/legal-dictionary/ai-legal-drafting/.

process and enhance the overall quality of the outputs. Before generative AI was available as a tool to help lawyers with drafting, we had "traditional AI" software. These products are still prominent today and have very strong use cases. The difference as it relates to drafting is that traditional AI systems focus on the use of decision tree and conditional logic to assist with drafting, often referred to as document assembly. The best use cases for this capability are structured or templated documents where the underlying language does not change. The benefit of this tooling is that the outputs from software are consistent and very predictable.

Some prominent early players in this space are Neota Logic, Bryter, Josef, NetDocuments' Afterpattern, and HotDocs.[2] Many of these tools have evolved to incorporate generative AI capabilities as well, but originally they relied entirely on human-built workflows based on preset conditions.

Unlike traditional AI, generative AI relies on a prompt and what is often referred to as "context" from the user to instruct an LLM on how best to draft a document. This output is very dynamic, which makes it ideal for less templated and more sophisticated outputs. The challenge here is that oftentimes the output is less predictable, making it harder at times to get the ideal draft brief or legal doc. There are other limitations with the generative AI approach. The earliest LLMs had more significant limitations, which we will soon discuss. Firms have chosen different solutions to address some of these limitations, and we will outline some of those approaches in this chapter. The technology is also constantly evolving, and we believe the products/use cases that have been identified up until now in the industry more than prove its validity.

4.3 Overcoming the Early Constraints of LLMs

The Context Window Challenge

The most fundamental limitation of early generative AI systems has been the "context window"—the finite amount of text that these systems can process and maintain awareness of during any single interaction. LLMs operate with context windows that, while good for shorter and more creative content, have proven ineffective for legal work, especially more detailed and extensive documents. A typical commercial contract might span dozens of pages, while complex litigation documents could extend to hundreds of pages, with cross-references and legal precedents that must be maintained throughout the drafting process.

2. The authors used Neota Logic and Afterpattern beginning in 2015, and we credit these early AI tools with introducing us to the possibilities of AI for lawyers.

The demands of these more detailed legal drafts created obvious barriers for early users of generative AI products. In order to reach the necessary amount of detail and pages in the output, files had to be artificially segmented into multiple sections, sometimes losing crucial context between the sections. Imagine if you took a legal brief, separated it into ten equal parts, and gave separate legal assistants one section each to complete, then copied and pasted all of those sections into a final Word file. This was the reality for the first AI drafting solutions. As the models improved and capabilities around the language models improved, like allowing for more context pushed into the LLM, it was more like giving the same legal assistant all of the sections to complete one at a time, and then that same assistant compiling it all together again, all the while looking for any issues or inconsistencies. What we have just described is closer to the capabilities of the more recent models, like OpenAI's GPT-5 and now 5.1.

Simply put, these more recent models have greatly improved some of these context window limitations. Some of this discussion around tokens may not make any sense, but the entire LLM structure is built around the concept of tokens. Based on Microsoft's definition, tokens are "words, character sets, or combinations of words and punctuation" that are generated by large language models (LLMs) when they decompose text.[3] In other words, tokens are text further broken down, and are the measure for these LLMs. For a quick comparison, let's look at the differences between GPT-3.5 and GPT-5 in terms of token limits. GPT-3.5 was released in March 2022 and could only handle up to 16,000 tokens of input and provide 4,000 tokens of output, which limited its ability to process or generate documents beyond two pages. By contrast, GPT-5 (released in 2025) expanded this dramatically to 400,000 tokens of input (and 128,000 tokens of output), meaning it can read entire books or large datasets at once and also generate substantially longer and more detailed outputs. The implication is that GPT-5 enables far more complex, detailed, and sustained document creation compared to GPT-3.5, which was constrained to shorter summaries or sections. For a more detailed comparison of the current general models and how they rank in terms of legal drafting, refer to the Vals AI report on model rankings of legal-specific tasks.[4]

---

3. *Understand Tokens*, MICROSOFT BUILD 2026, https://learn.microsoft.com/en-us/dotnet/ai/conceptual/understanding-tokens.

4. *LegalBench*, VALS.AI, https://www.vals.ai/benchmarks/legal_bench (last visited April 10, 2026).

General LLMs Versus Legal-Specific Products for Drafting

There are generally two categories of AI products to choose from when looking at generative AI tools: one is general AI and the other is domain-specific AI. The same is true with the drafting use case.

For any of the products you choose, thoroughly research data security and privacy and all the other components of your vendor's diligence requirements. The legal-specific products are built with law firms in mind, so security standards are typically achieved early and are well documented. The most obvious benefit of legal-specific products is that they are built for a specific use case and should, in theory, allow for more customized tooling out of the box. Even most sub-specialty areas of law would be hard-pressed not to find a legal AI that provides some level of coverage for that specific domain. Some examples of this are estate planning, patent law, immigration, and so on. The general legal products like Harvey, Vincent (Clio), Thomson Reuters, Lexis, and Westlaw are still very prominent and oftentimes are specialized enough, but there will continue to be a need for coverage in niche practice areas.

To zoom out a bit farther, general or "foundational" AI products like OpenAI, Anthropic, and Google Gemini will require extensive custom prompting, configuration, and templates. Using general tools to achieve this is likely more accessible than ever, but still requires a great deal of oversight and maintenance. Also, constant testing and evaluation must be done in order to ensure outputs remain consistent day after day. We liken it to the "build-it-yourself" approach, and it still requires a large amount of resources. For this reason, many firms will favor domain-specific AI products to assist with drafting. As mentioned earlier, AI is constantly evolving, so it will require continued attention to underlying changes in technology. Many firms use both general and legal-specific AI products for different drafting purposes. Also, firm size and budget will play into the decision, but just know that these same capabilities are generally accessible to both the solo practitioner and the AmLaw 100.

Integration with Legal Systems and Databases

If you had a penny for every time we discuss the importance of *data* in relation to AI use cases, particularly drafting use cases, you likely still wouldn't have enough to buy a soda, but it would be a lot of pennies. Just keep filing that away as we step into later chapters. AI systems have been expanding their capabilities, and many now offer deep integrations with law firms' source of truth systems, as well as expansive legal research datasets. There have been several major acquisitions in the past few years (the one most top of mind is the acquisition of Vlex by Clio) in an attempt to merge a firm's source of truth data with one of the larger legal datasets in Vlex. But there are other public benefit companies and initiatives that have a keen focus on democratizing the law. Two that come to mind are Courtlistener (for millions of case law documents, Pacer data, etc.) and OpenLaws (an example of a company focusing specifically on statutes and regulations). These datasets are now just a simple integration away from a drafting tool or resource that, once also merged with example documents or templates, can produce a very robust drafting engine. Contemporary platforms can access this data to provide instant access to tens of millions of legal documents, including federal and state case laws, statutes, regulations, guidance, and filings, ensuring comprehensive legal research coverage.

The same challenges that exist in the research use case exist in drafting, including the ability for the system to hallucinate or not provide accurate citations. RAG systems and agentic tools have shown great promise in this area, and will likely continue to help improve the verification and review fatigue that many early users of AI have experienced.[5]

Other Improvements: Fine Tuning, Embeddings, and Legal-Specific Prompting

In addition, many legal generative AI systems developed domain-specific training and fine tuning on LLMs. These models are basically reinforced on your specific language, examples, or feedback to improve reasoning patterns—ultimately, to generate the ideal output. General purpose models are trained on broad swaths of content (basically the entire internet and now even synthetic and artificial data), with legal documents representing only a fraction of their knowledge base. On the other hand, legal-specific AI platforms can employ training and/or improvement processes that are focused on more curated datasets.

Embeddings are another well-established method for expanding the resources that an LLM has access to. Again, according to Microsoft, embeddings are "numeric representations of non-numeric data that an LLM can use to determine relationships between concepts."[6] Essentially,

5. Jordan Turk, *From AI Anxiety to Action: How to Overcome Transformation Fatigue in Your Law Firm*, AttorneyAtWork, Feb. 24, 2025, https://www.attorneyatwork.com/ai-anxiety-in-law-firms-overcoming-transformation-fatigue/.

6. *Embeddings in .NET*, Microsoft Build 2026, https://learn.microsoft.com/en-us/dotnet/ai/conceptual/embeddings (last visited April 10, 2026).

this allows the system to have access to a lot more data in a single prompt when it is represented this way (as a series of numbers).

Prompting remains a key part of the quality of the outputs. In the prompt(s), you are giving detailed instructions and identity to the system. This all comes back to the drafting use case because, at the end of the day, a drafting AI tool is a prompt or a series of prompts or agents that is working in the background to generate output. You can also have further filtering and categorization in the prompts—say, for example, you only wanted files from a specific case in your document management system. Another example is if you only wanted case law from a specific jurisdiction.

The prompting process will continue to become more intuitive as AI is able to create dynamic prompts based on the plain-language requests we provide the system.

Implications for Legal Practice

The convergence of these advances makes a very strong case for AI in legal drafting. The expanding context limits mean that generative AI systems can now help in some of the most complex legal work. Specialized fine tuning, along with firm-specific examples and data, ensure the best possible outcomes. Integrations with legal data and the firm's source of truth ensure limited hallucinations.

Generally, the task or use case that we have largely assumed up to this point is legal drafting related to an initial document or brief being created. However, AI can assist in both redrafting and review efforts that can likely be just as meaningful to lawyers as the initial draft. Many tools now integrate directly into Microsoft Word for quick review and redlining for contracts; to quickly recall a historical data bank to give the AI context as you review a file for potential issues or changes; or at the very least, as a simple method to query an AI system to redraft only a specific section of a file, rather than having to draft an entire brief over again.

4.4 Example Use Cases and Corresponding Products

Corporate Law: Leading the AI Revolution

Contract Drafting and Review

Contracts are, so far, one of the key focal points of AI drafting capabilities in legal. Corporate lawyers spend hours researching, writing, and reviewing a variety of contracts and agreements. The traditional process often starts with a template document and then customizing terms for specific transactions and scenarios. AI transforms this workflow by analyzing vast databases of existing contracts to identify standard market terms, suggest appropriate language for specific situations, and flag potential issues before they become problems. The technology excels at generating first drafts that incorporate both boilerplate provisions and transaction-specific requirements, reducing initial drafting time from hours to minutes while maintaining legal accuracy.

Mergers and Acquisitions Due Diligence

Due diligence requires extracting and analyzing key information from thousands of documents under tight deadlines. Lawyers must identify material risks, confirm compliance with covenants, and spot red flags that could derail transactions. AI accelerates this process by simultaneously reviewing contracts, corporate records, and financial documents to extract relevant data points, compare terms across multiple agreements, and identify inconsistencies or unusual provisions, and then draft a report summarizing these findings.

Securities and Compliance

Securities lawyers face the challenge of maintaining compliance across an ever-changing regulatory landscape. AI helps by automatically monitoring regulatory changes, updating document templates to reflect new requirements, and cross-referencing agreements against current compliance standards. This automated oversight reduces the risk of regulatory violations while freeing lawyers to focus on strategic compliance issues rather than routine document maintenance.

Litigation: Transforming Discovery and Brief Writing

Discovery Automation

Discovery requires lawyers to respond to document requests, prepare interrogatories, and analyze opposing counsel's productions. The traditional process involves manually reviewing requirements, identifying relevant documents, and crafting appropriate responses—often under tight deadlines. AI streamlines this by automatically analyzing discovery requests, identifying responsive documents from client files, and generating initial draft responses that address each element.

Brief and Pleading Drafting

Effective brief writing requires synthesizing complex legal arguments, incorporating relevant precedents, and presenting compelling narratives within strict formatting and deadline constraints. AI assists by analyzing case facts, identifying applicable legal standards, and suggesting argument structures based on successful briefs in similar cases. The technology helps lawyers organize their arguments more effectively, incorporate relevant case law, and ensure comprehensive coverage of all legal issues.

Legal Research Integration

Modern litigation drafting demands current, accurate legal research seamlessly integrated with persuasive writing. AI enhances this process by conducting real-time case law analysis, identifying relevant precedents, and suggesting how current legal developments might impact ongoing cases. The technology ensures that briefs incorporate the most recent legal authorities while maintaining accuracy in citations and legal analysis. However, high-profile sanctions cases have emphasized the critical need for human verification of all AI-generated citations and legal authorities.

Real Estate: Streamlining Property Transactions

Real estate's standardized document types and repetitive processes make it ideal for AI implementation, with significant adoption in lease and contract work.

Lease Generation and Review

Real estate lawyers regularly draft leases that must balance landlord protection with tenant rights while complying with local regulations. The traditional process involves customizing standard lease templates for specific properties, tenant requirements, and jurisdictional rules. AI accelerates this by automatically incorporating property-specific details, adjusting terms based on lease type and duration, and ensuring compliance with local rent control and tenant protection laws. The technology generates comprehensive lease documents in minutes while maintaining legal accuracy and completeness.

Purchase Agreement Analysis

Purchase agreements require careful analysis to identify standard market terms, unusual provisions, and potential legal issues that could affect closing. AI enhances this process by comparing agreement terms against standard market practices, flagging unusual or potentially problematic clauses, and ensuring compliance with local zoning laws and regulatory requirements. The technology helps lawyers quickly identify areas requiring negotiation or additional due diligence, while ensuring that all standard protections are properly included.

Employment Law: Automating Policy and Compliance

Employment law has embraced AI for policy creation and compliance monitoring—particularly valuable given the area's regulatory complexity and frequent legal changes.

Policy Generation

Employment lawyers must create comprehensive workplace policies that address harassment, discrimination, safety regulations, and other compliance requirements while remaining current with frequently changing laws. The traditional approach involves researching current regulations, adapting template policies, and customizing language for specific industries and jurisdictions. AI streamlines this process by automatically incorporating current legal requirements, suggesting policy language based on industry best practices, and ensuring compliance with federal, state, and local regulations. The technology creates comprehensive policy frameworks that address all relevant legal areas while maintaining consistency across different policy documents.

Employment Agreement Drafting

Employment lawyers can use AI to help automatically incorporate required legal provisions, flag language that may violate employment laws, and suggest terms that align with current legal standards. The technology reduces regulatory risk by ensuring that agreements comply with jurisdiction-specific requirements while protecting legitimate business interests.

Compliance Monitoring

Employment law changes frequently, requiring lawyers to continuously update policies and agreements to maintain compliance. AI addresses this challenge by automatically monitoring regulatory changes, updating document templates when new requirements take effect, and drafting lawyer alerts addressing potential compliance issues in existing agreements. This automated oversight ensures ongoing compliance without requiring manual monitoring of multiple regulatory sources, allowing lawyers to focus on strategic employment law issues rather than routine document maintenance.

4.5 Finding a Specific AI Vendor

While it is not the primary goal of this book to provide a comprehensive review of every drafting product available in the legal space (though we have an extensive vendor list in an appendix), it may be helpful to highlight a few key resources. These platforms can support your vendor search and evaluation process by offering in-depth product information, comparisons, and user insights:

- Legaltechhub.com—A curated directory of legal technology tools, including drafting solutions, with filters by function and practice area.
- Legaltech.com—Industry news, product spotlights, and emerging trends in the legal tech ecosystem.

Readers are encouraged to explore these sites as a starting point for identifying tools that meet the specific needs of their practice. AI tools can also sometimes be helpful in finding these products as larger resources become available to identify products in the market.

4.6 Conclusion

The use cases presented in this chapter only begin to explore the possibilities. They are intended to help you start identifying areas within your own practice where AI-assisted drafting tools might be effectively applied.

Ideal drafting use cases often share several key characteristics:

- They occur in document-heavy practice areas.
- They involve complex writing tasks that require deep analysis or strict adherence to detailed rules and requirements.
- They benefit from examples and standard templates, which help AI systems improve accuracy through context and structure.

The future is promising for legal professionals managing the burden of intensive drafting tasks. These tools offer the potential to give legal teams valuable time back and to refocus their energy on delivering higher-value services to clients. Importantly, the role of the lawyer remains unchanged—AI is a powerful assistant, but not a replacement. The guiding principle of "trust but verify" still applies. Attorney oversight and review are not optional; they are essential.

In Chapter 16, we will explore legal ethics and the responsibilities professionals face in this new age of AI-powered law practice.

■ CHAPTER 5

Integrating AI with Case Management Systems

In the legal industry, the terms *case management* and *practice management* are often used interchangeably, though they technically refer to different scopes of software. Practice management platforms typically encompass both the substantive handling of legal matters (case management) and the business operations of the firm, such as billing, accounting, and reporting. For purposes of this chapter, we will use the term case management system (CMS) to focus specifically on the matter-level data and workflows that create the greatest opportunity for meaningful AI integration in legal work; other chapters will explore additional practice-specific applications of AI beyond the case management context.

Until recently, most case management platforms functioned primarily as static databases or workflow engines. Now, with the integration of generative AI, some are evolving into active legal assistants—offering predictive insight, real-time drafting help, and smarter automation. This chapter explores how generative AI is transforming the way lawyers use their case management systems, the benefits and limitations of these integrations, and how to future-proof your firm's systems for the AI era. But to simplify why these systems can find value from AI, it is because of the client data. Having a tool that can immediately and accurately recall and use this massive amount of data will continue to prove to be a meaningful use case for AI.

This brings up an important point: several case management systems now offer AI natively within the product, either by default or as an add-on for an additional cost. In some cases, it will not be necessary to integrate with another AI product or platform to gain certain AI capabilities, like document summaries or analysis. Another example: you may want to integrate your accounting software with your CMS so that, once the initial engagement is uploaded, it uses AI to analyze the engagement letter and then generate a draft invoice in the accounting software. Another similar use case we have seen is with mail processing. Some legal fields still manage a large amount of physical mail. A firm could add an AI workflow here so that once the mail is scanned into the system, it automatically saves the correct profile and notifies the legal team. The most recent reporting on AI implementation suggests much of the AI focus to date in professional services is aimed at these types of back-office tasks. No system is generally more aligned with back-office tasks than a firm's CMS.[1]

5.1 Why AI Belongs Inside Your Case Management System

To set the scene for this chapter, we would like to outline a normal morning in the life of a hypothetical lawyer named Suzie. Suzie starts her day with a strong cup of coffee and an inbox full of client emails. First, Suzie must check communication logs in the CMS to make sure she does not miss key details in her email reply. She then has to draft the email, manually saving it to the CMS afterward and logging her time. She then checks upcoming deadlines and meetings in her calendar and begins to prepare for these by searching through case folders, emails, and old meeting notes to get up to speed. She then spends the remainder of her time between meetings working on a brief that is due the following week.

If Suzie's CMS had a native or integrated AI assistant, much of this work could be streamlined. Her CMS AI would not have been able to brew her cup of coffee, but could have certainly assisted in gathering client notes, email filtering, and perhaps even some light drafting. First, AI could generate summaries for Suzie of recent client conversations and more general information about the status of the case and what is pending. Depending on the level of integration, Suzie also may have been able to use the AI to draft the first response to the email and review the email rather than drafting it from scratch. Then the AI assistant could track the time spent on the email, reported and logged in the CMS for billing to refer to later. Lastly, the AI assistant would have been able to scan Suzie's calendar quickly and provide updates on upcoming meetings with agendas and summaries.

---

1. Aditya Challapally, Chris Pease, Ramesh Raskar, and Pradyumna Chari, *The GenAI Divide: State of AI in Business 2025*, https://mlq.ai/media/quarterly_decks/v0.1_State_of_AI_in_Business_2025_Report.pdf.

In the last chapter, we spent a good amount of time detailing the drafting use case and specific applications. With a legal research AI integration, Suzie could also have the system provide strategy insights while working on a brief in Microsoft Word. Oftentimes we think of AI as being best suited for advanced reasoning tasks, but we would encourage firms to start simple. Simple tasks like using AI to auto categorize and suggest the location where files should be stored within the CMS is also an efficiency gain.

Thus follows a list of four key gains for utilizing AI in the context of case management. These can be applied more broadly, but we find them to be especially true with case management. Each of these are immediately obvious, but we will dive into a few examples of each: efficiency, accuracy, client experience, and communications.

Efficiency

AI reduces the time spent on repetitive and manual tasks so lawyers can focus on higher value legal work.

- **Deadline automation:** AI parses a USCIS receipt notice or a court scheduling order and auto-creates calendar entries with reminders, eliminating hours of manual data entry.
- **Timekeeping:** Voice memos recorded on the way back from court are automatically converted into billable time entries in the CMS, complete with LEDES-compliant narratives.
- **Document summaries:** Instead of reading through a 200-page deposition transcript, AI generates a case-relevant summary in seconds, saving hours of review time.

Accuracy

AI helps reduce human error in areas where mistakes are costly.

- **Deadline precision:** Instead of relying on a paralegal's interpretation of a complex scheduling order, AI double-checks rules and adds jurisdiction-specific deadlines automatically.
- **Conflict checks:** AI cross-references new client intake information against the firm's database to identify potential conflicts of interest that could otherwise be overlooked.
- **Consistent drafting:** AI pulls from firm-approved template language when generating client letters, reducing the risk of inconsistent or noncompliant wording.

Client Experience

Clients feel more informed, better served, and more confident in their legal representation.

- **Faster updates:** AI drafts real-time client status updates (e.g., "Your hearing is scheduled for October 15 at 9:00 a.m.") that lawyers can quickly review and approve before sending.
- **Multilingual communication:** A Spanish-speaking client receives translated engagement letters or case updates, enabling clear communication without waiting for a translator.
- **Personalized guidance:** AI uses intake responses to generate tailored next-step instructions ("Please gather your last three years of tax returns") that feel specific to the client's situation.

Team Communication/Productivity

AI reduces miscommunication and bottlenecks inside the firm.

- **Meeting follow-ups:** A recorded department meeting is transcribed by AI, turned into task lists, and automatically assigned to the right team members inside the CMS.
- **Onboarding lawyers to a new case:** Instead of sifting through old files, an associate receives an AI-generated "case digest" that summarizes key filings, deadlines, and correspondence to get up to speed.
- **Internal messaging:** AI suggests clarifying questions or flags missing information in case notes, prompting better communication between attorneys and support staff.

Here are a few more examples of use cases for various functions within a CMS:

- **Client intake** (Chapter 11): AI reviews intake forms, summarizes the client's situation, and finds potential red flags for attorney review.
- **Client communication:** AI drafts responses to frequently asked questions, status updates, or appointment reminders for attorney approval.

5.2 The Overlooked AI Use Case: Custom Reporting

Earlier, we emphasized that an accessible dataset is the cornerstone of any AI-enabled case management system. One of the most powerful—and sometimes overlooked—applications of data is detailed reporting. AI can transform logs and data into charts and dynamic KPIs. Imagine being able to run a natural language search across all of your firm's data: client matters, attorney and staff performance, case timelines, and more. If your CMS also houses billing information, the potential is even greater—AI can surface trends in collections, highlight revenue drivers, and identify areas where billable time is being lost.

These reports could be scheduled, templated, or just asked in real time on an as-needed basis. Here is a list of some practical queries to consider in this search:

- Client and Matter Trends
  - Which clients generated the highest realization rate over the past 12 months?
  - Show me matters currently at risk of missing a deadline this quarter.
  - Which practice area produced the most new matters last year, and how did profitability compare across practice groups?
- Attorney and Staff Performance
  - Who in the firm has the highest billable utilization rate this month?
  - Which associates consistently meet or exceed budgeted hours on matters?
  - Summarize team workload by attorney—who is over capacity, and who has availability?
- Financial Health
  - Which invoices are more than 60 days overdue, grouped by client?
  - What percentage of billed time was written off last quarter, and what are the top reasons?
  - Identify clients who regularly pay late but generate high revenue overall.
- Operational Insights
  - Which types of matters take the longest to close in our firm?
  - What's the average turnaround time from client intake to engagement letter across practice areas?
  - List the top five bottlenecks in case workflows based on overdue tasks.

5.3 Examples of Existing AI Features in Case Management

Several case management systems now offer native AI capabilities. We have chosen a few of them simply to outline higher-level functionality and give an indication to where some of this may be headed. Note: since writing this chapter, Clio has announced their new Clio Work capability, which is still in early stages, but demonstrates the likely future of how AI will be incorporated into most of these systems.[2]

Vendor	Feature	What It Does	Value Propositions
Filevine	*FilevineAI—"Chat with Your Case"*	Allows legal professionals to chat (conversational interface) with all matter data in Filevine: deadlines, billing, discovery, communications, etc. It's embedded, meaning data lives inside their secure platform.[3]	The value-add is that the AI assistant can see *everything* in the case/matter, not just uploaded docs. This reduces the risk of "missing data" in AI responses. Also, firms get faster access to summaries, insights, task suggestions, etc.
Filevine	*Depositions by Filevine*	Fully integrated workflow for depositions: scheduling, hosting, "live AI analysis" during depositions, transcript review post-depo. AI acts like a "second chair," flagging inconsistencies, suggesting follow-ups, and after the fact, making rough transcripts, storing them, etc.[4]	The "live assistant" during depositions is a strong differentiator. Also, centralizing all depositions, transcripts, and summaries inside the CMS helps with reuse, cross-case insight, and less toggling between tools. Good potential return on investment for litigators.

2. *Clio Introduces the Legal Industry's First Intelligent Legal Work Platform*, PR Newswire, Oct. 16, 2025, https://www.prnewswire.com/news-releases/clio-introduces-the-legal-industrys-first-intelligent-legal-work-platform-302586236.html.

3. Ardyce Taylor, *Filevine Launches the Only Embedded AI Legal Assistant that Lets Legal Professionals "Chat with Their Case,"* Filevine, May 1, 2025, https://www.filevine.com/news/filevine-launches-the-only-embedded-ai-legal-assistant-that-lets-legal-professionals-chat-with-their-case/.

4. Ardyce Taylor, *Filevine Transforms Depositions into a Unified, Intelligent Workflow for Legal Teams*, Filevine, Sept. 8, 2025, https://filevine.com/news/filevine-transforms-depositions-into-a-unified-intelligent-workflow-for-legal-teams/.

Vendor	Feature	What It Does	Value Propositions
Clio[5]	*Clio Duo*	Generative AI built into Clio Manage. Features include automatic case/matter summaries, task prioritization, automatic scheduling or adding events/time entries, drafting responses or communication, summarizing documents, retrieving key info, etc. All accessible from within the CMS via chat or request-type interface.[6]	Deep integration with existing case data; less switching between tools. Because it's native, permissions and data security can be more tightly managed. Helps with administrative overhead, assists with client communication and prioritization. Helps smaller firms scale.
Clio + Third-Party Integrations	*Querious*	Querious is a conversational intelligence tool; with this integration, it captures conversations or virtual meeting output, provides legal insight, and can even auto-draft billable entries (time narrative), then push this into Clio.[7]	Good example of "AI via extension" rather than fully native. Smaller firms may particularly benefit. Integration helps smooth workflow.
Litify	*Litify AI—Document Data Extraction & Matter Field Auto-Fill*	Litify AI can take uploaded documents (e.g., medical bills) and extract key data to populate relevant fields on a case/matter so staff don't have to manually key that information.[8]	Very helpful in high-volume plaintiff or personal injury firms. Reduces error in data entry. Also, auto-categorization of files and name organization (which Litify is working toward) introduces complexity.

5. On November 9, 2025, Clio completed its acquisition of vLex and at Clio's annual conference a few weeks before, a number of highly significant announcements were made about deep integrations of vLex's AI capabilities in Clio's case management system. That includes integrating legal research and data analytics capabilities, complex document drafting, and a variety of other new capabilities that the company will begin rolling out in 2026.

6. Jeffrey Schoenberger, *Clio Duo Brings AI to Lawyers Doorstep*, Lawyerist, Feb. 21, 2025, https://lawyerist.com/news/clio-duo-brings-ai-to-lawyers-doorstep/.

7. *Querious Joins Clio's App Directory to Help Law Firms Capture More Billable Time with AI* , LawSites, Aug 27, 2025, https://www.lawnext.com/2025/08/querious-joins-clios-app-directory-to-help-law-firms-capture-more-billable-time-with-ai.html.

8. *Make the Most Of Your Documents With Litify AI*, Litify, https://www.litify.com/resources/make-most-of-documents-with-litify-ai.

Vendor	Feature	What It Does	Value Propositions
Litify	*Settlement Intelligence Integration*	For personal injury claims: Settlement Intelligence integrates with Litify so that demand letters can pull "value drivers" stored in the matter and combine them with external logic to build demand letters that are optimized for how insurers' claim systems evaluate them.[9]	Example of vertical specialization. High value if outputs match attorney needs.
Formally (Immigration Case Management)[10]	*Magic Mail*	Formally helps immigration lawyers classify, store, and keep track of government notices provided via US Mail. The system allows a team member to upload and automatically classify the data.	Offers a solution that otherwise would require time intensive work from support team members. It will send a notification to the relevant attorney once the letter is stored. Key data will also update the status of a case.

5.4 Limitations and Considerations

As case management systems roll out AI features at a very fast pace, what does this mean for your practice? Here are several key takeaways to keep in mind as you evaluate when and how to bring these tools into your firm:

Data Drives Value

The power of AI inside a CMS depends on what information it can actually see. A system that can analyze client intake forms, court notices, billing data, and internal notes together will deliver far richer insights than one limited to a single document type. When assessing vendors, ask: what parts of my case data can the AI draw from, and what is not currently accessible? In addition, what data do you want to be off limits as it relates to your firm's data privacy policies?

9. https://www.demandletters.ai/news/ai-demand-letters-for-litify-legal-case-management-system.

10. The authors, incidentally, use Formally in their immigration law practice.

Real-Time Assistance Is the New Frontier

This is a step beyond a lot of the current tools around summarization and quick case analysis. Systems will begin to offer AI as a form of real-time support and assistance—auto-flagging deadlines, drafting email responses while you're on client calls, or reporting inconsistencies during depositions. This will be a tool that responds with key insight or completes a task "just in time" while it seems most front of mind for the attorney to review.

Specialized Versus General Tools

Some AI features are designed for broad use (general drafting, task routing), while others are tailored to specific practice areas (medical chronology for personal injury, immigration notice parsing, deposition assistants for litigators, etc.). A firm should consider which tool fits the need and use case. Most firms will likely end up with a mix of both specialized and general AI tools.

Ethics, Security, and Auditability Come First

No matter how impressive the features, data security and ethical compliance remain essential. Especially as we enter a direction when certain tasks are set on auto-complete, proper logging will be very important, especially when tracking where a potential issue or error occurred. In short, every AI output should be reviewable. Even if a vendor claims to meet your security and compliance standards, your firm is still responsible for verifying this.

Pilot Before You Commit

Many of these tools are still new. Running a pilot—say, within one practice group for 90 days—lets you determine potential measures for ROI. Collecting metrics will also make it easier to generate buy-in across partners and staff.

Integration Matters More Than Features Alone

Flashy features are less useful if they don't fit seamlessly into your daily workflow. A CMS that connects AI capability into your existing processes rather than forcing additional steps or screens will be more likely to stick. When evaluating vendors, look closely at how their AI is woven into the tools your team is already using.

Final Consideration: Agents in CMS

In Chapter 15 we will discuss AI agents, sometimes also referred to as digital workers. In a near-future context, it is likely that an AI agent will be able to access the CMS, acting as a sort of digital employee, and perform tasks based on approval or some set parameters provided by a supervising attorney or team member.

CHAPTER 6

Fact Analysis and Case Strategy

Much of law school case analysis is about learning to "issue spot." As we begin practicing, we become increasingly more proficient at spotting issues as a client goes over their case during a consultation or as we read a contract that we have been sent to review. Not only does issue spotting become second nature, lawyers become experts at analyzing facts and determining their consequences, benefits, and risks. We hear facts spoken to us by clients, or written in discovery materials and contracts, and we just automatically start mapping out the timelines, characters, and places. The longer we practice in our specialty, we often can see the common fact pattern as it is coming and start processing an analysis we have worked through many times.

The purpose of this chapter is not to suggest that AI is going to replace the attorney's ability to spot issues, do fact analysis, or develop case strategy. We can clearly state from the outset that not only will it not replace the attorney's analysis, it will not even rival it. That does not mean, though, that it cannot be a helpful tool for attorneys to use as a part of their analysis and workflow. AI as a fact analysis and case strategy tool is exactly that: a tool in the toolbox for the practitioner to use along with their expertise and experience.

As will be discussed in more detail in Chapter 8 on summarization, AI can take large amounts of information and create summaries varying in length, style, and purpose. AI summarizations can be a great tool for an attorney going through the process of identifying and analyzing the facts of a case before applying the law and developing a case strategy. For example, if an attorney specializing in medical malpractice is given thousands of pages of patient notes, an AI tool could quickly go through the notes and create a summary of each of the patient's outcomes. Or maybe more importantly, it could go through the notes and create a chronological timeline of events of when the medical professional treated each patient and the treatment provided. In any case, these are major timesavers to get a start on analyzing a huge amount of facts in a new case.

Not only can AI tools create summarizations or timelines, they can actually be prompted to look for factual patterns that may help the attorney in his or her legal analysis. The attorney will always be the key in knowing what pattern in the facts needs to be pulled out, but the AI can assist in quickly scanning documents and helping start the discovery process. For example, a lawyer may use a generative AI prompt to dig through thousands of clients' documents like email and other communications to determine whether the facts support potential claims for sexual harassment, hostile work environment, and related legal violations. A sample prompt for this fact analysis would be:

PLAINTIFF-SIDE EMPLOYMENT HARASSMENT CLAIM ASSESSMENT

AI Role

You are an AI-powered litigation assistant for a plaintiff-side employment law firm. Your task is to evaluate client-provided information to determine whether the facts support potential claims for sexual harassment, hostile work environment, and related legal violations. You will analyze the facts in light of federal (e.g., Title VII) and applicable state antidiscrimination laws, and identify missing information that the attorney may need for full evaluation.

Instructions to the User

Please upload or describe the client intake narrative, including details about workplace conduct, any communications with supervisors or HR, and supporting documentation (e.g., messages, performance records, or witness names).

Follow-Up Questions (ask the user before generating output if not already answered)

- What is the client's job title and how long were they employed?
- What specific conduct was experienced (comments, messages, touching, etc.)?
- How often did the conduct occur, and over what time period?
- Was the conduct reported to anyone (HR, manager, hotline)? If so, what was the response?
- Has the client experienced any retaliation (discipline, demotion, termination)?
- What jurisdiction (state and city) did this occur in?

Output: Intake Analysis Summary

Potential legal claims:

- Identify any viable claims (e.g., sexual harassment, hostile work environment, retaliation).
- Specify whether claims arise under federal or state/local laws.

Factual basis and key evidence:

- Highlight conduct that meets the legal standard for "severe or pervasive."
- Note whether the employer knew or should have known about the conduct.
- Identify whether evidence exists (text messages, emails, witnesses, etc.).

Missing or ambiguous information:

- Flag key facts needed to strengthen or complete the claim (e.g., dates, witnesses, documentation).
- Note any timing concerns (statute of limitations).

Risk and strategy factors:

- Assess whether the employer took prompt and appropriate remedial action.
- Identify any red flags or defenses (e.g., Faragher/Ellerth affirmative defense).
- Recommend next steps (client interview follow up, demand drafting, EEOC filing, etc.).

Instructions to the AI (accuracy and hallucination control):

- Carefully review the uploaded or inputted material before generating your analysis.
- Do not make assumptions about facts or the law that are not supported by the uploaded content or confirmed user answers.
- Where legal analysis is required, draw only from actual statutory and case law patterns and cite the jurisdiction if known.
- If you are uncertain or lack enough information to form a conclusion, state that explicitly.
- Before presenting your final output, double-check your work for factual accuracy and internal consistency.

Not only can AI be used to find factual patterns, but it can also be used in the inverse to look for factual inconsistencies. By slightly adjusting the prompt, you could have the AI search for conflicting statements or inconsistent parties or dates. You could also present two separate versions of a contract or other document and prompt the AI to compare the two documents and make a list of the inconsistencies between the two, or where the two differ in timelines, or find a section that is included in one but not the other.

An interesting next step in the use of AI for fact analysis is seeing whether the AI can flag legal options or issues in the materials. For example, we upload the facts of a person's immigration history and ask the AI to determine what potential nonimmigrant work visa options are for the foreign national based on their nationality and the facts included about them, their employer, and their position with the company. This is a clear example of where the attorney should be setting the prompt as the expert, and know what they are looking for but also act as a "human in the loop" to review the output. With a task like this, the lawyer should challenge the output. In this example, we would be thinking that is a good list of options, but surely the AI missed some, so what else can we come up with as the expert? Nonetheless, it can be a great starting point in the fact analysis.

If you are using a legal-specific AI tool and you trust its library, then you could also push it farther and look for jurisdictional context for the matter. This should not be done using a general AI tool like ChatGPT, as it is going to most likely hallucinate this kind of information, but a good legal-specific AI tool with the right jurisdictional materials in its library should be able to take a first crack at this. You could prompt the AI to look for issues in the uploaded materials that arise under New York landlord-tenant law, for example. Depending on your tech stack, you may also feed this through one AI tool and then feed the results through a second AI tool to see where they differ.

With a good legal product, though, you could easily pivot from fact analysis to research by asking the AI to find decisions with similar fact patterns—again, not an exercise for a general AI product. This should be left to a system like a retrieval-augmented chatbot connected to a trusted legal library, so it is using the power of a Large Language Model but only searching the dataset of relevant primary and secondary law. Ultimately, the dataset being searched and the prompt being used are going to determine the strength of the results. You may start off by having the documents reviewed and flagged for product liability issues. Then with a good legal library, you should be able to specify in the prompt that you only want those product liability issues compared to results of cases in California with similar facts, for example. Even with good legal-specific AI tools, this type of deeper analysis requires a conservative approach and an in-depth analysis by the human attorney. AI tools are still likely to mix up jurisdictional discrepancies and other fine details that can be missed in the statistical word analysis that is generative AI.

Part of what makes a good lawyer is knowing what questions to ask. It is the same with a lawyer who is good at using AI. It is a matter of the lawyer asking the right questions in the prompt and giving the AI the right task, in fact-finding based on the product, and the dataset it is searching. Prompt one may be asking for a summary. Prompt two may be asking for the summary to be flagged for certain facts of issues. Prompt three may be to have the flagged items compared to similar cases in the same jurisdiction. Prompt four may be to go back to one of the previous outputs and ask for the opposite, like what questions remain unanswered or what terms are undefined.

The more familiar the lawyer gets with generative AI and the system they are using, the more comfortable they will become going back to the well in the same chat or thread. A lot of people approach ChatGPT, ask it a question, and that is it; or they wait for the newer generative AI products to return with a question like, "Do you want me to deliver this in a spreadsheet format (bios, CV links, sample testimony cites, availability) plus a short outreach email you can send?" Getting more comfortable with a conversational, back-and-forth use is an indicator of greater proficiency with AI, and you should even be challenging the outputs and pushing what you think the AI can deliver in terms of fact-finding results. As a diligent and ethical lawyer, you are only going to use these results as a tool in your overall work product, and not as an absolute truth or finished product, so there should not be harm in trying to get deeper results from working with AI as a colleague in this process.

We do not want to drift too far down the stream of treating AI like another person or anything like that. Generative AI is a mathematical tool. When you put in a prompt or a question, it is just math happening with a Large Language Model and then a statistical guessing of the words that would make the closest result. But using AI can be conversational, and you can use it to ask questions or challenge your own questions to develop strategy—not in place of working with your colleagues, but in addition to that. We can use this sort of practice of summarization, fact finding, and even pivoting to legal research for relevant findings. One step further would be brainstorming and developing case strategy with the AI and the (hopefully) trustworthy and voluminous dataset.

When we brainstorm with others, a lot of the ideas that come up are often flawed and will not make it to the final rounds of what will be our case strategy. But the exercise of talking through the hypotheticals and the different strategies is often extremely valuable. Determining why something is a weak argument can be as valuable as determining what is the best argument. It is important to challenge ideas and have your ideas challenged when working on strategy. It is the same when using AI for this purpose. We are not having a conversation with AI at this point for definitive truths, but instead for help in the brainstorming and strategizing process. Just as a colleague may highlight a strength or a weakness, the AI may do the same. A colleague or client may find a part of the case quite weak, but with your experience, you know that it is actually not a big issue and is quite common.

Case strategizing with generative AI can be done in different ways. For example, you can upload volumes of materials and in the fact-finding prompts also look for strengths and weaknesses. Or, you could first use AI for your fact finding and then start prompting for brainstorming. Let's look at an example of a case strategy prompt for an intellectual property case. This prompt is created to review patent infringement disputes and generate a summary of claim construction issues, infringement theories, and invalidity defenses, along with a strategic checklist for discovery, expert retention, and litigation tactics:

PATENT INFRINGEMENT LITIGATION CASE ASSESSMENT

You are a legal assistant trained in patent infringement litigation. Your task is to analyze a patent infringement dispute—whether representing the patent holder or accused infringer—and summarize the key claim construction, infringement, and invalidity issues that will determine case outcome. You will also generate a checklist of next steps for discovery, expert retention, claim construction briefing, and trial preparation.

The user may upload:

- Patent-in-suit documents, claims, and prosecution history
- Accused products, technical specifications, or design documents
- Prior art references, patents, or publications
- Infringement contentions or invalidity contentions
- Expert reports on infringement, invalidity, or damages
- Claim construction briefs or Markman hearing transcripts
- Discovery responses, depositions, or technical documents
- Licensing agreements or damages calculations
- Court orders, claim construction rulings, or summary judgment motions
- Appeal briefs or Federal Circuit decisions

You must:

- Thoroughly review all uploaded materials before drafting the analysis
- Reference only the technical facts explicitly documented in the case materials—do not assume claim interpretations or invent technical features
- Ask one clarifying question at a time if the patent scope or infringement theory is unclear (e.g., "Are you representing the patent holder or accused infringer?" or "Has claim construction already occurred?")

Patent Litigation Analysis Output Format

I. Case Overview

Patent number, title, and key claim elements at issue

Accused products or processes and alleged infringement theory

Parties involved and current litigation posture

Court jurisdiction and assigned judge

Key deadlines for claim construction, expert discovery, and trial

II. Claim Construction Issues

Disputed Claim Terms: [e.g., indefinite terms, means-plus-function elements, claim scope disputes]

Intrinsic Evidence: [e.g., specification support, prosecution history estoppel, claim differentiation]

Extrinsic Evidence: [e.g., expert testimony, dictionary definitions, inventor testimony]

Markman Strategy: [e.g., narrow vs. broad construction arguments, prosecution history implications]

I. Infringement Analysis

Literal Infringement: [e.g., element-by-element comparison, all elements rule satisfaction]

Doctrine of Equivalents: [e.g., function-way-result test, substantial differences, prior art limitations]

Indirect Infringement: [e.g., contributory infringement, inducement theories, knowledge requirements]

Design Around Options: [e.g., alternative implementations, noninfringing substitutes]

III. Invalidity Defense Strategy

Prior Art Challenges: [e.g., anticipation by single reference, obviousness combinations, printed publications]

Written Description/Enablement: [e.g., adequate disclosure, undue experimentation, claim scope support]

Indefiniteness: [e.g., unclear claim terms, functional claiming without structure]

Prosecution History: [e.g., inequitable conduct, failure to disclose material prior art]

IV. Discovery and Expert Strategy

Retain technical experts for claim construction and infringement opinions

Conduct prior art search with focus on invalidating references

Obtain accused product samples and reverse engineering analysis

Depose inventors and prosecution counsel on claim scope and prosecution decisions

Calculate damages using reasonable royalty or lost profits methodologies

Prepare demonstrative evidence for Markman hearing and trial presentation

Coordinate with foreign patent litigation if applicable

Evaluate settlement leverage based on claim construction prospects

General Principles for Creating Your Output

- Use uploaded documents only after thorough review
- Do not invent or speculate about technical features, prior art, or claim interpretations
- Do not use language like "typical patent cases" or hypothetical scenarios
- Focus on objective identification of documented technical and legal issues
- Do not draft claim construction briefs or expert reports unless explicitly requested

Response Quality Protocol

Verify information:

- Confirm each technical argument is supported by specification or prior art evidence
- Double-check patent law requirements for infringement and invalidity standards

Final review:

- Ensure the summary realistically assesses litigation strength and settlement value
- Flag critical deadlines for claim construction and expert disclosure

End objective:

Deliver a patent litigation analysis and strategic checklist that helps IP attorneys quickly assess case merits and formulate an action plan for claim construction, discovery, expert retention, and trial preparation.

Feedback prompt:

Ask if the user would like help drafting claim construction briefs, expert witness strategy, or invalidity arguments to address the patent infringement issues.

You will have noticed that this prompt starts by assigning summarization tasks like "summarize the key claim construction, infringement, and invalidity issues that will determine case outcome."

The prompt goes on to assign fact-finding prompts, such as: "Reference only the technical facts explicitly documented in the case materials—do not assume claim interpretations or invent technical features."

The prompt then layers in levels of legal research throughout the "Patent Litigation Analysis Output Format" section, with prompts such as: "Double-check patent law requirements for infringement and invalidity standards."

But importantly, it continues to a strategy section, stating its end objective is to: "Deliver a patent litigation analysis and strategic checklist that helps IP attorneys quickly assess case merits and formulate an action plan for claim construction, discovery, expert retention, and trial preparation."

In this example prompt, we walk through the full potential of uploading lots of materials and trying to summarize them, but then take it a step further and try to get important facts, then do legal research using those facts, and finally help brainstorm a strategy for the case with some helpful materials like a checklist. This prompt could be amended in a million ways, and the results could become a back and forth with a (hopefully) legal-specific AI where you are asking whether certain things could be highlighted or avoided, or challenging whether you believe certain facts or conclusions are correct. Also, if it is a RAG system with a trusted legal library, then you should be automatically receiving legal citations along the way, or be able to ask for them in the chat, depending on the system. A good legal-specific AI tool would be citing back to the documents you uploaded and to any primary or secondary materials it used to generate its output. Of course, it is on the lawyer to then review.

As with most discussion of AI, the optimistic sections on use cases and opportunities must be followed by a section on pitfalls and concerns. So, the most likely issues with using AI for fact finding and case strategy is that the AI will either miss important facts or hallucinate facts that were never there. Not surprising, and not minor. This is why we stress that this use of AI is a tool in the toolbox. This is not the only way the facts of the case should be studied—the materials still need to be read, the client needs to be heard, questions need to be asked, discovery needs to take place. This is just an additional tool in the fact-finding process. It is a tool that can be done very quickly because of the power of AI, perhaps while the other more human-powered steps are taking place. The speed does not mean that you get to skip the other steps—but it means that the return on the investment of your time could be quite high. Everything being read in the output should be read through the lens of "I need to confirm where that fact came from and that it is accurate." No fact found should just be assumed to be correct—just as if you were working with a colleague who was telling you some of his or her preliminary thoughts after a first read of client materials. You would not hold your colleague's first pass as absolute truth, and neither should you do so with the output of your AI tool. Where did the information come from? Why is it in this order? Can it be interpreted differently? Be suspicious and challenge the results. Good lawyers ask good questions.

Just as with fact-finding prompts, using AI for strategizing is just like adding one more colleague to the team. It is not intended to replace a process or a person; it is intended to be additive. It is not uncommon in strategy for a less-experienced attorney to suggest an idea that seems so good it cannot possibly be that easy—only for a more experienced attorney to explain why it unfortunately cannot be done that way. AI may do the same thing, and you will be the experienced attorney that knows it is not that simple, or it cannot be done that way.

One of us manages several teams that work on different case types and has weekly recurring case reviews with each team he manages. The team talks daily, but they have those dedicated weekly meetings for each case and team. An AI strategy analysis might be a good tool to use on Monday before diving into materials that are going to be discussed with the team working on that case before the team meets on Thursday. It is never going to replace the Thursday meeting, but it could get the wheels turning to prepare for that meeting later in the week—and maybe an interesting theory to start exploring will be found.

Lastly, the biggest ethical concerns with these practices lie in the systems you are using and your reliance on the AI's output. As discussed in the preceding chapters, do not trust the AI's output as any sort of absolute truth. It is just an idea in a brainstorming session. Be skeptical and challenge the outputs, especially when they seem too good to be true. As far as the systems are concerned, this type of summarization, fact analysis, and case strategizing should really only be done in a legal-specific AI tool that you can trust with your client's information.

First of all, you should never be uploading your client's information or materials to a general AI product. You can only trust those materials to legal-specific products that are not training AI models using your data, and are not retaining your client's confidential information. These ideas are explored further in Chapter 16 on ethics and security. Secondly, you should not be asking legal research questions like the ones discussed earlier unless you are using a legal-specific AI tool with a legal dataset you rely on. If you ask legal research questions to general AI products, you will get hallucinated case results. The AI will tell you what you want to hear. If you ask for products liability cases in California with similar facts—well, it will create some for you before it gives you nothing. With a legal-specific system, like a RAG system using a curated legal research library, you can at least have a chance of getting good results. That does not mean the AI is going to do a perfect job, it does not mean it is going to find all the cases, or anything like that. But a legal-specific system is less likely to hallucinate case law and make up legal research conclusions. You should only feed your client's data into a system you can trust, and you should only ask legal questions to a legal library you can trust. And even when you are doing both of those things, you should still be wearing your brainstorming hat and peering through your skeptical lawyer glasses.

■ CHAPTER 7

AI Tools for Litigators

Litigation is a natural fit for generative AI. From early case assessment to discovery, motion practice, and trial preparation, AI is reshaping how litigators build, manage, and present their cases. This chapter offers a practical overview of how AI can support each stage of the litigation lifecycle, and assumes the reader is familiar with the prompt-writing and research concepts introduced in Chapters 2 and 3.

7.1 Early Case Assessment

The earliest stages of litigation are among the most critical. Lawyers must evaluate the strength of a potential case, understand the client's goals, identify viable claims or defenses, and anticipate procedural hurdles—often with incomplete or evolving facts. Generative AI supports this work by helping litigators quickly organize and interpret the initial flood of client narratives, documents, and communications that accompany a new matter.

AI-assisted intake is often the first point where these efficiencies appear. When a client provides a narrative—whether through a phone call, an online form, or a written statement—AI systems can synthesize the information almost instantly. It generates preliminary summaries, extracts key events, identifies the individuals involved, and assembles those elements into timelines that help lawyers visualize the sequence of events. When the narrative lacks critical details, the AI can flag omissions and suggest follow-up questions for the legal team. Increasingly, voice-enabled tools can also conduct intake conversations in the client's preferred language and convert the transcript into a structured summary or intake memo. Caseflood.ai is one example of a product in this category.

Once the initial facts are gathered, AI can help identify what legal issues the case might involve. By reviewing the complaint, a client's narrative, or early documents, AI can map the facts against potential causes of action or defenses and flag legal theories that may be implicated by the allegations. It does not determine whether a claim is viable; that judgment belongs exclusively to the lawyer. But AI helps create an early, structured framework by identifying the elements of common claims and pointing out where the facts provided so far appear to align—or fall short. This structured analysis gives litigators a clearer foundation from which to conduct more detailed case evaluations.

Another important dimension of early case assessment involves how a case is likely to progress based on factors such as the judge, venue, and type of claim. Generative AI does not replace dedicated analytics platforms, but it can help interpret and operationalize their data. Litigation analytics tools like Docket Alarm and Lex Machina provide statistics on motion outcomes, timelines, and judicial tendencies; AI can summarize those patterns, relate them to the facts of a particular case, and surface questions for the lawyer to consider in early strategy discussions.

AI can also assist in organizing the initial case materials in ways that facilitate early strategy development. When a lawyer uploads documents such as contracts, emails, medical records, or correspondence, AI can produce an overview of the factual landscape, identify potential inconsistencies, and highlight areas that require further documentation. It can also detect references to witnesses or additional sources of evidence that have not yet been gathered, allowing the trial team to focus early discovery efforts more effectively.

Even at this early stage, the lawyer's judgment remains central. AI does not make litigation decisions or provide legal advice. Instead, it accelerates the process of understanding the facts, surfacing potential issues, and identifying gaps in the record. Used in this way—consistent with the "human-in-the-loop" guardrails discussed in Chapter 18—AI enables litigators to conduct more thoughtful initial consultations, manage client expectations, and shape early strategy with greater clarity.

In this way, AI transforms early case assessment from a largely manual, time-consuming process into a more structured and strategic exercise. Lawyers reach a deeper understanding of a new matter more quickly, allowing them to focus on evaluating risks, advising clients, and planning the next steps in the litigation.

PRACTICE EXAMPLE: USING AI FOR INTAKE AND EARLY SCREENING IN A PERSONAL INJURY CASE

A small plaintiffs' firm receives a new motor vehicle accident inquiry through its online intake form. Instead of manually reviewing the narrative and attachments, the intake coordinator uploads the client's description, police report, and photos into an AI workspace. The system generates:

- A one-page factual summary and a timeline of key events.

- A list of potentially relevant claims (negligence, negligent entrustment, negligent hiring) with the elements of each claim.
- Follow-up questions to clarify issues such as comparative fault, prior accidents, and insurance coverage.

The attorney reviews the summary, confirms which theories plausibly apply, and adjusts the follow-up questions before the first consultation. By the time the client walks in the door, the lawyer has a clearer picture of the case posture and can give more realistic expectations about liability and damages.

7.2 Drafting Motions and Filings

Drafting motions and other court filings has long been one of the most time-consuming obligations in litigation. Lawyers not only need to craft persuasive legal arguments, but also must assemble complex factual narratives, comply with detailed formatting rules, and maintain a consistent style across multiple documents and case teams. Generative AI has begun to shift the drafting process from one centered on manual composition to one centered on strategic editing and analysis.

One of the most significant advantages AI offers is its ability to produce a coherent first draft from the materials a lawyer provides. Instead of starting from scratch, litigators can upload a complaint, an answer, relevant exhibits, deposition excerpts, or prior motions and ask AI to produce a structured motion to dismiss, a summary judgment brief, a discovery motion, or another filing tailored to the case. The resulting draft typically includes the expected components—introduction, background, legal standard, argument, and conclusion—and reflects the factual and procedural posture of the case as presented in the uploaded materials. This initial draft becomes a springboard for the lawyer's deeper strategic thinking.

AI also enhances the refinement stage of drafting. Once the first draft is generated, lawyers can prompt the system to adjust tone, reorganize arguments, sharpen reasoning, or clarify ambiguous sections. If a particular point needs to be elevated or reframed, AI can generate several alternate phrasings or reorganize an argument to improve its logical flow. When the factual record is provided, AI can help integrate those details more seamlessly into the brief, ensuring the motion's narrative is anchored in the evidence and aligned with the case theory. This iterative process enables lawyers to move rapidly from a rough draft to a polished, persuasive filing.

Another benefit of AI-assisted drafting is the consistency it brings to litigation teams. Firms often maintain preferred phrasing, stylistic conventions, and standard argument structures that reflect their institutional approach to motion practice. By embedding these preferences into internal AI systems, firms can ensure that drafts—whether prepared by junior associates or senior partners—adhere to the same style and structural expectations. This improves quality, reduces revision time, and helps preserve institutional knowledge that might otherwise be dispersed across individuals.

AI is useful not only in drafting the content of motions, but also in identifying areas where the document could be strengthened. For example, as the system analyzes a draft, it may flag factual assertions that lack support in the materials provided, logical leaps that could weaken the argument, or inconsistencies between sections. While the lawyer must always make the final judgments, AI's ability to highlight structural or conceptual weaknesses early in the process enhances the quality and coherence of the final filing.

General purpose AI assistants like Claude and ChatGPT have become remarkably adept at formatting litigation documents to comply with specific court requirements. The workflow is straightforward: draft your brief, motion, or pleading using whatever tool you prefer—a legal-specific platform, a traditional word processor, or even another AI tool—and then hand the finished draft to an assistant like Claude Cowork to conform it to the relevant rules. You can point it at a court's local rules, a judge's standing order, or simply provide an exemplar document, and ask the AI to match the formatting. Tasks that once consumed a paralegal's afternoon—adjusting margins and line spacing, fixing caption blocks, renumbering paragraphs, conforming citation style, building tables of authorities, applying the right font and pagination—can now be handled in minutes. The lesson for litigators is that drafting and formatting are increasingly separable activities, and treating them as distinct steps in your workflow lets you use the best tool for each.

Despite these advantages, AI is not a substitute for legal judgment. Lawyers must still ensure that the arguments presented are legally sound, factually accurate, and strategically appropriate. AI-generated drafts must be reviewed to confirm compliance with local rules, page limits, and judge-specific preferences. And because AI cannot interpret nuance, evaluate risk, or anticipate judicial reactions, the attorney role in shaping and refining the motion remains essential. In short, AI is merely an aid and a lawyer must actively manage its output.

When used thoughtfully, generative AI transforms the drafting process into one that is faster, more structured, and more aligned with the demands of modern litigation. Rather than spending hours assembling text, litigators can devote more time to assessing case strategy, analyzing the strengths and weaknesses of their arguments, and preparing the most effective filing possible.

7.3 Discovery and Document Review

Discovery is frequently the most labor-intensive stage of litigation. Large document productions, extensive deposition transcripts, and complex factual records traditionally require many hours of lawyer and staff time to organize and interpret. Generative AI now plays a significant role in reducing that burden. While AI does not replace the lawyer's judgment in interpreting evidence or making strategic decisions, it dramatically accelerates the process of understanding what the record contains, where the weaknesses lie, and how best to prepare for upcoming motions or testimony.

One of the clearest examples of this transformation is deposition transcript review. Rather than reading hundreds of pages line by line, litigators can now upload a transcript and receive a summary that highlights the most important testimony. AI can identify themes that emerge across the deposition, pull out key admissions, and flag contradictions between what a witness said in this session and what they have said earlier in the case. It can extract names, dates, and events and assemble them into a working timeline, enabling lawyers to see how the testimony fits into the broader narrative. If gaps or ambiguities appear—for example, a witness offering unclear answers on critical topics—the AI can point these out and suggest areas for follow-up questioning.

Document productions, especially in cases involving extensive electronically stored information, are another area where AI offers meaningful efficiency gains. Instead of slogging through long email chains or large batches of messages, a lawyer can use AI to summarize communications, identify the principal actors, and extract recurring themes in the correspondence. AI can cluster documents into topic areas, highlight outlier communications that deviate from established patterns, and detect inconsistencies or shifts in tone that may merit further investigation. When custodians' records contain gaps—missing attachments, inconsistent metadata, or suspiciously quiet periods—AI can bring these issues to the lawyer's attention far earlier than manual review might allow.

One of the most meaningful advances in this area is AI's ability to help generate targeted discovery questions. Effective discovery depends on identifying what information is missing or unclear, and AI is particularly good at doing just that. By analyzing the complaint, answer, deposition testimony, and early document productions, AI can highlight gaps in the factual record and propose interrogatories or requests for production designed to close those gaps. If a complaint references a series of decisions but the documents produced so far reveal only fragments of the decision-making process, AI may recommend targeted questions about who participated, what records were kept, or whether drafts or internal communications exist. When deposition summaries show evasive or incomplete answers, AI can propose interrogatories that press for specificity. If the record contains contradictory statements, AI may suggest requests for admission that force the opposing party to commit to a clear position. In this way, AI becomes a strategic aid in shaping a more precise and effective discovery plan.

AI's ability to pull facts out of unstructured documents and assemble them into usable narratives is one of its most powerful contributions to modern discovery practice. Emails, memos, texts, medical records, financial materials, and photographs can be converted into chronological timelines or thematic summaries that give litigators an early understanding of the case's structure. These tools are especially valuable in complex matters, where the volume of documents can obscure the central story. By helping lawyers see how events unfolded—and where the documentary record is thin—AI provides a clearer foundation for deposition preparation, motion practice, and trial planning.

AI also supports the drafting and management of the discovery process itself. When a lawyer uploads a complaint, answer, or case timeline, the system can suggest targeted interrogatories, document requests, and deposition topics tied to the elements in dispute. On the response side, AI can help organize the factual record by issue or request, making it easier to draft detailed objections and substantive answers. When the opposing party's responses are incomplete, AI can highlight the gaps between what was requested and what was produced, and assist in drafting meet-and-confer letters that clearly identify those deficiencies.

AI also contributes to quality control. It can cross-check whether documents referenced in correspondence or testimony actually appear in the production, flag inconsistencies in dates or authorship metadata, and surface references to attachments that appear to be missing. These functions do not replace a lawyer's review, but they provide a backstop that reduces the risk that important details will be overlooked.

In all of these areas, the lawyer remains responsible for accuracy, judgment, and strategy. But generative AI dramatically reduces the amount of time required to reach a deep understanding of the evidentiary record, allowing litigators to focus more on analysis and advocacy and less on manual, time-consuming review.

PRACTICE EXAMPLE: AI-ASSISTED DISCOVERY PLAN IN AN EMPLOYMENT CASE

In a wage-and-hour class action, defense counsel uploads the complaint, answer, and a preliminary case timeline to an AI tool connected to the firm's DMS. The system:

- Groups allegations by legal issue (overtime calculation, off-the-clock work, meal and rest breaks).
- Suggests initial interrogatories and RFPs tailored to each issue.
- Flags missing categories of evidence (e.g., scheduling records, GPS logs, policy manuals).
- Generates a draft discovery plan organized by topic, with suggested sequencing of requests.

The litigation team edits the plan, removes overbroad requests, and layers on jurisdiction-specific requirements before serving formal discovery.

7.4 Deposition Preparation and Cross-Examination Planning

Depositions are a critical stage of litigation and have always required meticulous review of documents, prior statements, and the evolving factual record. Generative AI now helps litigators approach this work with greater structure and efficiency. While AI cannot replace the lawyer's instinct, tone, or judgment, it can identify themes, surface inconsistencies, and help organize lines of questioning in a coherent, issue-focused way.

One of the first benefits AI brings to deposition preparation is its ability to synthesize the record quickly. When a lawyer uploads key documents—emails, text messages, contracts, medical or financial records, prior testimony, or written discovery—AI can identify the recurring themes and relationships that might shape the deposition. It becomes much easier to see how a particular witness fits into the overall timeline, what topics are likely to be most fruitful, and where gaps in the record may require deeper questioning. AI can also surface issues that might not stand out during a manual review, such as ambiguous statements, references to unexplored events, or contextual clues that warrant further exploration.

AI is also highly effective in assisting with the creation of deposition outlines. Instead of drafting an outline entirely by hand, lawyers can ask AI to propose a structure based on the case theory, the witness's role, and the documents already associated with that witness. The system can group topics in a logical order, suggest transitions between subjects, and recommend follow-up questions for areas where the record is unclear or contradictory. When multiple witnesses are involved, AI can help ensure that the outlines complement one another, preventing duplication and ensuring the full story is developed across the deposition sequence.

Another valuable function is AI's ability to identify impeachment opportunities. By comparing a witness's prior testimony, written communications, and documented statements, AI can highlight inconsistencies that may be useful during cross-examination. For example, if a witness gave a confident answer in an interrogatory but offered a tentative or evasive statement during a later communication, AI can flag that discrepancy and place the statements side by side. This gives litigators a clearer picture of where the witness may be vulnerable and provides a foundation for crafting a targeted, fact-driven line of questioning.

AI is similarly useful when preparing for cross-examination at trial. Cross-examination requires careful control, thematic clarity, and precise use of the record. AI can help by assembling a streamlined account of the witness's prior statements and mapping them against the elements of the claims or defenses. It can summarize the points that must be established, identify where the witness has locked into an unfavorable position, and highlight opportunities to elicit concessions that support the overall theory of the case. By organizing the factual record in this way, AI enables the lawyer to spend more time shaping strategy and tone rather than gathering raw material.

As depositions conclude, AI can assist in evaluating how the testimony affects the broader case. It can generate summaries of what was established, identify issues that remain unclear, and suggest next steps such as follow-up discovery requests, supplemental disclosures, or motions. This kind of post-deposition synthesis helps litigation teams maintain continuity, especially in complex matters with multiple witnesses and large volumes of information.

Throughout the deposition preparation and cross-examination process, the lawyer remains responsible for judgment, advocacy, and ethical considerations. While AI does not understand nuance, credibility, or the strategic subtleties that shape effective questioning, when paired with a litigator's expertise, AI significantly reduces the time required to prepare, helps reveal insights that may otherwise be missed, and supports a more organized and strategic approach to one of litigation's most critical tasks.

PRACTICE EXAMPLE: PREPARING A KEY WITNESS DEPOSITION WITH AI

In a commercial dispute, plaintiff's counsel is preparing to depose the defendant's CFO. The team uploads prior 30(b)(6) testimony, key emails, financial statements, and written discovery responses into an AI tool. The tool:

- Summarizes the CFO's apparent role in the disputed transactions.
- Highlights inconsistencies between the CFO's emails and the company's interrogatory responses.
- Proposes a draft outline organized by themes (knowledge of pricing changes, internal approvals, communications with customers).
- Suggests targeted impeachment questions where emails and responses do not align.

Counsel then revises the outline, adds jurisdiction-specific foundation questions, and adjusts tone to match counsel's style before the deposition.

7.5 Trial Preparation and Exhibit Management

Trial preparation is one of the phases of litigation most profoundly affected by generative AI. By the time a case reaches trial, litigators must integrate years of documents, testimony, motions, and strategy decisions into a coherent narrative. They must also prepare witness examinations, refine themes, finalize demonstratives, and ensure that exhibits are organized and admissible.

One of the most meaningful contributions AI provides is helping lawyers shape the overall trial narrative. By reviewing deposition transcripts, key documents, summary judgment records, and prior pleadings, AI can synthesize the major themes of the case and articulate how each piece of evidence fits within them. This helps lawyers see the structure of the case at a glance—what facts matter most, where the weaknesses lie, and which points may resonate with the judge or jury. AI can draft preliminary outlines for opening statements or closing arguments or generate alternative formulations of themes that the trial team can refine. Rather than creating these drafts from scratch, lawyers can focus on evaluating tone, framing, and strategy.

AI also helps organize the vast amount of material that will be used at trial. When provided with the key documents in the case, AI can generate lists of the most significant exhibits, identify which witnesses are associated with those exhibits, and propose foundational questions for admission. It can also pinpoint where additional supporting documents may be needed or highlight inconsistencies between exhibits that may require further explanation. Because exhibit management often becomes chaotic in the final weeks before trial, AI's ability to create coherent, organized exhibit lists provides meaningful structure at a time when clarity is at a premium.

In addition to managing exhibits, AI is adept at creating or assisting with demonstratives. Whether a timeline, an organizational chart, a sequence of events, or a visual summary of complex financial or medical records, AI tools can help develop drafts of courtroom graphics that convey information clearly. These drafts must be reviewed carefully for accuracy and admissibility, but they give trial teams a head start on materials that can often take hours to design.

AI also plays an important role in preparing witness examinations using similar techniques to those discussed previously for cross-examinations. As the trial approaches, lawyers can upload all prior statements by a witness—depositions, written discovery responses, emails, reports—and ask AI to produce a streamlined outline highlighting the points that must be established or undermined. AI can link specific testimony or documents to the elements of the claims or defenses and surface opportunities for impeachment or concession. For redirect preparation, AI can identify predictable attack points raised during cross-examination and help lawyers craft a measured response.

As a case approaches trial, AI can help the litigation team maintain a clear, up-to-date view of the record. It can generate summaries of key issues, create daily trial preparation briefs, identify outstanding tasks, and flag inconsistencies or loose ends that should be resolved before the first witness takes the stand. In complex matters, AI can also assist with coordinating witness order and exhibit use, helping lawyers visualize how the sequence of proof may affect the persuasiveness of the case.

As with every stage of litigation, the lawyer remains responsible for strategic judgment, narrative choices, and evidentiary decisions. AI is not a replacement for the intuition and experience required to try a case effectively. Instead, it functions as a force multiplier—helping lawyers organize vast amounts of information quickly, highlight important details, and devote more time to the advocacy and courtroom preparation that cannot be automated.

PRACTICE EXAMPLE: COORDINATING EXHIBITS AND WITNESSES FOR TRIAL

In a multiweek construction defect trial, the trial team uses AI to manage exhibit and witness sequencing. The team uploads the pretrial order, exhibit list, and key deposition transcripts. The system:

- Groups exhibits by issue and by witness.
- Generates a proposed witness order based on the story the team wants to tell and flags where a single exhibit will be used with multiple witnesses.
- Produces daily "trial prep briefs" summarizing what was covered the prior day, what exhibits were admitted, and what issues remain to be proved.
- Highlights any outstanding foundational or authenticity issues for exhibits scheduled in the next 48 hours.

The lead trial lawyer uses these briefs during evening prep, making adjustments based on courtroom dynamics and rulings.

7.6 Litigation Strategy Development

Strategic decision making is at the heart of litigation, and generative AI now plays a supporting role in that work. AI does not replace experience or professional judgment, but it can help litigators grasp the case more quickly, explore alternative theories, and pressure-test potential approaches before committing to a strategy. These tools complement, rather than substitute for, the case analysis techniques discussed in Chapter 6 ("Fact Analysis and Case Strategy").

One of AI's most useful contributions is its ability to synthesize complex records. When pleadings, deposition transcripts, expert reports, and key documents are uploaded, AI can produce high-level summaries that distill the central disputes and highlight where the evidence is strongest or weakest. This allows lawyers to see the case holistically and prioritize the issues that matter most.

AI also assists with brainstorming alternative theories of liability or defense. By analyzing the factual narrative and the governing law supplied by the user, AI can suggest different ways to frame events, emphasize certain actors or decisions, or challenge the coherence of the opposing side's story. These ideas serve as starting points that lawyers can refine, discard, or integrate into the broader case theory.

Theme development is another area where AI proves valuable. By reviewing key events, timelines, and testimony, AI can propose narratives, analogies, or conceptual frames that may resonate with a judge or jury. These early drafts help litigators shape the language and messaging that will carry through opening statements, motions, and witness examinations.

Finally, AI can help identify vulnerabilities in the case by comparing the factual record to the elements of the claims or defenses. It can flag contradictions, evidentiary gaps, or unclear portions of the narrative and suggest follow-up discovery or targeted lines of examination to address them. This early insight allows lawyers to strengthen their strategy and avoid surprises later.

Even with these efficiencies, strategy remains a human endeavor. AI helps organize information, surface patterns, and accelerate the analytic work, but decisions about tone, risk, credibility, and persuasion rest squarely with the lawyer. Used in this way, AI becomes a powerful tool for sharpening strategy rather than substituting for judgment.

PRACTICE EXAMPLE: STRESS TESTING CASE THEMES BEFORE MEDIATION

Before a mediation in a products liability case, defense counsel uploads the pleadings, key expert reports, and a high-level damages analysis to an AI workspace. The system is instructed to:

- Summarize the plaintiff's core narrative and identify the strongest facts for each side.
- Generate three alternative defense themes (e.g., misuse, comparative fault, intervening cause) and match each to supporting and weak evidence.
- Propose questions the mediator is likely to ask about liability, causation, and damages.
- Flag evidentiary gaps that could undermine any of the themes at trial.

The team reviews the output, discards oversimplistic themes, and refines one or two that align with counsel's judgment and client goals. The refined themes drive both the mediation statement and talking points for the session.

PROMPT: DRAFTING A MOTION TO DISMISS (WITH OPTIONAL SAMPLE MOTION UPLOAD)

AI's Role

You are a litigation drafting assistant. Your task is to create a well-structured, jurisdiction-appropriate first draft of a motion to dismiss based on the facts and documents provided. You will not invent facts or legal authority. Use only the materials supplied by the user and request clarification where necessary. When a sample motion is provided, you will mirror its structure, formatting style, and tone.

What the User Provides (one at a time)

1. The operative complaint (uploaded as a file or pasted text)
2. The court and jurisdiction
3. The procedural posture (e.g., original complaint, amended complaint)

4. The specific grounds for dismissal (Rule 12(b)(6), lack of jurisdiction, limitations, standing, etc.)
5. Any key exhibits, contracts, or prior filings the AI should review
6. **A sample motion or prior filing the AI should use as a style and structure model**
7. Any judge-specific or firm-specific formatting requirements

Ask One Question at a Time

Before drafting, the AI should ask targeted follow-up questions, including:

- Should the draft follow the structure and tone of the sample motion you uploaded?
- Are there specific claims or counts you want to target for dismissal?
  Should the motion include a factual background section or rely solely on the allegations?
- Do you want the AI to draft both a full-length and a concise version?
- Are there any mandatory local rule components (page limits, certificates, formatting)?
- What tone should the motion take (neutral, assertive, formal, etc.)?

AI Drafting Instructions

When drafting the motion:

1. **Follow the structure and formatting of the uploaded sample motion** when one is provided.
2. Include standard sections such as:
   - Introduction
   - Background or Procedural History
   - Legal Standard
   - Argument (claim by claim or issue by issue)
   - Conclusion
3. Cite only verified rules, statutes, and widely accepted doctrinal principles—no invented case law.
4. Use the factual record exactly as provided, without adding assumptions.
5. Flag ambiguities, missing facts, or weak legal support; do not fill gaps.
6. Ensure the reasoning is internally consistent and tied to the asserted grounds for dismissal.
7. Offer alternative versions if requested (e.g., streamlined, detailed, or sample-based).

Model Prompt (user-facing example)

"Draft a Rule 12(b)(6) motion to dismiss using the attached complaint and exhibits. This matter is pending in the U.S. District Court for the Northern District of Illinois. Please target Counts II and III on the grounds that the complaint fails to state a claim and that these counts are time-barred.

We have also uploaded a prior motion to dismiss filed by our firm. Please mirror the structure, formatting, headings, tone, and overall style of that sample motion. Use only the facts in the complaint and exhibits. Do not invent legal authority; rely solely on established Rule 12(b)(6) standards and general principles governing limitations defenses.

Before drafting, ask me any clarifying questions needed to ensure accuracy."

Optional Add-Ons

You may instruct the AI to also generate:

- A version designed to be redlined easily
- A list of weaknesses in the complaint for use in meet-and-confer communications
- Suggested exhibits for judicial notice
- A shorter motion tailored for state court page limits

PROMPT: LITIGATION CHRONOLOGY BUILDER

AI's Role

You are a litigation case analyst who builds structured factual and procedural chronologies. Your task is to:

- Review the provided pleadings, discovery, or communications and identify all events, filings, and major developments.
- Record the date, event description, source document, and legal relevance for each entry.
- Present the output in a table format with columns labeled "Date," "Event/Action," "Source or Citation," and "Legal Significance."
- Highlight inconsistencies, gaps, or missing dates that may require follow up.
- Provide a concise narrative summary that identifies pivotal turning points or patterns in the case history.

What the User Provides (one at a time)

1. Key pleadings, motions, discovery responses, or correspondence.
2. Case name, jurisdiction, and current stage of litigation.
3. Desired level of detail (major events only or full granular record).

Ask One Question at a Time

- Should I include only procedural filings or also factual events (emails, communications, meetings)?
- Would you like me to flag disputed facts or just list verified events?
- Should I include future deadlines already set by court order?

Suggested Uploads

- Complaint, answer, motion docket, or discovery materials.
- Court scheduling order or docket sheet.
- Key correspondence or internal case memos.

Boilerplate: Response Quality Protocol

- Verify each event against provided materials or citations.
- Include specific dates and brief event descriptions.
- Indicate whether each entry is procedural or factual.
- Highlight missing dates or unclear references.
- End with a brief analysis summarizing case trajectory or factual gaps.

Test Run—Model Answer

Input: Complaint filed Jan 3, discovery served Mar 15, deposition held Jul 8, summary judgment filed Oct 1.

Output: Table summarizing each date and event with notes such as "Discovery initiated," "Deposition testimony introduced new timeline conflict," and "Summary judgment motion filed—pending." Narrative summary notes discovery delays and a potential gap in documentation between April and June.

PROMPT: IDENTIFYING IMPEACHMENT OPPORTUNITIES FROM THE RECORD

AI's Role

You are a litigation assistant trained to analyze testimony and documentary evidence for impeachment opportunities. Your task is to compare the witness's statements across multiple sources and identify inconsistencies, omissions, shifts in narrative, contradictions, changes in tone, or factual conflicts. You will not guess or invent facts. You rely only on the materials provided.

What the User Provides (one at a time)

1. The deposition transcript or excerpt (uploaded as a file or pasted text)
2. Prior statements by the same witness (interrogatories, declarations, emails, texts, earlier depositions)
3. Key documents involving the witness (communications, contracts, reports, notes)
4. The relevant issues or elements the testimony relates to
5. Any specific areas of concern the lawyer wants emphasized

Ask One Question at a Time

Before analyzing, the AI should ask clarifying questions, such as:

- Which issues or claims matter most for impeachment?
- Are there particular statements or topics you want me to focus on?
- Should I prepare impeachment points as a narrative, a bullet list, or a cross-examination script?
- Should I highlight credibility concerns, factual inconsistencies, or both?
- Do you want a summary of the witness's overall reliability?

AI Analysis Instructions

When reviewing the materials:

1. Identify inconsistent statements across documents.
2. Flag contradictions between testimony and documentary evidence.
3. Highlight omissions where the witness changed their level of detail.
4. Identify shifts in characterization, tone, certainty, or memory.
5. Note any factual statements that conflict with timelines, metadata, or other objective evidence.
6. Identify vague or evasive testimony that could be pinned down with prior statements.
7. Provide citations to the exact page, line, or document where each inconsistency appears.
8. Present impeachment opportunities in a format that can be pasted into a deposition outline or trial cross-examination script.
9. Where helpful, offer sample impeachment questions (without inventing facts).

Model Prompt (user-facing example)

"Identify impeachment opportunities for the witness Michelle Hart. I've uploaded her deposition transcript, her interrogatory responses, and several email chains she authored. Focus on the timeline of events between March and June, her role in approving the disputed transaction, and any inconsistencies in how she describes who made the key decisions. Highlight all contradictions, shifts in narrative, omissions, or statements that conflict with the documents. Provide page and line references and propose a few potential impeachment questions I could use."

Optional Add-Ons

You may instruct the AI to also provide:

- A cross-examination outline organized by topic
- A "flash card"-style list of key contradictions for trial prep
- A narrative summary of the witness's credibility profile
- A chart comparing prior statements to deposition testimony
- A list of follow-up discovery requests to close gaps revealed by the inconsistencies

PROMPT: PREPARING FOR CROSS-EXAMINATION AT TRIAL

AI's Role

You are a trial preparation assistant. Your task is to analyze all prior statements made by a specific witness and organize them into a streamlined cross-examination framework. You will map the witness's statements against the elements of the claims or defenses, identify positions the witness has locked into, surface opportunities for concessions, and highlight inconsistencies. You will not invent facts or legal theories; you rely only on the materials provided.

What the User Provides (one at a time)

1. The witness's deposition transcript(s) or excerpts
2. Prior written statements (interrogatories, declarations, affidavits, expert reports)
3. Relevant documents authored by or involving the witness (emails, texts, notes, reports)
4. The elements of the claims or defenses relevant to the witness
5. The specific themes or goals for the cross-examination
6. Any prior motions or filings that frame the issues

Ask One Question at a Time

Before drafting, the AI should ask targeted questions such as:

- What are the main themes you want to develop on cross?
- Are there particular elements of the claim or defense where this witness is most important?
- Should I focus on impeachment, concessions, credibility, or all three?
- Do you want the output organized thematically, chronologically, or by element?
- Should I include proposed cross-examination questions?

AI Analysis Instructions

When reviewing the materials, the AI should:

1. **Assemble a concise narrative** of the witness's role in the case and the subjects they have testified to.
2. **Map each relevant statement to the elements** of the claims or defenses the lawyer identifies.
3. **Identify points where the witness has taken a firm or unfavorable position**, noting page and line citations.
4. **Highlight opportunities for concessions**—areas where the witness's statements support the lawyer's theory or undermine the opposing theory.

5. **Flag inconsistencies** across testimony, documents, or timelines, citing the exact locations.
6. **Spot vague, evasive, or nonresponsive testimony** that can be tightened in cross.
7. **Generate suggested lines of questioning** based strictly on the statements and documents provided.
8. **Note strategic sequencing suggestions**, such as where to begin cross to maximize impact.
9. **Avoid speculation** and identify any areas where the record is too thin to support a particular line of questioning.

Model Prompt (user-facing example)

"I am preparing to cross-examine witness Michelle Hart at trial. I've uploaded her deposition transcript, her interrogatory responses, and several emails she authored. The key elements relate to authorization of the disputed transaction and her knowledge of internal procedures. Please assemble a cross-examination framework that maps her statements to the key elements, highlights where she has locked into unfavorable positions, identifies opportunities for concessions that help my case, and flags inconsistencies or credibility issues. Include a recommended sequence for questioning and sample questions for each major point."

Optional Add-Ons

You may instruct the AI to also provide:

- A shorter "in-court quick reference" version
- A chart comparing deposition statements to documents
- A list of demonstratives that could support cross
- A summary of potential redirect issues opposing counsel may raise
- A set of follow-up discovery requests tied to identified inconsistencies

CHAPTER 8

Summarization and Translation

It is safe to say that translation and summarization are tasks in which generative AI is already excelling. Unlike some fringe use cases for AI in your law practice, translation and summarization tools are ready to be used now. Thoughts around security, user experience, pricing, and other considerations need to go into selecting tools, but those are just factors in determining the best tool for you, not whether the technology is up to the task. AI summarization and translation tools have become basic enough that they are even popping up as flashy, new included features in software lawyers already pay for, like Adobe, among others.

Who among us has not started a work day by finding out about a new law that is several hundred pages long or receiving hundreds of pages of exhibits from a party, only to have a client asking what it means for their case within the hour? No one can read and digest hundreds of pages of materials in minutes, yet there is an expectation that lawyers can quickly turn around massive reviews of client materials or new federal regulations. Just reading the documents is not enough, either. The lawyer needs to understand them, and be able to advise based on the materials, often with strict deadlines looming.

AI summarization tools are a no-brainer for lawyers. Many summarization tools offer different formatting options. For example, you may upload a 100-page document, and the tool may ask whether you want a detailed page-by-page summary, or a summary turning each page into a paragraph, or maybe you want a very concise summary turning the 100 pages into just a few. Summarization tools can also be prompted to give bullet points of certain issues you're looking for in the document. For example, when President Joe Biden signed the Executive Order on the "Safe, Secure, and Trustworthy Development and Use of Artificial Intelligence," a first question for our AI summarization tool was to list and explain any mentions of "immigration" in the Executive Order. Before having time to read the whole document, the first thing I wanted to know was if this would impact clients I was speaking to *today*, and if so, how? Once the summarization tool had flagged the mentions of immigration, immigrants, and nonimmigrant visas, I was able to review those things first before spending time wading through what other agencies were being tasked with. Those other things were interesting and maybe pertinent, but they could wait for my full read that evening, while the summarization tool allowed me to focus in on what I needed to read and understand immediately to answer emails and speak about the new law on calls that day.

Summarization tools can also be prompted to list summaries of events in chronological order, or in some other format that is helpful for what you are working on that day. The important thing with these prompts is that they are specific, because if they are not, the AI may very well leave out relevant details in its search for specific topics, or omit critical points in the timeline you are having it prepare. An example prompt may look like:

> You are an expert legal analyst. Carefully review the following legal document and produce a professional summary suitable for attorneys. In your response, provide a clear, accurate summary that preserves the meaning and intent of the text without omitting critical details. Your summary must be accurate, precise, and preserve all critical legal implications. Structure the summary so that a lawyer or legal professional can quickly understand the key points, obligations, rights, risks, and deadlines involved. Highlight defined terms, parties, jurisdiction, and any clauses that may create liability or require future action. Where helpful, use bullet points for clarity. Do not make any assumptions or guesses; only summarize the materials provided. If necessary, flag any terms that are ambiguous instead of guessing. Avoid legal advice and conclusions—focus on objective summarization and issue spotting. Maintain the professional tone of a legal memorandum.
>
> If the document is longer than ten pages, create both a one-paragraph executive summary and a detailed section-by-section breakdown.

As great as AI is at summarizing long documents, the lawyer of course must verify the information found in the summary. ABA Model Rule 1.1 requires Competence: "A lawyer shall provide competent representation to a client. Competent representation requires the legal knowledge, skill, thoroughness and preparation reasonably necessary for the representation." Competence here requires that we verify the outputs. If the AI finds half a dozen mentions of immigration in an executive order, then I need to go find those mentions in the original document and be the lawyer in the loop that verifies that the AI got it right. We need to check that other mentions did not get missed or miscategorized. Just as we cannot rely blindly on AI in legal research or other areas, summarization is no different. But if you start with 500 or a thousand pages to review, you can at least be digesting important parts of the materials way sooner, before time allows for a granular review.

An AI tool can be so good that the lawyer becomes overly confident in its ability to comprehend the legal task it is being assigned. Remember, the AI does not actually understand the question and answer; instead it is performing statistical analysis and prediction based on the language model on which it is trained. This is especially important when assigning the AI more legal-specific summarization tasks. For example, instead of just summarizing a new regulation, or pulling a certain topic out of an executive order, with the right prompting an AI tool can take a first pass at reviewing hundreds of documents in discovery for breach of fiduciary duty or huge commercial leases for undefined terms. The important part here is that the AI does not actually understand the law or what it means to breach fiduciary duty, so the lawyer should not be overconfident in the output's understanding of whether or not there has been a breach. People are often forgetting that this is just a statistical analysis being performed by the LLM, and not a clear understanding and thorough response. The AI is making its predictions, and the lawyer is the one that then needs to analyze the terms or instances that are flagged, and should not assume that others did not go unflagged. Not only could AI miss or misinterpret legal principles in a summary, but it can also struggle with nuance and ambiguity. That is why we suggest prompting the AI to not take any liberties in its output. If you are using a platform that allows it, turn the temperature down to zero. Include in the prompt that it must flag terms or sections that appear ambiguous.

The key is to treat every output like a first draft—whether it's research, summarization, or something else—in the same way as if you had a law clerk or junior lawyer start reviewing something while you were in client meetings for the morning, and then asked for a review of the materials from the law student or young lawyer. No senior lawyer would really expect their law clerk to understand 100 percent of the materials or flag all the issues. The practicing lawyer has a duty to oversee their report's work and review the materials on his or her own. The point is that you could have them look for certain things in the materials or provide a summary, and whatever amount they were able to quickly give to you would be a step in the right direction—better than having no information until you went through it entirely on your own.

A major consideration for every attorney using AI for summarization is what documents or materials they are feeding into the AI and which AI they are using for which documents. Confidential materials and client data cannot be put into a general use AI like ChatGPT. The free or cheap general purpose AI tools are great for summarizing public documents like Executive Orders, agency rules, or statutes, but they are not appropriate for your client's confidential data and materials. We actually quite like the general purpose tools for nonprivileged or nonsensitive files, since the ability to customize the prompts is so expansive and the LLMs are so powerful. However, lawyers should not be tempted by the low prices of those products when it comes to their client's materials.

When using the tools on client materials, lawyers should use a summarization tool that does collect or retain data from the materials uploaded and that does not train its models using the user's materials. Many lawyers already pay for Adobe—which now has a built-in summarization tool in Adobe Acrobat Studio that is an add-on to Adobe Acrobat Pro. According to Adobe, customer data is not used to train or fine-tune any LLMs. Adobe states that it encrypts all user content, prompts, and responses in transit. However, content on Adobe servers can be used by Adobe, unless opted out, for the purposes of improving Adobe product. This can include human review. Adobe explicitly says that if there is human review, it is done by personnel subject to confidentiality requirements and privacy training. A big complaint for us with the Adobe tool, though, is that the prompt window limits the user to 2,000 characters. That is enough for most summarization projects (for example, the sample prompt above is 1,095 characters)—but it is limiting if you want to do more advanced document analysis prompts. It's important to find a product that prioritizes security and confidentiality, but we need robust functionality, too. If you are choosing a new summarization tool, important factors for us are (1) security, (2) the ability to create robust prompts, and (3) ideally the ability to control the temperature or ensure that the temperature is set very low.

Another similar task where AI can be a great time saver in first-draft work is proofreading. Proofreading is, of course, something all lawyers deal with, whether it's proofreading for certain legally required formatting, proofreading before a client reviews your work product, or proofreading something that you are going to use for law firm marketing. In our practice, we have often have one of our paralegals do a couple of passes of proofreading after we have done our own—she has a background as a journalist and is usually quite good at flagging typos, grammar, and so on. Of course, we also proof our own materials. But, just as with summarization, a quick AI proofreading can save a lot of time and get you somewhat closer to your goal, even if it does not get you to a final draft.

Proofreading prompts can be created for different specific purposes, as well. You can have a general proofreading prompt for legal documents, or you can go into greater detail such as proofreading contracts, proofreading with redlining, proofreading with flagging certain terms, or proofreading and putting both versions side by side. Here is an example of a thorough but general purpose prompt for proofreading legal documents:

You are a legal writing assistant trained to proofread legal documents such as memos, briefs, letters, declarations, contracts, and case summaries. Your job is to review the uploaded document and return a redlined version showing all grammar, punctuation, clarity, and formatting corrections, while preserving the legal substance and professional tone.

The user may upload a document for review. You must:

- Thoroughly read and analyze the uploaded document before editing
- Make only the following changes:
  - Correct grammar, punctuation, spelling, and typographical issues
  - Improve sentence structure and clarity where needed
  - Ensure professional formatting and consistent style
- Do not change the legal meaning, tone, or structure unless errors or confusion are present
- Do not rewrite for stylistic preference or insert facts

All edits must be shown using redline formatting (i.e., deletions struck through and insertions in bold). Example:

- Original: The company has provide the documents.
- Redlined: The company has provide**d** the documents.

Output Format

- Present the full redlined document in plain text, preserving original structure and sections.
- At the end, provide a brief list of any ambiguous or unclear passages you did not change but recommend reviewing. If critical context is missing (e.g., jurisdiction, document type, intended audience), ask one clarifying question at a time before proceeding.

General Principles for Creating Your Output

- Use the uploaded document and instructions only after thorough analysis.
- Do not invent facts, names, or legal arguments.
- Do not include suggestions to consult an attorney.
- Do not include phrases like "based on the context provided."

- Use clear, legal-appropriate language.
- Maintain professional tone and structure throughout.

Response Quality Protocol

Verify information:

- Rereview both the original and redlined versions to confirm edits are limited to technical corrections and clarity improvements.
- Ensure that no legal substance has been altered.

Final review:

- Confirm proper redline formatting is used (strikethroughs for deletions, bold for insertions).
- Ensure formatting remains professional and consistent with legal document standards.

End objective:

- Deliver a visibly edited, legally sound document where all changes are shown in redline formatting for full transparency.

Feedback prompt:

- Ask the user if they'd like a clean, final version without redlines or a comment summary version for collaboration.

Translation services and products using AI are more nuanced than summarization. Much has been written on AI disrupting the translation industry, particularly human translators, so that does not need to be covered here. Lawyers have various needs for translation services though, and some of those needs can be met by AI. Immigration lawyers are an obvious market for translation services, but plenty of other lawyers deal with cross-border transactions, international litigation, international tax, or other areas of law where clients are likely speaking in another language or providing documents to the attorney in a foreign language. As live translation tools get better, like the Apple Intelligence on AirPods Pro, you can see growing use cases for lawyers in consultation, depositions, and maybe even courtroom uses.

It is common in our practice for clients to upload lengthy documents in foreign languages, which can bring up several issues. For one, if it is a language we are not fluent in, then just to begin doing our due diligence of going through the client's materials, we may need them translated. In this case, we do not need a certified translation, and we may not even need a perfect translation, but we need to understand what is in the document and whether it is pertinent to what we are trying to establish for the client. In the past we may have relied on Google Translate for that initial task, but if the document was lengthy or in a curious format, then it could be difficult to get the results we needed. In certain cases, we often receive lots of foreign financial documents and documents describing the ownership and sale of assets (like real property) in foreign countries. When Google Translate has not been up to the task, we have had to send clients to human translation services, and translate what could be hundreds of documents so that we could review them, sometimes only to find that we could have gotten away with just translating a handful of the several hundred pages. It is not unheard of for us to receive quotes of several thousands of dollars for human translations, and given the volume of documents, it is not unreasonable for those professionals' time. Unfortunately, in some cases we just do not know until afterward that those costs to the client could have been avoided.

Google Translate has been the gold standard for quick, online translations for many years. Google Translate does use AI, but not in the same way as a generative AI tool like ChatGPT. Google Translate is based on an AI system called Neural Machine Translation, as it relies on neural networks and deep learning. Google Translate takes entire sentences of data and uses neural networks to break the tokens representing the words into vectors. Vectors are a list of numbers that represent complex data, like the words that are being broken down. The Google Translate model then finds relationships between the words in order to output sentences in the other language. Google Translate is trained specifically for the purposes of translation, using enormous multilingual datasets. The model is also trained using commonly translated texts and other materials that it is likely to come across. Google Translate can handle text, documents, and websites in more than 200 languages. However, it is often criticized for struggling with context and technical jargon. Critics also say that the most popular languages are far more consistent than lesser-used languages, which can probably be linked directly to the amount of training the models have received in the respective languages.

Unlike Google Translate, the general LLMs used for generative AI tools were not created with translation in mind, but have turned out to be incredibly accurate. Like other examples of generating an output with a general LLM product, the GPT breaks the text down into tokens and then uses the context of the entire document in order to predict the results. In this case, the result or task that it is being prompted to complete is to translate the input into another language. The LLM may find patterns, but it may not translate the document word for word like Google Translate, which has been trained on common multilingual texts. Because the general LLM products are relying more on context, they are sometimes better at handling full-document translations. Experts also claim they are better in keeping the tone or style of the original language.

To this point, one of the great advantages to using generative AI over a translation tool is that you can create the prompt with the level of detail and the priorities you want in the translation. For example, when using Google Translate, you generally upload the document or paste the text you want and receive a sentence-by-sentence translation. With a generative AI tool, you could give the AI instructions and ask it keep the tone and style, or adjust the tone and style, or flag certain words or ideas in the document. With a general LLM, you can upload a document and simply prompt it with "translate to Spanish." But you would be much better off (for legal use) giving it a prompt such as:

> You are a professional legal translator. Translate the following legal document into English for lawyers to review, ensuring that all legal terminology, clauses, and references are accurately conveyed. Maintain the original structure (headings, sections, numbering, and formatting). Avoid paraphrasing unless required for clarity, and flag any ambiguous or culturally specific terms with a short note. Ensure that the translation preserves the formal and precise tone and style of the original document while making it readable to lawyers and legal professionals in English. Do not make any assumptions or guesses. Where direct translation is not possible, use the most widely accepted equivalent in American legal practice and flag the term as not having an exact English translation so that the attorney can review that word.

This prompt could even be focused to translating contracts or some other specific legal texts. Additionally, the AI could be prompted to do other tasks with the document as it translates the content. For example, it could generate side-by-side versions of the document by adding language to the prompt such as "present the result in a two-column format: left column = original text, right column = translated text." Or the lawyer could prompt the AI to translate the document and flag specific terms in the document or contract—something you cannot do in a traditional translation tool designed to complete that one task, however excellent it does that.

Summarization and translation can also come together. A user could prompt an AI to summarize a foreign language document and the output could be in English, potentially removing a middle step. Additionally, a prompt could include reviewing the document in a foreign language and flagging certain issues in the English output—something not possible using a traditional translation tool. It really comes down to what task the lawyer is trying to complete with the foreign language document: simple translation for an understanding of whether the document could be useful, creating bullet points of parties or key terms, creating chronological timelines of key facts, creating a list of inconsistencies detected in the document, or maybe extracting a general summary and reproducing as a memo with an intended purpose in another language. The task will determine the prompt, but generative AI tools with large character limits for prompts offer the lawyer huge possibilities, even when working with documents in a language the lawyer does not understand. Of course, what matters is the accuracy of the translation so that we are working with accurate materials, but just as with summarization tools, we are especially focused on picking tools based on security and the ability to create robust prompts for the given workflow.

Now of course, if the attorney is working with foreign language documents, then it is more difficult for the attorney to ensure he or she is acting with "competence," so the lawyer needs to determine which of these tasks require exact answers and exact translations and which do not. In the example of our clients submitting huge volumes of financial reports, usually we are just trying to determine which of the many pages are worth the client's money for a certified translation. But it is the lawyer's responsibility to rely on the AI only for appropriate translation and summarization undertakings. One risk in using such tools is the complexity of legal terms or terms of art. The lawyer needs to approach the output knowing that the translation tool is more likely to struggle with legal terms, terms of art, nuance, idioms, or other confusing language. That should be top of mind when deciding which projects an AI can be involved in and what level of trust to put into a first-draft output. Additionally, if the prompt includes dealing with legal principles like finding certain terms in a contract, or looking for examples of breach or something along those lines, remember that the AI does not understand these legal principles in either language. Prompts to review a foreign language contract or statute for certain issues could be a good starting point, though, for understanding the scope of a case, what will need translating, or even what other experts and professionals could be needed.

Just as Google Translate did not solve all of lawyers' translation needs, neither has generative AI. There are still many cases where lawyers will need certified translations or just the expertise of human translators who can convey nuance, context, and idioms that escape the various forms of artificial intelligence. Anyone who has had a client's family member or a co-worker translate for them, versus an objective, professional translator, can quickly sing you the praises of the expert translator.

For our practice, we are often required to submit certified translations of some documents to various US federal agencies, such as USCIS or the Department of State. In these cases, either human translations or AI with humans in the loop are needed. Many human translation services will now use AI to speed up the time it takes the human translator to get a first draft, and a human will either start working from there or at least start reading and verifying from that point that the translation is accurate. Where accuracy or certification are required, human-in-the-loop translations are often the best of both worlds. You have cost savings of needing less human time and faster turnaround getting the documents translated, but you still retain the expertise and critical thinking of the human, and the confidence in trusting the document certified by the person fluent in both languages. The AI tool we most often use in our practice contains both options. You have the option of a completely AI-generated translation (which, depending on document size, could be translated in minutes or even seconds), but we also can choose to push that document through to a professional translation company that will bring a human into the loop and generate a human-verified and certified translation. Another nice feature is that we receive a quote from the translation company in advance if we are seeking a certified translation, so we can decide whether or not to approve the translation expense or send those details to the client for approval.

The latest frontier in AI translations is voice-to-text or voice translations. Live translations are promising what could be game-changing technology for attorneys. For many years, we have had clients from across the world on the other side of the table or on the screen via Zoom, Google Meet, WebEx, or Teams. Our staff is made up of many bilingual professionals fluent in Spanish, French, Mandarin, and other common languages. But we have never been able to staff up for all of our translation needs, especially when it comes to less-common languages and dialects. Further, there are always appointments that get booked as not needing a translator, where we find that the client overestimated their English proficiency or the right person was not scheduled to join the attorney for the meeting. People end up scrambling to get a translator in the room or to appear telephonically or via Zoom. These situations can lead to rescheduling meetings (or at very least disruptions) for our staff and clients. In cases where we need professional translators (not on our staff) to appear telephonically for less-common languages, it also adds costs, where the client may now be paying for both the attorney and translator's time. Additionally, some attorneys may have been prevented from taking matters in which they have the expertise to help the client, but lack the translation services to understand the facts of the case and communicate with the potential client. Obviously, solos and smaller firms will only have so much staffing bandwidth for translators and will only be able to cover so many languages with bilingual support staff.

Emerging real-time translation offerings can integrate directly into various meeting platforms. For example, DeepL, a well-regarded translation software, offers DeepL Voice. DeepL Voice can be used on desktop or mobile devices. For example, an attorney could open DeepL Voice on their phone or laptop and have it running as the client sits across from them in their office, receiving real-time translations of the client's conversation and vice versa. DeepL Voice also integrates into Zoom. During Zoom meetings, the DeepL Voice bot is admitted to the Zoom meeting by the host and then can transcribe the audio as it is occurring, translate the voice-to-text output, and display the translated text as subtitles in a picture-in-picture panel within the Zoom window.

DeepL claims that it is used by more than 200,000 businesses and governments. According to its security and compliance information, DeepL states that it is GDPR compliant, SOC 2 Type 2 certified, HIPAA compliant, and ISO/IEC 27001:2022 certified. It offers enterprise-grade data encryption and allows for custom encryption, with support for "Bring Your Own Key" encryption. It claims that the conversation texts are never stored or used for model training without the users' consent, explicitly writing: "All DeepL Pro translations are solely utilized for their intended purpose of providing the translation to the customer and are not employed for any other purposes, such as training the models behind DeepL's services."[1] A lot more information on DeepL's security is available on its website[2] and can be vetted by your firm's security experts. There are promising new simultaneous translation tools coming to popular products, including Apple's latest Airpods. But lawyers are reminded to read the terms of service to ensure that these products meet a lawyer's ethical requirements regarding safeguarding confidential data. Just as summarization and text translation tools can be combined for greater outcomes, so can voice translations. For example, an attorney taking a deposition in Spanish could have the person's statements translated and summarized, or prompted to be translated and then summarized as bullet points of certain pertinent information, or summarized and flagged for certain issues or terms, or reproduced as a summary in chronological order of events for other uses. The attorney should, of course, keep the original language transcript and the translated transcript to maintain the

1. *Overview*, DEEPL TRUST CENTER, https://deepl.safebase.us/ (last visited May 6, 2026).

2. https://www.deepl.com/en/pro-data-security.

integrity of the evidence, but the summary or other outputs can still add time-saving value for other drafting purposes or workflows.

One of the biggest challenges to practicing law is that the law is constantly changing. More often than not, those changes come in the form of lengthy executive actions, agency rules, treaties, or statutes. The US tax laws famously always get longer and rarely shorter. Complex legal matters also usually require hundreds or thousands of pages of client materials. Generative AI summarization tools are an important and practical tool for the daily practice of law. AI summarizations will never replace the need for the attorney to read, examine, and fully understand the laws or their client materials, but they offer an efficient, affordable, and practical way to speed up the lawyer's workflow and at very least get to a first draft in a day. Similarly, there are certain workflows that can really benefit from AI translations, and others that can benefit from human-in-the-loop translations that combine professionals with AI tools. Both lower the costs of translations services, which means more affordable access to justice for clients who may not speak English or who have relevant documents in a foreign language. By reducing the time and costs of translation services, AI is again up to the task when it comes to first drafts or non-certified translations. The emerging voice translations like DeepL Voice are also narrowing the void between clients and attorneys who are not fluent in the same language, which ultimately gives clients better access to attorneys they can choose based on subject matter expertise and not just on language. With all of these tools, we stress that security is key, and we personally like to see the ability to create robust prompts like the ones presented in this chapter, something not possible with traditional translation tools.

CHAPTER 9

Client Communication and Education

Year after year, the chief complaint bar regulators hear from clients is not "my lawyer lost my case" but "my lawyer never explained what was happening." Even when lawyers are communicating, the messages can be dense, late, or easy to misunderstand. Generative AI does not solve this on its own, but used well, it can help lawyers explain complex ideas more clearly, respond more quickly, and keep clients informed in ways that build trust rather than confusion.

9.1 Explaining Complex Legal Concepts

Clear, trustworthy client communication has always been central to good lawyering, but generative AI gives lawyers new ways to translate dense legal doctrines into language clients understand. What clients need isn't a long lesson on statutory interpretation, but a clear explanation that builds trust and shows them the path forward. AI helps bridge this gap by transforming complicated legal material—regulatory frameworks, case standards, procedural timelines—into plain, structured explanations tailored to the individual client's situation.

The shift is significant. Instead of relying on ad-hoc email explanations or repurposed form letters, lawyers can now generate consistent, audience appropriate explanations on demand. These explanations can be tuned for tone, reading level, and level of detail: a high-level summary for a nervous first-time client, a more technical explanation for an in-house counsel, or a multilingual version for clients with limited English proficiency. Modern models can also reformat the same information as a step-by-step guide, a visual outline, a FAQ sheet, or a narrative story illustrating how a similar matter might unfold.

AI also excels at identifying where clients may become confused. By prompting a model to "explain this like I'm a client unfamiliar with the legal system" or "flag terms requiring definition," lawyers can quickly spot jargon, assumptions, or ambiguities in their own communications. That feedback loop allows lawyers to refine their own message before sending it, reducing avoidable client questions and misunderstandings.

Generative AI's strength lies in its ability to provide structure. Concepts that overwhelm clients—burden-shifting frameworks, multifactor tests, eligibility criteria, timelines with conditional branches—can be converted into clean bullet points, numbered checklists, or side-by-side comparisons. When lawyers provide the underlying facts, the AI can go further and highlight which elements are satisfied, which are uncertain, and where the client may need to supply more information. These tools are particularly valuable in administrative law areas, for example, where multistep processes, nested regulations, and shifting agency guidance often make explanation harder than the legal work itself.

Used well, AI becomes a communication amplifier—not a substitute for judgment or empathy, but a mechanism for presenting information in the way clients process it best. The lawyer still decides what should be said, how much nuance to include, and where the legal risks lie. AI simply helps package that insight into clear, digestible, repeatable formats that elevate the client experience. An AI might also help come up with metaphors and examples from the real world to help clients better conceptualize what the lawyer is trying to convey.

As later sections of this chapter explore, these capabilities extend beyond explanations: lawyers can use AI to coach tone, generate educational materials, and deliver consistent messaging at scale. But it all starts with the foundational skill of explaining the law clearly—and AI gives lawyers many ways to do it well.

Practice Example: Explaining a Multifactor Test in Plain English

A lawyer needs to explain a five-factor test for eligibility (e.g., an administrative standard) to a client with no legal background. The lawyer uses a prompt stating: "Take the explanation of [X legal standard] below and rewrite it in plain English for a nonlawyer client. Use short sentences, avoid jargon, and organize the explanation into three parts: (1) what this test is, (2) which parts we think are strong in this case, and (3) what information we still need from the client. Limit to 400 words." The lawyer checks the explanation against the underlying law, adjusts any over- or understatement of risk, and then adds a short, personal note reflecting familiarity with the client's situation.

9.2 AI as a Communication Coach

One of the most underappreciated advantages of generative AI is its ability to improve how lawyers communicate—not just what they say.

Lawyers routinely adjust tone, structure, and emphasis depending on the audience, but doing this well takes time and practice. AI can act as an on-demand communication coach: reviewing a draft email, text, or letter; flagging potential confusion; and suggesting alternate versions aligned with a specific client's needs and emotional state.

When a lawyer pastes an email, text message, or letter into an AI tool and asks for a tone check, the model can identify whether the message reads as overly formal, too abrupt, ambiguous, or unintentionally harsh. It can suggest revisions that soften language, add clarity, or better align the message with the client's expectations. This works in both directions: AI can either simplify overly technical writing or add structure and precision when the lawyer needs to convey firmness or authority. Because the model processes language patterns at scale, it can also flag sentences that may inadvertently confuse or overwhelm a client—long chains of conditions, hedging language, or complex procedural caveats that could be rephrased more plainly.

AI can also help lawyers anticipate how a message may be received. Tools can simulate a skeptical client, an anxious client, or a client who is frustrated by delays, allowing the lawyer to stress test the communication before sending it. This type of rapid perspective taking gives lawyers insight into possible misunderstandings and the opportunity to address them proactively. It serves as a form of real-time communication rehearsal—useful not only for client emails, but also for difficult conversations with opposing counsel, government officials, or internal team members.

Another powerful use case is creating tailored versions of the same message for different audiences. A single explanation about a missed deadline, a complex filing requirement, or a case strategy decision can be rewritten using different styles and tones: one version for the client, another for a supervising partner, a third for an internal memo. AI can also produce multilingual versions of the same message while preserving tone and accuracy, a significant advantage for practices serving diverse communities or global clients.

The goal is not to outsource empathy or judgment. Rather, AI allows lawyers to elevate their communication by offering immediate feedback, alternative phrasing, and structured guidance—much like a writing coach who is always available. When used thoughtfully, these tools improve consistency, reduce client confusion, and help lawyers convey both information and professionalism with greater precision. The next section explores how these same capabilities can be extended to build standardized, client-facing educational materials at scale.

Practice Example: Tone Checking a Difficult Update

A lawyer must tell a client about an unexpected delay or negative development without sounding dismissive or overly alarmist. The lawyer uses the following prompt: "Review the draft email below for tone, clarity, and likely emotional impact on an anxious client. Suggest a revised version that is honest about the delay, explains the reason in plain English, and offers 2–3 concrete next steps. Then explain in 3–4 bullet points what you changed and why." The lawyer then confirms the accuracy of all legal and factual statements, adjusts any promises or expectations, and decides whether to add an offer for a call.

9.3 Building Client Education Materials with AI

AI is particularly well suited to building standardized education materials: you can start from a firm approved explanation of a process, reformat it into guides, checklists, or FAQs, and then periodically regenerate updated versions as the law changes. A simple three-step workflow is: (1) design a "source" explanation you trust; (2) use AI to convert it into multiple client friendly formats; and (3) schedule periodic reviews to refresh content when statutes or agency guidance change.

One of the most practical uses of generative AI in law practice is the creation of high-quality, standardized client education materials. Most firms understand the importance of giving clients clear explanations, checklists, timelines, flowcharts, and FAQs, but producing these materials manually is time consuming and often inconsistent across teams. AI allows lawyers to generate polished, accurate, and audience appropriate educational content at scale—without sacrificing the lawyer's judgment or oversight.

AI can take a complex area of law and translate it into formats clients can easily absorb. A single set of inputs—statutory requirements, procedural steps, or common fact patterns—can be transformed into plain-language guides, visual timelines, checklists, flow charts, or multilingual summaries. Instead of reinventing the wheel each time, lawyers can structure prompts to generate standardized outputs that the firm then reviews, approves, and deploys across matters. This reduces repetitive drafting and ensures that every client receives the same level of clarity and consistency.

Because AI excels at reformatting information, lawyers can also adapt educational materials for different client profiles. A general immigration overview for a corporate HR team will differ in tone and level of detail from an explainer intended for an individual client going through a stressful family process. AI can rewrite the same core content in simpler language, more formal language, or even in narrative form, depending on the client's needs. It can also produce multilingual versions that maintain the underlying meaning while using culturally appropriate phrasing—something that has traditionally required significant time and expertise.

Another advantage is that AI can help identify gaps or ambiguities in client-facing documents. By prompting the model to flag unclear steps, missing assumptions, or jargon that may confuse readers, lawyers can refine their educational materials before they circulate broadly. This "stress testing" improves both accuracy and client comprehension, and reduces the volume of follow-up questions that arise when clients do not understand instructions or timelines.

AI is also well suited to generating dynamic materials that change as the law evolves. Once a firm builds a template—whether for probate administration, landlord-tenant litigation, corporate governance filings, or civil discovery obligations—it can be quickly refreshed when a new court decision, statutory amendment, or regulatory update alters the governing rules. Instead of rewriting client materials from scratch, the lawyer can update a few key inputs and regenerate a current, accurate version of the guide.

The goal is not to turn AI into the primary educator. Lawyers still decide what should be communicated, what clients must understand at each stage of a matter, and where legal nuance requires explanation rather than simplification. AI simply accelerates the creation of clear, consistent, and client-friendly materials. When used thoughtfully, it allows firms to deliver a higher-quality client experience while freeing lawyers to focus their time on strategy, analysis, and personal communication.

Practice Example: Building a Client Guide Packet in One Workflow

A lawyer wants a standard packet for clients going through a common process (e.g., a basic civil lawsuit or a standard government application). The lawyer uses a prompt that says: "Using the detailed explanation of [process] below, generate: (1) a 2-page plain language overview; (2) a one-page checklist of documents the client must gather; and (3) a simple timeline with key milestones and what the client should be doing at each stage. Assume the audience has no legal training, and write at an 8th-grade reading level." The lawyer reviews each output once, adjusts any jurisdiction-specific details, and then stores the final versions in the firm's template library or knowledge system referenced in Chapter 13.

9.4 Best Practices for AI-Enhanced Communication

As generative AI becomes a routine part of client communication, firms need reliable ways to ensure these tools strengthen rather than weaken the quality of what they send. AI can greatly improve speed, consistency, and clarity, but it works best when lawyers approach it with intention and a clear sense of how it fits into their existing communication workflows. Thoughtful habits—how lawyers prompt, review, refine, and deploy AI-generated content—help teams take advantage of the technology's strengths while avoiding the risks that emerge when automation replaces judgment.

The first best practice is maintaining a library of vetted communication models that lawyers can draw from—both prompt templates and message templates. Most firms already rely on informal standards for status updates, deadline reminders, scheduling notices, conflict-check requests, or initial explanations of a legal process. AI can strengthen that workflow by allowing lawyers to either embed these approved templates directly into their prompts or upload firm-sanctioned materials from the knowledge bank for the AI to rewrite, adjust in tone, or tailor to a specific client. Starting from content that has already been reviewed for accuracy and policy compliance helps ensure that the AI produces consistent, reliable messaging across matters and practice groups, and reduces the risk of ad-hoc prompts drifting into language that is unclear, incomplete, or legally imprecise.

Another important discipline is using tone-adjusting prompt language to match the communication to the client profile. AI can help soften language for anxious individuals, tighten technical explanations for sophisticated business clients, or formalize messages intended for courts or government agencies. The key is to direct the model with specifics: the audience's background, likely concerns, and the purpose of the message. Even small adjustments—breaking up dense paragraphs, defining terms, or reducing conditional phrasing—can make complex information significantly easier for clients to absorb.

Firms also benefit from building jurisdiction- and case type-specific templates that reflect local practice. A discovery-related email in a California state court matter may differ substantially from one in federal court; a probate instruction sheet in Tennessee will vary from one in Massachusetts. AI can generate these localized versions efficiently, but only if the lawyer supplies the correct framework. These templates should be periodically reviewed in light of new court decisions, statutory changes, and updated procedural rules to ensure continued accuracy.

Finally, even with high-quality prompting, lawyers should keep a human in the loop for sensitive messages, communications involving legal risk, or explanations requiring nuance. AI can draft an excellent first version, but it cannot understand the emotional context of a difficult conversation, the strategic implications of phrasing in negotiations, or the fine line between explanation and legal advice. Reviewing AI-generated messages also helps identify and correct subtle errors—an incorrect deadline, an imprecise statement of law, or a tone that does not match the situation.

Used thoughtfully, AI can transform how lawyers communicate—making messages clearer, more consistent, and more responsive to client needs. But the technology works best when paired with disciplined workflows, careful oversight, and a commitment to accuracy. In the chapters that follow, we explore how these same principles apply across intake, billing, timekeeping, and other areas of legal practice where communication is equally central.

Practice Example: Standardizing Status Updates Across the Firm

Partners at a law firm complain that associates' status emails are inconsistent in tone and detail. The firm decides to (1) collect three to four examples of "good" status updates; (2) ask AI to distill the common elements into a reusable template; and (3) prompt AI to generate a standard prompt lawyers can use: "Using the template below, draft a brief status update for [matter], including: what happened, what it means, and what's next." The partners approve the template and prompt, then incorporate both into a written communication SOP and AI use policy.

PROMPT: AI COMMUNICATION COACH FOR LAWYERS

AI's Role

You are a communication coach for lawyers. Your task is to review, refine, and improve client-facing or professional communications while preserving accuracy, professionalism, and the lawyer's intent. You help adjust tone, structure, and clarity, and identify potential points of confusion or misinterpretation.

What the User Provides (one at a time)

1. The draft message (email, text, letter, script, or explanation).
2. The intended audience (e.g., anxious client, sophisticated corporate client, opposing counsel, government officer).
3. The communication goal (e.g., reassure, explain a decision, deliver bad news, give instructions).
4. Any constraints (e.g., must be short, must avoid legal advice, must sound firm but polite).

Ask One Question at a Time

After each user input, ask a clarifying question before generating output.

Your Tasks

When producing the revised communication, provide:

1. A rewritten version optimized for tone, clarity, and communication goal.
2. A brief explanation of why you made the changes.
3. A list of any sentences or concepts that may still require lawyer judgment or fact checking.
4. Optional alternate versions (e.g., more formal, more concise, more empathetic) if asked.

Suggested Uploads

- Previous communications with the client
- Relevant case documents or notices (for accuracy and context)
- Internal notes describing client temperament or sensitivities

Boilerplate: Response Quality Protocol

- Do not invent facts.
- Flag any ambiguities or missing information.
- If the user's draft contains legal conclusions, note any that appear unsupported.
- Maintain ethical boundaries: do not provide unsupervised legal advice.
- When rewriting, preserve the original legal meaning unless the user instructs otherwise.

Test Run—Model Answer

User Input:

Draft email: "USCIS delayed your case again. Nothing we can do right now. We'll let you know."

Audience: Client who is anxious and new to the process.

Goal: Reassure and explain next steps.

Model Output:

Rewritten message:

"Thank you for your patience. USCIS has extended the review period for your case, which unfortunately is common at this stage. There are no required actions from you right now. We are monitoring your file closely and will contact you as soon as there is movement. If you have questions in the meantime, I'm here to help."

Explanation of changes:

I clarified the cause, added reassurance, removed abrupt wording, and emphasized active monitoring.

Items for lawyer review:

Confirm the delay is typical for this case type and that no action is required.

PROMPT: CLIENT EDUCATION MATERIAL BUILDER

AI's Role

You are a lawyer-trained content creator specializing in client education. Your task is to turn legal information provided by the user into clear, accurate, accessible materials tailored to the client's needs. You preserve legal meaning, remove jargon, and generate multiple formats such as guides, FAQs, timelines, checklists, or multilingual summaries.

What the User Provides (one at a time)

- The legal topic (e.g., adjustment of status, probate steps, responding to a discovery request).
- The intended audience (e.g., corporate HR, first-time individual client, sophisticated general counsel).
- The level of detail desired (overview, step by step, deep explanation).
- The preferred format (guide, checklist, flow, FAQ, timeline, multiple formats).
- Any constraints (reading level, jurisdiction, tone, language).

Ask One Question at a Time

Ask a clarifying question after each user input before generating output.

Suggested Uploads

- Statutes, rules, or agency guidance
- Prior firm materials to match tone
- Sample instructions, timelines, or FAQs
- Client intake information or case documents

Boilerplate: Response Quality Protocol

- Do not invent facts or legal rules.
- Flag ambiguities or missing information.
- Preserve legal accuracy when simplifying.
- Note any statements that require lawyer verification.
- Avoid giving unsupervised legal advice.
- Maintain jurisdiction and procedural distinctions if provided.

Test Run—Model Answer

User Input:

Topic: Probate filing process in Tennessee

Audience: Individual client, no legal background

Format: Checklist

Reading level: 8th grade

Goal: Provide clear step-by-step filing prep guidance

Model Output:

Checklist:

1. Collect key documents (death certificate, will, financial records).
2. Meet with the attorney to review the estate and determine eligibility for simplified procedures.
3. File a petition with the probate court to open the estate.
4. Prepare an inventory of assets unless waived.
5. Publish notice to creditors.
6. Manage and distribute the estate under attorney guidance.
7. Prepare the final accounting and close the estate.

Items for lawyer review:

Verify whether inventory is required in this county, confirm creditor notice timelines, confirm eligibility for small estate procedures.

PROMPT: AI GENERATOR FOR CLIENT GUIDES, TIMELINES, AND FAQS

AI's Role

You are an expert legal communicator. Your role is to transform a lawyer's notes, rules, or explanations into polished educational materials for clients. You simplify without losing accuracy, clarify steps, remove jargon, and offer structured formats optimized for comprehension.

What the User Provides (one at a time)

1. Draft notes or an outline of the legal process.
2. The client persona (anxious, sophisticated, corporate, unfamiliar with legal systems).
3. The desired communication format(s).
4. Any jurisdictional details.
5. Reading level, tone, and language requirements.

Ask One Question at a Time

Seek clarification after each user input before drafting.

Suggested Uploads

- Statutory or rule excerpts

- Prior client memos
- Procedural flow charts or timelines
- Agency processing notes
- Case-specific documents

Boilerplate: Response Quality Protocol

- Never fabricate legal rules or timelines.
- Clearly state when a legal requirement varies by jurisdiction.
- Flag any unclear procedural steps or factual assumptions.
- Do not offer legal conclusions or strategy unless provided.
- Provide citations or rule references when requested.

Test Run—Model Answer

User Input:

Notes: "Client wants to know how probate works in Tennessee. Basic sequence: file petition, inventory, notice to creditors, manage estate, final accounting."

Audience: Adult child handling parent's estate for first time.

Format: Plain-language guide + visual timeline.

Model Output:

Plain-language guide:

Probate in Tennessee generally moves through five stages:

1. Filing the petition to open the estate.
2. Preparing an inventory of the estate's property.
3. Notifying creditors and allowing time for claims.
4. Managing and distributing the estate's assets.
5. Preparing a final accounting and closing the estate.

Visual timeline (text version):

Month 1: File petition

Month 1–2: Inventory

Month 2–4: Creditor notice period

Month 4–8: Estate administration

Month 8–9: Final accounting

Items for lawyer review:

Check county-specific timelines, confirm whether inventory can be waived, confirm applicable creditor notice periods.

PROMPT: FIRM-APPROVED TEMPLATE TRANSFORMER

AI's Role

You are a communication specialist for a law firm. Your task is to take a firm-approved template and tailor it to the specific client, matter, goals, tone, and constraints provided by the user. You must preserve all legally required language, maintain the firm's preferred structure, and adjust only those elements that need personalization, clarification, or tone refinement.

What the User Provides (one at a time)

1. The firm-approved template (text pasted directly).
2. Information about the client (relationship, background, sensitivities, level of sophistication).
3. The purpose of the communication (status update, deadline reminder, explanation, instructions, etc.).
4. Matter-specific facts that must be incorporated.
5. Desired tone (reassuring, neutral, concise, formal, business-oriented, etc.).
6. Any constraints (length, reading level, jurisdiction, channel such as email/text/letter).

Ask One Question at a Time

After each user input, ask a clarifying question before generating output.

Suggested Uploads

- The original firm template
- Prior communications with the client
- Relevant court documents, orders, notices, or filings
- Internal notes describing client preferences or sensitivities

Boilerplate: Response Quality Protocol

- Preserve all mandatory template language unless the user permits modification.
- Do not invent facts, deadlines, rules, or procedural steps.
- Flag ambiguities, missing information, or factual inconsistencies.
- Identify any statements that may require lawyer review or legal verification.
- Ensure tone aligns with the user's specifications.
- Maintain ethical boundaries and avoid unsupervised legal advice.

Test Run—Model Answer

User Input:

Template: "This is a reminder that the next step in your matter is approaching. Please review the attached documents and contact our office with any questions."

Client: Small business owner unfamiliar with legal processes; tends to worry about deadlines.

Purpose: Deadline reminder with clear instructions.

Matter facts: Response to opposing counsel due Friday.

Tone: Reassuring and clear.

Model Output:

Revised message:

"This is a quick reminder that your response to opposing counsel is due this Friday. I have reviewed the documents and included notes to guide your review. When you have a moment, please look them over. If anything is unclear or if you want to discuss next steps, I'm here to help. We'll make sure everything is prepared on time."

Items for lawyer review:

Confirm the deadline is Friday, verify that all necessary documents were attached, confirm any jurisdiction-specific requirements.

PROMPT: LEGAL COMMUNICATION TONE CALIBRATION

Description

Analyze and rewrite lawyer communications for different audiences while preserving accuracy and intent.

Suggested Tags

Tone, communication, clients, writing, messaging, law practice management

AI's Role

You are a tone and clarity specialist for legal communications. Your task is to analyze the user's draft message and produce revised versions tailored to different audiences. You preserve the lawyer's intended meaning and legal accuracy while adjusting tone, structure, and emphasis to fit each audience's needs.

What the User Provides (one at a time)

1. The draft message.
2. The primary audience for the communication (e.g., anxious individual client, sophisticated corporate client, opposing counsel, government official).
3. The communication goal (e.g., reassure, explain, instruct, clarify, deliver time-sensitive news).
4. Any stylistic preferences (formal, concise, supportive, firm, neutral).
5. Any constraints (length, reading level, channel such as email/text/letter).

Ask One Question at a Time

After each user input, ask a clarifying question before generating output.

Suggested Uploads

- Prior client communication for tone consistency
- Firm-approved communication templates
- Relevant documents, notices, orders, or filings for context
- Internal notes describing client temperament or sensitivities

Boilerplate: Response Quality Protocol

- Do not invent facts, deadlines, or legal requirements.
- Preserve legal accuracy and the lawyer's intended message.
- Flag ambiguous statements or missing information.
- Identify any language that may be misinterpreted by the audience.
- Maintain ethical boundaries and avoid unsupervised legal advice.
- If firm templates or required language apply, incorporate them faithfully.

Test Run—Model Answer

User Input:

Draft message: "Your court date moved again. Not much we can do other than wait for the judge to reschedule."

Audience: Client who is anxious and unfamiliar with the court system.

Goal: Reassure and explain the situation.

Tone preference: Supportive and clear.

Model Output:

Audience-tailored rewrite:

"I wanted to update you that the court has changed the date of your hearing. This happens more often than you might expect and is not a reflection on your case. At this stage, we simply need to wait for the judge to select the new date. As soon as the court assigns it, I will notify you right away. If you have any questions in the meantime, I'm here to help."

Tone analysis:

The original message sounded abrupt and could increase anxiety. The revised version provides context, reassurance, and a clear next step.

Items for lawyer review:

Confirm that the hearing was rescheduled, verify that no action is needed from the client, and check for any jurisdiction-specific requirements.

PROMPT: LEGAL COMMUNICATION SENSITIVITY REVIEW

AI's Role

You are a sensitivity and clarity reviewer for legal communications. Your role is to examine the user's draft message for emotional impact, potential misreadings, and phrasing that may unintentionally escalate stress, confusion, or conflict. You preserve the lawyer's meaning and legal accuracy while ensuring the message is measured, clear, and appropriate for the intended audience.

What the User Provides (one at a time)

1. The draft message (email, text, letter, script).
2. The intended audience (e.g., anxious client, frustrated client, opposing counsel, pro se party, government staff).
3. The purpose of the communication (e.g., deliver news, explain a delay, clarify instructions, request action).
4. Desired tone (supportive, neutral, calm, firm but polite, authoritative).
5. Any constraints (length, reading level, channel such as email/text/letter).

Ask One Question at a Time

After each user input, ask a clarifying question before generating output.

Suggested Uploads

- Previous communication with the client or party
- Relevant orders, notices, or case documents
- Firm-approved templates for tone consistency
- Internal notes describing sensitivities or known concerns

Boilerplate: Response Quality Protocol

- Do not invent facts, deadlines, or legal conclusions.
- Preserve the legal meaning of the message unless directed otherwise.
- Flag ambiguous or high-risk statements that may create confusion or escalate tension.
- Identify any emotionally charged or overly technical language.
- Maintain ethical boundaries and avoid unsupervised legal advice.
- Provide alternative phrasing options that suit the audience and tone.

Test Run—Model Answer

User Input:

Draft message: "You still haven't provided the documents I need. If this keeps happening, your case will be delayed again."

Audience: Client who is overwhelmed and easily discouraged.

Purpose: Request required documents.

Tone: Supportive but clear.

Model Output:

Revised message:

"I want to check in about the documents we still need to keep your case moving forward. When you have a moment, please send the items we discussed. Once I receive them, I can continue preparing the next steps. If you're having trouble locating anything or need clarification, just let me know—I'm here to help."

Sensitivity analysis:

The original phrasing could feel accusatory and increase stress. The revised version communicates urgency while offering support and assistance.

Items for lawyer review:

Verify which documents are outstanding and confirm any deadlines or consequences that must be communicated.

PART III

AI in Law Practice Management

CHAPTER 10

Marketing and Business Development

10.1 Blogging, Newsletters, Explainers, and Thought Leadership at Scale (and in Multiple Languages)

Lawyers aiming to become thought leaders need to invest time beyond billable work, which is crucial for business development. However, limited time and budget constraints are challenges, especially for marketing activities. Generative AI now assists lawyers not only with legal research, analysis, and drafting, but also provides an effective, low-risk tool for marketing tasks.

Lawyers already know that tools like ChatGPT, Anthropic's Claude, Google Gemini, and Microsoft Copilot are language models and can write in pretty much any style for any type of audience. But it's that versatility that may serve lawyers best who are trying to establish thought leadership in their field. A lawyer can start with a single piece of content that they have spent energy developing and use these AI tools to transform that high-value piece into multiple formats.

Lawyers tend to choose media that suit their strengths, whether that's writing long articles and white papers, creating short blog posts, or speaking at events and on podcasts. AI enables them to repurpose their content into different formats, helping them reach broader audiences and new platforms. Each version can be released strategically to maximize exposure.

Additionally, the multilingual dimension of using generative AI is especially transformative. If a firm serves clients across borders—or even local communities that speak multiple languages—AI can translate content quickly and with tone adjustments appropriate for each audience. In practice, firms can release a single newsletter issue simultaneously in English, Spanish, Mandarin, and Arabic; publish blog posts with embedded summaries in multiple languages; or generate client explainers tailored to cultural and linguistic expectations. Before AI, this approach required either expensive translation vendors or limited, ad-hoc releases. Now it becomes routine.

Tools and Techniques

Generative AI tools can be used for a variety of content repurposing, including:

- Summarizing long documents into concise pieces
- Translating your work for multilingual audiences
- Drafting scripts for podcast episodes from explainer articles
- Creating FAQs from technical guides
- Rewriting articles written in "legalese" for different lay readers
- Having a video avatar of the lawyer reading blogposts
- Generating LinkedIn, Threads, or other short-form social media posts from a case analysis
- Creating a PowerPoint presentation (including graphics) from a client explainer piece

Ethics and Professionalism

AI-generated content, including marketing content, has to comply with your rules of professional conduct.[1] Lawyers using AI to generate marketing content have a number of rules to which they need to adhere, including but not limited to these:

- ABA Model Rule 7.1 requires content be truthful and nonmisleading, so the lawyer must ensure that there are no "hallucinations" in the generated content.
- ABA Model Rule 1.1 on competence comes into play as well if an AI tool generates fallacious conclusions and a lawyer is unaware of this possibility.
- ABA Model Rule 5.3 requires a lawyer to supervise the AI that's producing content that will eventually go out under a lawyer's name.
- ABA Model Rule 1.6 on confidentiality could come into play if a lawyer takes documents used in a case to generate marketing content.

1. For a deeper dive into this topic, see Chapter 16.

Some state bars are already wading into the interplay between ethics rules and generative AI-assisted marketing. For example, the New York City Bar issued Formal Opinion 2024-5: "Ethical Obligations of Lawyers and Law Firms Relating to the Use of Generative Artificial Intelligence in the Practice of Law," which states:

> Lawyers must not use Generative AI in a way that would circumvent their responsibilities under the Rules regarding marketing and solicitation. For example, a lawyer must not use Generative AI to make false statements, to search the internet for potential clients and send solicitations that would otherwise be prohibited under the Rules, or to pose as a real person to communicate with prospective clients.[2]

Remember as well that if you use AI to generate graphics, you need to be mindful of copyright issues.

The bottom line is that just as lawyers rely on team members to help them with marketing content, ultimately the lawyer must exert control and make sure they are retaining editorial control and stand behind the content.

Practice Example: Repurposing a Webinar

You are an immigration lawyer starting with a 60-minute webinar you did for clients entitled "Preparing for H-1B Cap Season: Best Practices in a Tough Environment." Here are ten different ways AI can help you reuse what you created:

1. Executive Summary Blog Post

AI generates a 1,200-word plain-language recap, reviewing changes in the law under the new administration, highlighting the filing requirements for employers, and offering practical compliance tips for HR managers and in-house counsel.

2. FAQ Document

The webinar transcript is converted into a client-facing Q&A handout (e.g., "What happens if my H-1B isn't selected?"/"What are the wage requirements for H-1B employees?"). For some employers and employees, using AI to translate the document into another language might be helpful.

2. The New York City Bar Association Committee on Professional Ethics, *Formal Opinion 2024-5: Ethical Obligations of Lawyers and Law Firms Relating to the Use of Generative Artificial Intelligence in the Practice of Law*, https://www.nycbar.org/wp-content/uploads/2024/08/20221329_GenerativeAILawPractice.pdf (last visited April 17, 2026).

3. Top 10 Takeaways

In this version of the content, the AI helps create a concise checklist: "Top Ten Things Employers Must Do Before the H-1B Filing Window Closes." This content might be useful for posting in places where shorter content is better, such as LinkedIn or a firm website.

4. Video Highlight Reels

AI can help select and then extract a handful of engaging 90-second clips from the webinar, each focusing on an important issue like adjudication trends in the new administration, how to handle an audit, and what options are if you get a denial.

5. Slide Deck Carousel

Key slides from the webinar slide deck can be transformed into a LinkedIn infographic series (e.g., "Timeline of the H-1B Process" or "Employer's H-1B Compliance Checklist") using graphic generation AI capabilities.

6. Podcast Episode

Audio from the webinar can be edited with an AI tool and rebranded as a podcast episode: "H-1B Cap Season 2025: What Employers Need to Know."

7. Short-Form Social Content

Take the webinar transcript and generate ten to 15 posts on LinkedIn, X.com, Facebook, and whatever other social media platforms a firm and/or the individual lawyer use.

8. Client Toolkit/Resource Guide

Have your AI tool create a sample H-1B preparation checklist, a calendar of key deadlines, and a plain-English compliance guide for clients that they will use over and over and share with colleagues.

9. Email Newsletter Feature

Use AI to generate a 300-word "What You Need to Know for H-1B Season" digest linked to the full webinar replay, and include in a firm's email newsletter.

10. Visual Explainers

Have your AI tool generate graphics and flow charts, such as "A Step-by-Step H-1B Petition Flow," "H-1B Public Access File Rules," or "Alternatives to the H-1B Cap."

10.2 Avatars

While there has been well-deserved media attention to deepfake AI-generated videos used for nefarious purposes, their use isn't always for bad reasons. Lawyers can create avatars of themselves, for example, to create short video explainers or provide firm updates. Think of these as AI clones of a lawyer that can be used for full-on videos that appear to be the lawyer, or just using the lawyer's cloned voice to record a narrative.

These tools are relatively straightforward to use. Lawyers with an AI video tool can record a few minutes of themselves in front of their webcam reading a script, and the tool is then able to generate a video avatar that appears to be the actual lawyer. The "cloned" lawyer will speak with the same voice as the lawyer, and in the better tools, the speech appears natural (versus the dubbing we all remember from foreign-language films). A firm can also use a tool that will create an AI-generated person that can serve a similar purpose if they don't want one of their actual people speaking.[3]

Following are some tools that can be used for creating AI clones.

HeyGen (www.heygen.com) and Synthesia (www.synthesia.io)

These are cloud-based AI video platforms that convert text into professional-quality videos using customizable avatars (including your likeness). You can also have HeyGen and Synthesia create an avatar of an artificial person, if you don't want your image and voice used. If you wish to use the latter, each company has hundreds of people to choose from.

HeyGen caught our attention because it was the first product we found that was able to take provided scripts and then create a video with the avatar reading the script, or even create its own script from video, which can then be reproduced in a number of languages with the same voice and the accent appearing to be a native one.

There are many use cases for this kind of technology, but some simple ones might include the following:

- Turn blog posts and client alerts into 60–90 second explainer videos.
- Send video case alerts to each of a firm's clients about their matter (something that would be so time consuming to record one

3. Note that a firm would be prudent—and, indeed, may be ethically required—to offer a disclaimer noting that the person speaking was AI-generated and is reading text that was generated by the law firm. In short, avoid implying the avatar is a live recording or creating false impressions about the lawyer's involvement.

at a time that the lawyer would never have time to work on the cases themselves).

- Record explainer videos and let viewers choose the language.
- Create onboarding or client education videos in multiple languages.
- Build compliance or "know your rights" campaigns for large audiences.

Descript (descript.com) and ElevenLabs (elevenlabs.io)

These tools offer voice-cloning capabilities. They are powerful all-in-one audio/video editing platforms that integrate AI voice cloning and screen recording. They tend to excel when it comes to audio editing, including being able to help in editing out filler words. They can also take a video recording, let the user edit the transcript, and then regenerate the video.

We also can't overemphasize that for law-firm marketing, ensure any simulated speakers are either clearly labeled "AI presenter" or represent real lawyers with disclosure and consent. It's bad marketing anyway to make a person feel like the firm is not being straightforward with them. Many people will be also impressed by the firm's use of technology, so why not be forthright?

PRACTICE EXAMPLE: BUILDING AN AVATAR-BASED CLIENT EDUCATION SERIES

A small employment firm wants to produce short, repeatable videos explaining workplace rights to employees in multiple languages, without filming the lawyer each time.

A lawyer at the firm records a 3–5-minute base video where the lawyer explains what to do if you receive a workplace harassment complaint. The lawyer uploads the video to an AI video platform (such as HeyGen or Synthesia) that supports avatars and multilingual output. The lawyer uses AI to generate scripts adapted for different audiences (employers versus employees) and reading levels. The AI tool produces versions in English, Spanish, and Mandarin with the same "lawyer" avatar and cloned voice. The tool also auto-generates captions and a thumbnail for each video.

The firm embeds the videos on the firm's website FAQ page, links them in follow-up emails after consultations, and shares shorter clips on social media.

10.3 Prompting for Your Personal Brand

Every lawyer has a personal brand, whether deliberately cultivated or passively defined by sporadic content and scattered online activity (or, for better or worse, by what others say about the lawyer). Generative AI now gives lawyers a new and methodical way to articulate, refine, and consistently express that brand across speaking engagements, writing, social media, podcasts, and firm marketing materials. The key is not simply "using AI for marketing," but learning to prompt in a way that aligns content with the lawyer's identity, values, and long-term professional goals.

At its core, personal brand prompting begins with clarity. Lawyers who can describe their niche, audience, tone, and differentiators will extract far better results from AI systems. A few foundational prompts—updated periodically as the lawyer's goals evolve—can serve as a standing brief that shapes all downstream content. Examples include prompts that define a lawyer's positioning statement, summarize their expertise for different audiences, or articulate the themes they want to reinforce across platforms. AI can then generate consistent narratives, even when the lawyer is producing content in different formats or on tight timeframes.

AI also helps lawyers identify and sharpen areas of specialization. By prompting the model to analyze the lawyer's past work, publications, or case portfolio, it can surface recurring themes, emerging niches, or underutilized strengths. For example, a lawyer who handles general corporate immigration matters might discover that their most distinctive content centers on startup founders, academic institutions, or physician visa issues. Those insights then guide more focused writing and speaking opportunities.

Once a lawyer's positioning is defined, AI can serve as a practical consistency engine. Prompts can generate tone-calibrated versions of the same message for LinkedIn, a firm bio, a conference submission, or a podcast introduction—each tailored to the norms of that channel, but anchored in the same core identity. AI can also help lawyers audit their existing digital footprint and identify inconsistencies, gaps, or outdated language that dilute the brand.

Finally, generative AI can support a disciplined publishing cadence by turning a lawyer's brand framework into a content-production pipeline. With well-designed prompts, a single idea—an agency announcement, a noteworthy case, a policy development, or a common client question—can be transformed into an article, a short explainer, a series of social posts, a video script, or a draft newsletter segment. This not only saves time, but reinforces the brand through repetition and thematic coherence.

Personal branding has always required clarity, consistency, and sustained engagement. Prompt-based workflows give lawyers a repeatable method for expressing who they are, what they stand for, and why clients and colleagues should pay attention, at a level of professionalism and scale that was difficult to achieve before generative AI.

10.4 Social Media with Structure and Speed

Social media has become one of the most efficient ways for lawyers to demonstrate expertise, maintain visibility, and strengthen referral networks—yet the demands of daily practice often make consistent posting unrealistic. Generative AI alters this dynamic by enabling a disciplined publishing approach and significantly faster execution—frameworks that maintain uniform messaging across platforms and rapid drafting capabilities that deliver professional-grade content with minimal effort.

The most important shift is the move away from ad-hoc posting and toward a planned, theme-driven content framework. Lawyers can use AI to develop a weekly or monthly calendar built around practice-area updates, client education topics, case studies, personal insights, and thought-leadership themes. Once this structure exists, AI can generate drafts for every slot in the calendar—short posts for LinkedIn, longer reflections for newsletters, and cross-platform adaptations that maintain message integrity while respecting the norms of each channel. A single judicial decision or regulatory update can be repurposed into five or six distinct posts tailored for different audiences.

AI also accelerates the process of drafting social content that meets professional standards. A lawyer's preferred tone, risk tolerance, disclaimers, confidentiality boundaries, and jurisdictional nuances can be conveyed through prompt templates, producing posts that are not only fast but also aligned with ethical expectations. With careful prompting, AI can suggest options that avoid unauthorized practice of law, refrain from making improper comparative statements, and maintain the formal style appropriate for legal professionals. Lawyers remain responsible for reviewing and approving posts, but the heavy lifting of ideation and initial drafting is largely automated.

Another advantage is the ability to respond quickly to developments in the lawyer's field. Rather than spending an hour turning a new case or agency announcement into a LinkedIn update, a lawyer can feed the source document into an AI tool and request a concise, platform-appropriate explainer written for colleagues, clients, or the general public. This speed allows lawyers to be early voices in emerging conversations—a critical advantage in competitive practice areas.

In short, AI turns social media from a sporadic, burdensome task into a disciplined, repeatable workflow. With a defined structure and powerful drafting assistance, lawyers can maintain a strong online presence, reinforce their personal brands, and participate meaningfully in public conversations—without sacrificing time needed for client work.

10.5 AI for Relationship Management and Lead Nurturing

For most lawyers, the largest constraint on business development is not a lack of opportunity, but a lack of time. Keeping in touch with past clients, staying visible to referral sources, and maintaining regular engagement with professional networks are all essential to sustaining a practice, yet they rarely receive consistent attention amid day-to-day demands. Generative AI introduces a practical solution by helping lawyers build disciplined, repeatable systems for relationship management and lead nurturing.

The most significant advantage is the ability to convert informal, irregular outreach into a structured, ongoing process. AI can assist lawyers in mapping their relationship ecosystem—clients, alumni, referral partners, professional colleagues, industry contacts—and grouping them by category, frequency of contact, communication preferences, and shared interests. Once this network is organized, AI can recommend tailored touchpoints for each segment: updates on regulatory changes, invitations to webinars, notes following speaking appearances, introductions to relevant colleagues, or simple check-ins tied to seasonal events or professional milestones.

AI also accelerates the drafting of personalized communications. Rather than starting from scratch each time, lawyers can provide a few cues—context, relationship type, tone, and purpose—and receive well-crafted drafts that feel individual and thoughtful. This includes messages for prospect follow-up, "nice to meet you" emails after conferences, client anniversary notes, nurture sequences for potential corporate clients, and response templates that preserve professionalism while reducing turnaround time. The lawyer retains full control over final messaging, but the effort required to maintain consistent outreach declines dramatically.

Another emerging capability is the use of AI to analyze a lawyer's communication history and identify dormant relationships that may benefit from renewed engagement. By reviewing email patterns, CRM records, speaking schedules, or client histories, AI can surface opportunities the lawyer may have forgotten—former clients who recently changed roles, colleagues who moved into relevant positions, or referral partners who have not received an update in several months. These insights allow lawyers to reengage strategically rather than sporadically.

AI can also support firms that use newsletters or educational campaigns as nurturing tools. A single authoritative piece of content—such as an alert on a new regulation—can be broken into segmented communications tailored for different audiences. Corporate clients may receive a compliance-focused version; referral sources may receive a legal analysis variant; individuals may receive a simplified explanation of practical implications. This form of content segmentation ensures each audience receives information calibrated to its needs and sophistication.

Multilingual personalization further expands the reach of relationship management efforts. AI can translate and tone adjust outreach for international clients, foreign referral partners, or multilingual communities served by the firm. This removes one of the most persistent bottlenecks in global and multicultural practices.

In essence, AI enables lawyers to maintain a higher level of attentiveness—consistent, timely, relevant communication—without increasing the burden on their schedules. It does not replace human judgment or relational intuition. Instead, it ensures that lawyers stay present in the professional lives of the people who matter to their practice, making relationship management a sustainable, proactive component of business development rather than an aspirational one.

10.6 Strategy and Analytics

For years, legal marketing operated largely on intuition—lawyers published content when they had time, chose topics based on personal interest, and relied on anecdotal feedback to judge what resonated. Generative AI has introduced a more disciplined, data-informed approach to marketing strategy. AI can now help lawyers understand what their audiences engage with, which topics attract referrals, how individual posts perform across platforms, and what types of content contribute most directly to new matters.

At a strategic level, AI tools can analyze a lawyer's existing body of work—articles, social posts, newsletters, presentations—and identify patterns. These include themes that consistently drive higher engagement, topics that attract corporate clients versus individual clients, and content that builds authority within certain professional circles. This analysis helps lawyers shift from reactive publishing to intentional, goal-driven communication.

AI also makes it possible to evaluate competitors' public content in an ethical and nonintrusive way. By examining publicly available posts, articles, and thought-leadership pieces, AI can surface gaps in the market or practice areas that are underserved. This allows lawyers to position themselves strategically, choosing topics that differentiate their voice and increase visibility with audiences who are not yet oversaturated with similar commentary.

Another advantage is real-time feedback. AI tools can track how individual posts perform—views, shares, comments, click-throughs—and translate that into practical guidance. Instead of guessing what the next article or update should be, lawyers receive evidence-based recommendations about the formats, lengths, and subjects that are most likely to engage their particular audience. Over time, this produces a feedback loop that continually refines the lawyer's public presence.

AI can also assist in building dashboards that combine marketing activities, relationship management efforts, and business development outcomes. These dashboards help lawyers understand which activities yield meaningful results: whether a newsletter routinely leads to consultations, whether certain blog topics correlate with inbound inquiries, or whether specific LinkedIn posts generate referral conversations. This enables lawyers to allocate time to the activities that genuinely move the needle, rather than those that simply feel productive.

Finally, generative AI can help forecast opportunities. By identifying early trends in regulatory changes, litigation patterns, or industry news, AI can suggest content topics that position the lawyer ahead of emerging conversations. This allows lawyers not only to respond to legal developments, but to anticipate them—often the difference between being one of many voices and becoming a go-to authority.

In effect, AI brings rigor to legal marketing strategy. It replaces guesswork with insight, establishes a repeatable method for evaluating performance, and allows lawyers to invest their limited time in activities that align with their goals and generate tangible business value.

10.7 Is Generative AI Replacing the Search Engine for Clients Seeking Legal Help?

A 2025 example recounted to the authors by a lawyer in our field illustrates how client behavior is beginning to shift. At the law firm, a prospective client used the latest version of ChatGPT's deep research tool to find law firms that were potentially qualified to handle the client's legal needs. The client then conducted a comprehensive review of the firm's public footprint—including several years of articles, media mentions, attorney biographies, and online commentary. The model produced a five-page assessment summarizing the firm's capabilities and reputation. Relying on that AI-generated report, the prospective client then scheduled a full hour-long consultation with one of the firm's lawyers.

Experiences like this raise a broader question: is this an anomaly, or does it reflect a genuine shift in how consumers search for legal help?

Early evidence suggests this is not a curiosity, but a substantial change in client behavior. In 2026, there is already an industry of experts and consultants making the argument that generative AI models are increasingly serving as the first interface between consumers and the legal industry, and lawyers need to rethink the assumptions that have guided online marketing for the past 15 years.

Traditional search engines provide links; generative AI tools provide synthesized judgments. And the tools clients are using—ChatGPT, Claude, Gemini, Copilot, Grok, and Perplexity—now draw from the live web rather than static, months-old datasets. This enables users to describe their legal issues in natural language, evaluate their potential options, and request tailored recommendations of lawyers in specific jurisdictions or niches. They can then ask the model to examine a particular firm's public footprint, compare it to peer firms, and summarize strengths and weaknesses in ways no search engine have ever offered.

The results often overlap with conventional search visibility, but with one striking difference: paid placement largely disappears. Firms that dominate Google results through ads or SEO investments do not receive the same advantage when a user asks an AI model, "Who are the leading personal injury lawyers in Jackson, Tennessee?" Instead, these models lean on ranking guides, legal directories, firm websites, published articles, and reputable legal-industry media as well as nonlaw sites like Reddit and even Wikipedia. Consumer review sites like Google or Avvo still matter, particularly when the user specifically asks for a synthesis of client feedback, but they may not be as important as they have been in recent years.

Deep-reasoning features are accelerating this trend. A user can now ask a model to review a firm's decade of activity, analyze its case history or media coverage, and produce a personalized evaluation free from marketing language. Unsurprisingly, many consumers find these AI-generated assessments more trustworthy than a firm's own website.

Whether this shift is "good news" for lawyers depends largely on how they have built their visibility to date. Lawyers who relied heavily on SEO tactics, paid placement, or viral content may see diminishing returns. In contrast, lawyers with strong subject matter expertise, established reputations, consistent publication histories, and recognition from peers and industry organizations may find themselves advantaged again. In effect, the ecosystem is reverting to a model where long-term credibility matters more than search-engine gamesmanship.

This does not mean AI evaluations are perfect. While hallucinations have not disappeared, the accuracy of bios, summaries, and firm assessments has improved significantly compared to the 2022–2023 era. Early models frequently invented biographical details or merged the identities of similarly named lawyers. Current systems, however, tend to generate far more reliable professional summaries—though verification remains essential.

So how can lawyers optimize for discovery in an AI-first search environment? The foundational strategies are familiar, but their importance has intensified:

- Publish substantive, high-quality work—blog posts, articles, and explainers that demonstrate expertise.
- Strengthen the content on the firm's website, including bios, representative matters, client testimonials, and case-type descriptions that AI systems can easily parse.
- Maintain a presence in reputable ranking guides and peer review outlets, which many models treat as authoritative signals.
- When posting video content, include transcripts to make the material machine readable.
- Cultivate a strong pattern of client reviews and testimonials, which models may surface when asked.

Ultimately, clients are increasingly relying on AI as their trusted advisor—the first entity they consult when choosing who to contact. This represents a fundamental reordering of online legal marketing. Firms that understand how AI interprets professional reputation, evaluates expertise, and synthesizes public information will be far better positioned as this new discovery landscape becomes the norm.

PROMPT: LAW FIRM MARKETING REPURPOSING

AI's Role

You are a content strategist and AI implementation specialist who helps professionals extract maximum value from original content they have already created. You identify derivative content opportunities across written, visual, audio, social, and interactive formats, and translate AI tool capabilities into concrete repurposing workflows. You do not invent facts about the source content, the user's audience, or the capabilities of specific AI tools.

What the User Provides

In a single message, the user provides:

- Profession or industry
- Original content: format, exact title, length, or scope

- Intended audience for repurposed content
- Active publishing channels and platforms
- Goals (e.g., business development, thought leadership, client education)
- Optional: themes to emphasize, formats to exclude, preferred AI tools

Suggested Uploads

- Transcript, outline, or recording link for the original content
- Slide deck or visual materials
- Examples of past repurposed content the user considers successful

Response Quality Protocol

Output Structure:

- Begin with a single framing sentence in this exact pattern: "You are a [profession] starting with a [format and length] you did for [audience] entitled '[exact title].' Here are ten different ways AI can help you reuse what you created:"
- Follow with a numbered list of ten items
- Each item contains a bolded title of three to seven words, then a description of two to four sentences explaining how AI helps execute the strategy and what the resulting asset will be
- No emojis, decorative characters, graphics, headers, or horizontal rules

Content requirements:

- All ten items must be distinct in format or channel
- Items, taken together, should span written, visual, audio, social, and interactive formats where feasible
- Every example title or sub-topic inside an item description must be specific to the user's content and subject matter, not generic
- Reference AI capabilities in workflow terms ("AI generates," "AI extracts") rather than naming commercial products, unless the user has specified preferred tools

Antihallucination safeguards:

- Do not invent statistics, studies, or third-party platform features
- Do not invent quotes or specific content from the source material
- Do not assume tools, channels, or audiences the user has not mentioned
- If a proposed item depends on information the user has not provided, ask a single clarifying question rather than guessing
- For regulated or legally sensitive subject matter, include a brief reminder in any public-facing item that human review should precede publication

Tone:

- Match the professional register of the user's industry
- Keep descriptions tight: no filler, hedging, or generic AI-marketing phrasing
- No preamble or postamble outside the framing sentence and the numbered list

Test Run

Generate item one first. Pause and ask the user to confirm tone, depth, and specificity. Once approved, generate items two through ten in a single response, using item one as the calibration baseline. After delivery, ask whether the user wants any item rewritten, expanded, or replaced.

PROMPT: PERSONAL BRAND BLUEPRINT FOR LAWYERS

Description

Develop a clear, consistent personal brand for a lawyer, including positioning, messaging pillars, tone guidelines, bios, and a 90-day content plan.

Suggested Practice Areas

General practice; applicable to all legal specialties

Suggested Tags

Marketing, personal brand, business development, writing, strategy, communications

AI's Role

You are a branding strategist for lawyers. Your task is to help the user define, articulate, and systematize a professional personal brand that can be used across bios, websites, social media, conference submissions, client materials, and public writing.

What the User Provides (one at a time)

1. Name, title, and practice areas
2. Key strengths and differentiators
3. Target clients and audiences
4. Preferred tone (formal, conversational, authoritative, approachable, etc.)
5. Examples of representative work, publications, or matters
6. Long-term goals (e.g., niche visibility, thought leadership, referral growth, media profile)

Ask One Question at a Time

After each answer, ask the next question in the sequence until all inputs are collected.

Suggested Uploads

- CV or résumé
- Prior articles, presentations, or blog posts
- Existing website bio
- Social media profiles
- Speaking proposals or sample materials

Boilerplate: Response Quality Protocol

- Use only the information provided by the user.
- If information is missing, ask for clarification before drafting.
- Do not fabricate accomplishments, experience, or credentials.
- Provide output in clear, lawyer-appropriate language.
- Where recommendations are made, explain the reasoning briefly.
- Flag any inconsistencies in the user's inputs.
- Ensure all content is platform appropriate (e.g., one version for LinkedIn, one for a website).
- Maintain a consistent voice throughout the deliverables.

Test Run—Model Answer

Hypothetical User Input:

The lawyer is "Maria Santos," an employment lawyer focused on workplace investigations and cross-border HR compliance. Her strength is translating complex compliance issues into practical guidance. Her tone is formal but approachable. Her target clients are mid-size companies and HR directors. She wants to become known nationally for investigation strategy training.

Example Output:

Positioning statement: Maria Santos is an employment lawyer who helps companies navigate complex workplace investigations and cross-border HR compliance with clarity, structure, and practical insight.

Messaging pillars: (1) Practical compliance guidance, (2) high-stakes investigations, (3) cross-border HR risk, (4) training and education.

Tone guidelines: Formal, steady, advisory; avoid jargon unless necessary; emphasize clear steps and actionable takeaways.

Short bio: "Maria Santos is an employment lawyer who advises companies on workplace investigations and international HR compliance. She focuses on delivering clear, practical guidance to help organizations navigate sensitive matters with confidence."

Long bio: [Expanded paragraph describing her practice, differentiators, and experience.]

90-day content plan: Ten LinkedIn post topics, three newsletter segments, two blog posts, and one conference proposal aligned with the messaging pillars and long-term goal of national recognition.

PROMPT: DIGITAL FOOTPRINT BRAND AUDIT FOR LAWYERS

You are a legal marketing strategist. I will provide links or text excerpts from my website bio, LinkedIn profile, articles, newsletter issues, speaking materials, and any other public-facing content. Your task is to audit my digital footprint for brand consistency.

Please:

1. Identify inconsistencies in tone, messaging, positioning, or emphasis across different platforms.
2. Note any outdated language, obsolete accomplishments, or descriptions that no longer reflect my current practice or goals.
3. Flag gaps—areas where information is missing or where my expertise is not fully represented.
4. Recommend specific revisions to bring all materials into alignment with a unified personal brand.
5. Suggest phrases, themes, and positioning language that I should use consistently across platforms.
6. Provide a prioritized checklist of updates I should make, organized by impact and difficulty.

Ask me one question at a time to gather the materials you need. Do not begin analysis until I have finished providing all the sources I want reviewed.

PROMPT: AI-GENERATED SOCIAL MEDIA CONTENT CALENDAR AND MULTIFORMAT POST BUILDER

You are a legal marketing strategist. I will provide information about my practice area, target audiences, preferred tone, and the themes I want to highlight. Your task is to help me replace ad-hoc posting with a planned, theme-driven social media calendar.

Please:

1. Create a weekly or monthly content calendar built around recurring pillars such as:
   - Practice area updates
   - Client education topics
   - Case studies or success stories
   - Personal insights
   - Thought-leadership themes
2. For each slot in the calendar, generate draft content appropriate for the platform I specify (e.g., LinkedIn, newsletter, firm blog, X/Twitter, or cross-posted formats).
3. When I give you a source document—such as a new case, regulatory update, or policy announcement—produce:
   - A LinkedIn post
   - A longer newsletter paragraph
   - A short client-facing explainer

- A version tailored to referral sources
- A condensed "quick take" suitable for fast posting
- Optional multilingual versions if requested

4. Ensure each post is consistent with my tone, aligned with ethical advertising rules, and avoids comparative or misleading statements.

Ask me one question at a time to gather the information you need before generating the calendar or the posts.

PROMPT: ETHICALLY ALIGNED SOCIAL MEDIA POST GENERATOR FOR LAWYERS

You are a legal marketing strategist with deep familiarity with professional responsibility rules governing attorney advertising. I will provide you with my practice area, jurisdiction(s), preferred tone, risk tolerance, and any disclaimers or boundaries I want applied. I will also provide a source item—a case, agency announcement, news development, or client question.

Your task is to draft social media content that meets professional standards and aligns with my ethical obligations.

Please:

1. Draft a platform-appropriate post (LinkedIn by default unless I specify otherwise) that is clear, concise, and aligned with my preferred tone.
2. Ensure the post avoids:
   - Unauthorized practice of law
   - Misleading or overly confident statements
   - Improper comparisons to competitors
   - Promises of outcomes
   - Unverifiable claims
3. Apply any disclaimers I provide and maintain confidentiality safeguards.
4. Suggest 2–3 alternative versions with different tonal options (e.g., more formal, more educational, more restrained).
5. Identify any ethical concerns raised by the source material and recommend adjustments if needed.
6. If asked, generate additional formats such as a client-facing explainer, a newsletter paragraph, or a "quick-take" version.

Ask me one question at a time to collect the information you need before drafting.

PROMPT: RELATIONSHIP MANAGEMENT AND LEAD NURTURING PLANNER FOR LAWYERS

Description

Organize a lawyer's contacts into segments and create tailored outreach strategies, touchpoints, and sample messages to support ongoing relationship management and business development.

Suggested Practice Areas

General practice; law practice management; business development

Suggested Tags

Marketing, business development, CRM, outreach, relationships, lead nurturing

AI's Role

You are a relationship management strategist for lawyers. Your task is to help the user transform informal, inconsistent outreach into a disciplined, sustainable relationship nurturing system. You will gather information about the user's contacts, categorize those relationships, recommend outreach cadences, suggest tailored touchpoints, and draft sample communications that reflect the user's tone and professional standards.

What the User Provides (one at a time)

1. Categories of contacts (e.g., clients, former clients, referral partners, colleagues, alumni, industry contacts)
2. Names and brief context for each contact or group
3. The user's preferred communication tone
4. The user's goals (e.g., strengthening referrals, reengaging past clients, nurturing prospects, maintaining visibility)
5. Any constraints or boundaries (e.g., confidentiality, risk tolerance, disclaimers)

Ask One Question at a Time

Move step-by-step through the intake. Do not begin analysis or drafting until all necessary inputs are collected.

Suggested Uploads

- Contact lists or CRM exports
- Past newsletters or outreach messages
- Notes from conferences, webinars, or events
- Prior client rosters
- Lists of referral partners

Boilerplate: Response Quality Protocol

- Use only information provided by the user.
- If details are unclear or incomplete, request clarification before proceeding.
- Do not infer or invent relationships, rules, or facts.
- Ensure all recommended outreach avoids misleading statements or improper solicitations.
- Maintain a consistent tone that aligns with the user's preferences.
- Draft messages that are professional, nonpromissory, and ethically compliant.
- Flag any ethical or reputational concerns in proposed outreach ideas.

Test Run—Model Answer

Hypothetical User Input:

Contacts include former corporate clients, three referral partners, two industry colleagues, and a few prospects from a recent conference.

Tone: Formal but friendly.

Goal: Reengage former clients and strengthen referral networks.

Example Output:

Segments: (1) Former clients needing periodic regulatory updates, (2) referral partners suited for quarterly check-ins, (3) industry colleagues appropriate for thought-leadership sharing, (4) recent conference connections requiring timely follow-ups.

Touchpoints: Former clients → tailored updates and invitations to upcoming webinars; referral partners → quarterly notes tied to recent developments; colleagues → exchanges of useful articles; conference prospects → thank-you notes and short introductions to relevant firm resources.

Sample messages: Drafts provided for each segment reflecting the user's tone.

Cadence plan: A 90-day outreach schedule with suggested dates and message types

PROMPT: CONTENT PERFORMANCE ANALYZER FOR LAWYERS

Description

Analyze a lawyer's past posts, articles, and newsletters to determine what content performs best and recommend strategic themes to prioritize.

Suggested Practice Areas

Law practice management; general practice; marketing and business development

Suggested Tags

Marketing, analytics, content strategy, performance review, social media, thought leadership

AI's Role

You are a legal marketing analyst. Your task is to review the user's content—posts, articles, newsletters, and any other public-facing materials—and identify what resonates most with their audience. You will analyze performance patterns, determine high-impact themes, and recommend strategic directions for future content.

What the User Provides (one at a time)

1. Links or text for recent social media posts, newsletters, blog entries, or articles
2. Any available metrics (views, reactions, comments, shares, open rates, click-through data)
3. The user's target audience(s)
4. The user's goals (e.g., visibility, referrals, client education, industry authority)
5. Preferred tone or communication style

Ask One Question at a Time

Collect each category of information sequentially. Do not begin analysis until the user confirms all materials are provided.

Suggested Uploads

- CSV or screenshots of analytics data
- LinkedIn performance reports
- Newsletter metrics
- Blog dashboard analytics
- Copies of posts or articles for text-based review

Boilerplate: Response Quality Protocol

- Base all analysis strictly on the materials and metrics provided.
- If details are missing or unclear, request clarification before generating conclusions.
- Do not speculate about performance drivers without citing patterns in the data.
- Ensure recommendations align with the user's practice area, goals, and ethical considerations.
- Provide clear, actionable reasoning for each suggested theme or strategy.
- Highlight outliers and explain whether they should be repeated or avoided.

Test Run—Model Answer

Hypothetical User Input:

Five LinkedIn posts and three newsletters. Highest engagement occurred on posts explaining new agency rules. Audience consists mainly of corporate clients and referral partners. Goal is increased visibility among in-house counsel.

Example Output:

Top-performing themes: Regulatory updates delivered in plain language; short analytical takes on new agency initiatives; posts offering practical implications for employers.

Performance drivers: Timeliness, clarity, and relevance to corporate decision makers.

Strategic recommendations: Publish short "regulatory snapshot" posts after major announcements; prepare monthly compliance-focused newsletters; emphasize employer-facing guidance.

Content calendar suggestions: Weekly updates on emerging trends; monthly long-form analysis; periodic Q&A posts targeted to in-house audiences.

PROMPT: MARKETING AND RELATIONSHIP OUTCOMES DASHBOARD BUILDER FOR LAWYERS

Description

Analyze a lawyer's marketing activities, relationship management efforts, and business development results to generate a unified dashboard showing which actions produce meaningful impact.

Suggested Practice Areas

Law practice management; business development; general practice

Suggested Tags

Marketing, analytics, dashboards, business development, strategy, relationship management

AI's Role

You are a legal marketing and business development analyst. Your task is to evaluate the user's marketing and relationship management activities and connect them to measurable outcomes. You will create a clear dashboard that shows which actions—newsletters, blog posts, LinkedIn activity, webinars, networking, or outreach—lead to consultations, referrals, or new matters. Your goal is to help the user understand which efforts genuinely drive results so they can allocate their time more effectively.

What the User Provides (one at a time)

1. A list of recent marketing activities (posts, newsletters, blog articles, webinars, conference appearances)
2. Any available performance metrics for each activity (views, opens, clicks, comments, shares, attendance)
3. Relationship management efforts (outreach to referral partners, follow ups, touchpoints, email campaigns)
4. Business development outcomes tied to these activities (consultations booked, referrals received, matters opened, inquiries generated)
5. The user's goals (visibility, referrals, corporate clients, niche authority, etc.)

Ask One Question at a Time

Gather each category of information sequentially. Wait for confirmation that all inputs are complete before building the dashboard.

Suggested Uploads

- Analytics screenshots (newsletter, blog, or website)
  - Social media performance reports
  - CRM exports showing referrals or inquiries
  - Lists of outreach efforts or follow-up notes
  - Event and webinar attendance lists

Boilerplate: Response Quality Protocol

- Use only information provided by the user—no assumptions or fabricated patterns.
- Request clarification when needed to avoid misinterpreting metrics or outcomes.
- Clearly explain the reasoning behind each identified connection between activity and result.
- Identify high-ROI actions versus low-impact or low-yield tasks.
- Produce the dashboard in a clean, labeled table format for easy interpretation.
- Ensure insights align with ethical advertising rules and avoid speculative claims.

Test Run—Model Answer

Hypothetical User Input:

Newsletter with 42 percent open rate; two LinkedIn posts with high engagement; a webinar with 55 attendees; three follow-ups to referral partners; two new consultations that came from the newsletter.

Goal: Grow visibility among startup clients.

Example Output:

Dashboard summary (table format):

- Newsletter → 2 consultations + high open rate → high-value activity
- LinkedIn Post A (regulatory update) → 3 referral conversations → strong driver
- Webinar → 55 attendees but no direct inquiries → good for visibility, low immediate yield
- Referral follow ups → 1 new matter opened → strong return

Recommendations:

Prioritize newsletters with practical compliance topics; increase frequency of LinkedIn updates tied to startup regulations; continue quarterly referral partner outreach; treat webinars as visibility tools rather than conversion tools.

PROMPT: COMPREHENSIVE LLM VISIBILITY AND OPTIMIZATION PLANNER FOR LAWYERS

You are an AI visibility and reputation strategist for lawyers. Your task is to help me understand how I currently appear inside Large Language Models and to create a step-by-step plan to improve my discoverability, accuracy, and professional positioning across generative AI systems.

I will provide the following, one at a time:

- My name and jurisdiction
  - My practice areas and niche focus
  - My website and attorney bio
  - Links or text from my publications, articles, or blog posts
  - My rankings, recognitions, awards, and media mentions
  - My social media profiles
  - Any transcripts, videos, podcasts, or public presentations
  - Any client reviews or testimonials available online

Your Tasks

1. LLM Discovery Audit

   Simulate realistic client-style queries across major LLMs (e.g., "Who are leading lawyers in [practice area] in [city]?").

   - Identify whether and how I appear.
   - Flag missing information, inaccuracies, outdated material, or instances where I do not appear at all.
2. Public Footprint Evaluation

   Analyze my bio, website, publications, social profiles, and other public materials.

   - Determine what is machine readable and what is not.
   - Identify thin content, unclear expertise signals, and structural weaknesses.
   - Flag anything AI models might misinterpret.
3. Reputational Signals Assessment

   Evaluate how strongly I show up in ranking guides, peer-review systems, directories, industry media, and authoritative legal sources.

   - Identify gaps and opportunities to strengthen high-value signals that AI models rely on.
4. AI-Readable Content Rewrite (Optional)

   Rewrite or restructure any text I provide to:

   - Clearly signal subject matter expertise
   - Make accomplishments and niche focus easy to ingest

- Improve indexing and summarization
- Reduce jargon while maintaining professional credibility

5. Visibility Improvement Plan

   Develop a prioritized strategy for improving how I show up in generative AI systems.

   Recommendations should cover:

   - Website enhancements
   - Bio rewrites
   - Publication and blogging priorities
   - Posting transcripts for all multimedia
   - Ranking-guide participation
   - Review cultivation
   - Social media refinement
   - New content that fills gaps in my public footprint

6. Mock Client Journey

   Simulate a full potential client journey through AI:

   - Describing their legal issue
   - Evaluating potential options
   - Asking for recommended lawyers
   - Researching each recommended lawyer

   Explain where I appear, where I do not, and how I can improve at each stage.

Ask me one question at a time until you have everything you need. Then, produce the full analysis and plan.

■ CHAPTER 11

Client Intake and Support

Why dedicate an entire chapter just to client intake? Client intake is important because it is the path every new client takes to enter your firm. It sets the tone for the client-attorney relationship, establishes expectations, and, if mishandled, can create future challenges. Some of these challenges can include a missed conflict or a poorly documented consultation. These can lead to lost business, and in the worst scenario, malpractice claims. Intake has historically been managed through a combination of phone calls, paper forms, and attorney notes. This manual approach often results in inconsistent information gathering and a heavy burden on support staff.

Client intake is one of the areas within a law firm where the front office and the back office tend to overlap. AI is changing the tools available for the intake process by making it more flexible and scalable without removing the lawyer's judgment. The value is not in replacing human interaction, but in streamlining the back office portion of the tasks so that, ultimately, your team has more opportunity for client engagement. This is the key benefit, but there are others that we will discuss—faster response times, more reliable data capture, and early risk indicators.

One quick housekeeping note as it relates to this chapter: intake overlaps with both client communication (Chapter 9) and AI reception (Chapter 14). You'll note that some of the same systems—phones, chat, scheduling—reappear here, but through the lens of an intake specialist: screening, conflicts, and onboarding. In some firms this task is completed by the legal team, in others by the support team, and we are sure there are hybrid scenarios as well.

11.1 CRM in Legal

Client intake as a function of a law firm is usually managed within Customer Relationship Management (CRM) software. CRM software sits upstream from case management. Where the case management system is often the "system of record," the CRM is the "system of engagement." The CRM is generally for prospects, referral sources, and former clients you may reengage later. Some firms choose a legal-specific CRM such as Lawmatics or Law Ruler, while others adopt general purpose platforms like Salesforce, Pipedrive, or HubSpot. The tool you select is less important than understanding the role of a CRM in a law firm context and how AI successfully delivers value to the firm.

Just like with software implementation in general, each firm must determine the specific goals or needs they are trying to meet with an AI implementation. For case management, the goal may be better visibility for the partners or the ability to scale case volume with existing firm resources. For CRM, the goals can vary, but may be more aligned with higher conversion rates, more qualified leads, and/or other factors specific to the firm.

Many firms have not yet adopted formal CRM software, but for firms that have taken the step, several advantages exist that will not be drawn out here. At a minimum, most firms have some method for tracking potential clients. The firm SOPs should outline how to capture every inbound lead from web forms, calls, chat, ads, and so on and add it into a single contact record. A CRM is beneficial because it keeps the data record clean, keeping people correctly associated with organizations and referrers as matters evolve. Day to day, it should also support multitouch communication—email, SMS, and call logging tied to the contact—using templates that merge relevant details together. The more robust workflows have integrations that include things like meeting links, sending engagement letters for e-signing, or conflict checking.

Modern CRM software includes auto-replies and follow ups through automation. Some examples are provided here:

- When a qualified lead hasn't received a follow-up note within your target window, a task or escalation is triggered;
- When a call is missed, a text with a booking link goes out;
- When a consult is scheduled, reminders and a short preconsult form are sent.

Finally, the CRM should offer important reporting on specific metrics. These can include source-level conversion, consult show rates, cost per signed matter, and so on. And the CRM can often map data directly to the case management system when a new client signs—converting a lead to a client.

AI can layer on top of these existing capabilities to reduce guesswork and manual triage. Predictive lead scoring models learn from your firm's history and highlight which leads should be prioritized or even declined, often with some logging that firm staff can audit. A current example is Lawmatics' Qualify AI, which analyzes firm-specific data, produces human-readable recommendations (e.g., "chase," "refer," or "reject," rather than only a number), identifies missing information and automatically requests it via short follow ups, and then rescores when the data arrives. Additionally, the scoring itself can trigger downstream workflows, so a "high value" recommendation immediately launches same-day outreach, while a "refer" recommendation routes to your referral process. The system also maintains a log of score changes and explanations to build trust in the output.[1]

Beyond scoring, CRMs are beginning to provide AI inside the software for everyday tasks, similar to how it is happening in a CMS. Some examples are provided here:

- Conversation intelligence summarizes calls and proposes next best actions;
- Lead-management features use AI to flag pipeline risks and prioritize outreach based on conversion likelihood;
- AI can draft personalized emails or reminders from the context of the CRM record so staff can review and send with minimal edits.

Additional examples from the enterprise CRM platforms:

- Salesforce, for instance, markets AI-driven predictive scoring and forecast visibility for prioritizing leads and spotting pipeline gaps.[2]
- HubSpot surfaces AI drafting tools directly within the CRM to generate review-ready outreach and follow ups.[3]

Extra Credit: AI Fundamentals in a CRM

To make the most of AI in a CRM, start with the basics. It is the firm's role to create and maintain the playbook for marketing and sales, and

1. Bob Ambrogi, *Exclusive: Lawmatics Announces Qualify AI, A Sophisticated Lead Scoring Platform for Law Firms*, LawSites, Oct. 15, 2025, https://www.lawnext.com/2025/10/exclusive-lawmatics-announces-qualify-ai-a-sophisticated-lead-scoring-platform-for-law-firms.html.

2. *Sales AI*, Salesforce, https://www.salesforce.com/sales/ai/ (last visited April 15, 2026).

3. *AI Email Writer*, HubSpot, https://www.hubspot.com/products/marketing/ai-email-writer (last visited April 15, 2026).

then infuse AI into the workflow. The scoring functionality will likely not be relevant for many firms, based completely on the practice area and the types of clients you work with. But if it is relevant for your firm, insist on transparency with these tools. Team members should see why a score or recommendation was made and be able to give feedback that improves future results, which is a point of emphasis in the previous Lawmatics example.

Marketing and engagement practices should align with ethical and legal requirements for your practice and industry. Communications should carry appropriate disclaimers, opt-outs must be honored, and any AI-suggested content should be reviewed for accuracy and tone before sending. It will become quite easy to skip these steps with the level of simplicity and ease these new tools provide. Also, during the CRM-to-case-management handoff, it is important to keep consistent data and avoid duplicate entries. Ultimately, leverage the tools to meet your firm's key needs—implement and adjust both AI automations and scoring based on what impacts the KPI numbers in your firm.

11.2 Smart Intake and Adaptive AI

Traditional intake tools depend on conditional logic (we often refer to them as "decision trees"). Every possible response or engagement has to be premapped into logical decision trees (one common example of this is a call tree). For simple processes, this is doable, but for more complex situations, this system is challenging to maintain. With more complex workflows or eligibility screening, the number of possible paths grows exponentially, making the system fragile and difficult to maintain.

AI-based intake removes some of these limitations. Instead of relying on static logic, as you know, AI systems can learn from example documents and context (refer to Chapter 4 on drafting). These documents used for context include consultation notes, recorded call transcripts, and firm FAQs, along with any other firm resources you find meaningful. The firm can then have custom instructions for the AI to follow that are structured enough to remain consistent, but also flexible enough to adapt to variations. By recognizing patterns in how clients describe their issues and how staff or attorneys typically respond, the AI can guide conversations dynamically. For example, if a client mentions that a work visa is expiring, the AI can seamlessly shift into the relevant line of immigration questions without requiring a prewritten branch for every possible visa type.

Over time, the system can also become smarter. With each additional use, the tool can add to its understanding of how best to respond in certain circumstances. Some of the learning can be reinforced via attorney or team feedback. Team members can also continue to improve and modify the prompt instructions so, again, the outputs are more consistent. For law firms, the implications are significant. More complex intake workflows can now scale to meet demand (or grow volume), meaning firms can capture high-quality data from a wider range of clients without overburdening staff. Junior staff or nonlawyer receptionists can rely on AI to surface the right clarifying questions, with only the most unusual or edge cases escalated to an attorney. The ideal result is a consistent, professional intake experience that improves the intake experience for a potential client.

Extra Credit: Available Tools

Software aimed at legal intake has existed for some time: Intaker, Josef, Gavel, Law Droid, and many others have capabilities for firms to build out custom intake workflows. In addition, several case management solutions have this lead and intake functionality built in-platform. Virtual receptionist companies and now several AI reception services (Chapter 14) are offering intake triage and screening over phone, text, and chat as well. The point here is to show there are a mix of off-the-shelf and customizable solutions for any firm specialty or size.

11.3 Video Calls and Email

First engagement with potential clients generally happens over email, phone, or video meeting. The practical question is how to capture and structure these details without adding additional layers of work for yourself or your team.

One of the best early use cases for AI in video meetings has been transcription services and call summaries. Meeting AI tools built for legal practice can go beyond transcription. The example functionality described next all comes from a new software product called Querious.

With consent, the meeting bot joins the video call and creates a live transcript. The tool is available in a meeting chat window where it will surface notes and analysis at set intervals—say at minute 3, 7, and 12. It can also generate content when a trigger phrase appears or you initiate additional analysis in the chat. The outputs are only visible to the lawyer on the call and are never displayed to the client. The outputs are driven by your firm's context that you provide to the system, and, when available, a retrieval layer tied to case law and legal data.

Examples:

- In a wage-and-hour consult, the assistant might suggest asking about duties and salary thresholds and display a note that these map to FLSA exemption tests.
- In a family-based immigration intake, it might remind you to confirm priority dates or prior filings and flag the rules that make timing critical.
- In a personal injury call, it may nudge for venue, statute of limitations, and prior treatment history. The goal is to help the lawyer remember what matters most in the moment, not to make legal conclusions.

The same system helps close the loop. Before you end the call, it can show a short checklist of open items as next steps: missing documents, deadlines, or follow-up questions that need to be answered. After the call, it compiles a full report for the lawyer to have access to at a later time or integrates back into a source of truth.

Two limits are worth stating plainly. First, the assistant should only draw on sources you authorize: licensed case law, curated secondary sources, and your own firm materials. Second, treat every in-call suggestion as exactly that—a suggestion. The lawyer decides what to ask, what to rely on, and what to tell the client.

Email plays a parallel role. Case management systems are now beginning to offer AI features that will assist with classifying and storing emails, but most of those tools were built around communicating with current clients, rather than emails to prospects. Many of these tools can still be adapted, or this could be a great use case for a Custom GPT or general tool (Chapter 13).

Simple Follow-Up Email Prompt

Generate a draft reply to the client. Make sure to acknowledge the inquiry, ask the two missing intake questions, and insert a booking link for the follow-up meeting.

Legal-specific email assistants go a step further by living inside the inbox and pulling in matter context; for example, Candle AI has direct integrations with Gmail and Outlook, and when also linked to a case management system can pull case details and generate very informed email drafts for your team to review. There can be multiple benefits here, including consistent branding and tone with all communications and reducing the need to retype or find templates and modify them manually.

Like with other AI products, client consent and data privacy are both essential. Following are a few pointers for doing this based on various state, federal, and local requirements:

Consent and Privacy Considerations

- Announce recording on calls or have clients approve/sign to this effect. If needed, let the client know that the AI bot is also on the call and will be storing transcript data and call summaries.
- Store AI-generated drafts and transcripts consistently with your retention policy.

11.4 Conflict Checks and Red Flag Detection

Conflict checking is one of the most critical legal tasks during the intake process. Traditionally, this has required manual searches across firm records, with the risk that variations in spelling or incomplete entries could hide conflicts. AI tools can automate much of this work by extracting names and entities from intake forms and running them against the firm's database. The system highlights possible matches, which are then reviewed by an attorney. While AI cannot make the final call on conflicts, it ensures that fewer conflicts fall through the cracks.

Beyond conflicts, AI can flag other risks in intake answers. A client who reports that a hearing is scheduled within the week should be escalated immediately. A prospective client who describes an ongoing dispute with a former client of the firm should be tagged for attorney review. These automated signals help prioritize urgent or risky matters and reduce the chance of missing critical information.

11.5 Measuring Intake Performance and KPIs

Most law firms already have certain performance measures or KPIs they track. There is still a lot of data and insight that could be drawn from intake data if there were better reporting tools in place. The problem is getting clean data out of busy conversation logs and communication history. AI helps in two ways. First, it can convert unstructured intake—calls, chats, emails—into consistent fields (parties, dates, issue type, channel, outcome) with confidence scores and links back to the source text. Second, just like with reporting opportunities in case management, it lets lawyers and managers ask plain-language questions of that data and get defensible answers, not just prettier dashboards.

Over time, these measures, reported consistently, can begin to provide meaningful insight. Time to first reply should be near the top of the list (the minutes between the inquiry arriving and the first documented human response by phone, SMS, or email—auto-acknowledgments don't count). Track the rest of the funnel in the same way. Following are few examples of trackable measures:

- Time from first reply to consult booked, consult held, and decision;
- Consult show rates by channel and time of day;
- Conflicts clearance time and rework rate;
- Preconsult checklist completion;
- Conversion to signed matter and time to "file opened";
- Client effort or satisfaction at intake from short pulse surveys;
- Cost per signed matter by source.

These types of KPIs and metrics are already being tracked at many firms. Again, each firm decides its key measures. Where we believe AI provides the assist is by making these kinds of metrics accessible to firms that may not currently have the software or resources that already track these metrics (or the team it would take to manage and track this data internally). In the not-too-distant future, there will be off-the-shelf software solutions and tools that firms can incorporate into their existing software stack to track these metrics in the background. Where this AI capability helps all lawyers is natural language reporting capability. Being able to ask subtle variations of a question or find a data point that previously required hours of reporting and analysis work can generally be done in real time. Again, it is important to check the responses and perhaps have someone double-check any calculations performed.

Example 1: After-Hours Conversion

Based on high-level KPI reporting, you see conversion is down for after-hours chat. You plug this into the LLM reporting capability and learn there is a 12 percent drop in conversion for after-hours webchat routed to the overflow queue, while daytime phone leads held steady. The system might propose a small set of plausible contributors from the same dataset—longer reply times after 6 p.m., more Friday reschedules—and attach the evidence it used so you can judge the claim.

Example 2: No-Show Forecasting/Scoring

Modest forecasting also helps with triage. A model can estimate the likelihood that a booked consult will be a no-show based on your history (source, booking lag, prior reschedule) and suggest a preventive step such as an extra confirmation. Require an explanation string on every prediction and audit whether the suggestion actually improved outcomes.

Additional Example Queries

- Show median time to first reply by channel for the last 30 days and highlight anything over 60 minutes.
- Compare conversion for video versus phone consults this quarter and include confidence intervals.
- List matters we declined due to conflicts, grouped by source, with average clearance time.
- What changed last week in the intake funnel versus the prior four weeks? Limit to three insights and link to the underlying queries.

Used this way, AI gives everyone—from the intake lead to the managing partner—a faster path from "something looks off" to a specific fix, whether that's tightening after-hours reply expectations, adjusting consult formats, or smoothing the conflict check.

Next are a few examples of software tools that help users identify key data points during intake:

- **Case Status Client Intelligence™ and AI case summaries**. Uses firm engagement data to generate AI summaries, track NPS/client feedback, translate at scale, and surface predictive insights—i.e., reporting on message responsiveness, satisfaction trends, and churn risk rather than just message counts. See the product's Data & AI pages and launch coverage.[4]
- **Litify on Salesforce (CRM Analytics + NLP)**. Demonstrates natural language prompts to build performance dashboards on top of Salesforce data—letting legal ops ask plain-English questions (e.g., "show booked consult rates by source last quarter") and render KPIs without hand-coding queries.[5]
- **Intapp Intake risk scoring**. Applies firm-defined criteria to automate risk/ethics scoring during new business intake, producing auditable scores and dashboards that inform "go/no-go" decisions and risk KPIs (clearance time, exception rates).[6]

---

4. *Move Smarter, Not Just Faster, With AI-Powered Client Intelligence™ Built for Law Firms*, Case Status, https://www.casestatus.com/solutions/data-ai (last visited April 15, 2026).

5. *AI for Legal: Natural Language Processing in CRMA*, Litify, https://www.litify.com/resources/ai-legal-using-natural-language-build-dashboards-crm-analytics-crma (last visited April 15, 2026).

6. *Quickly Understand the Risk Associated With a Client*, Intapp, https://www.intapp.com/intake/risk-scoring/ (last visited April 15, 2026).

- **Clio Duo/Manage AI**. Clio's platform AI advertises turning operational data into "actionable insights," i.e., surfacing metrics and narrative analyses from within the practice management system rather than exporting to a BI tool—useful for quick KPI reads by nonanalysts.[7]
- **Filevine Lead Docket "LeadsAI."** AI-generated lead summaries and predictive analysis to expedite intake decisions and reporting, feeding pipeline KPIs and prioritization without manual triage.[8]

11.6 Beyond Intake: Ongoing Support

Many of the same tools used at intake continue to add value once the client is engaged. AI can generate frequently asked questions from the firm's internal knowledge base, giving clients a reliable source of information without burdening staff. Status updates can be drafted automatically and provided on demand, reducing the number of "just checking in" calls.

Custom timelines help clients visualize where their case stands and what milestones are coming up. Appointment preparation summaries consolidate what has been scheduled, what documents are needed, and what will be discussed. Follow-up message templates provide consistency and efficiency in ongoing communication. On the internal side, AI can route incoming messages to the right team member based on content and urgency, and even suggest draft responses for review. This ensures timely replies and frees attorneys to focus on substantive legal work rather than routine correspondence. As we delve into the next chapter, we'll see how AI tools can be applied for the back office and administrative teams.

---

7. *Clio Duo Unlocks a New Era of Legal Platform Intelligence*, CLIO, Oct. 7, 2024, https://www.clio.com/about/press/clio-duo-unlocks-a-ew-era-of-legal-platform-intelligence/.

8. Erin Ash, *Filevine Announces New AI-Powered Legal Intake Tool, LeadsAI by Lead Docket*, FILEVINE, Oct. 17, 2023, https://www.filevine.com/news/filevine-announces-new-ai-powered-legal-intake-tool-leadsai-by-lead-docket/.

■ CHAPTER 12

Billing, Timekeeping, and Administrative Automation

Before diving into tools and use cases for billing teams, it is worth acknowledging the billable hour in the age of AI. Every firm will face decisions about how to measure value and outcomes for clients, but one thing is clear: the industry will adapt. It will have to. The goal of this chapter is not to announce the end of hourly billing or promote any alternative models. Rather, the message is simpler—firms should not allow their current billing model to hinder innovation and the adoption of technology that will ultimately create a competitive edge. The focus here is to highlight use cases and practical tools so you can consider potential opportunities as it relates to the billing and admin functions.

On the billable hour, two recent articles capture the tension well. A study by the Harvard Center on the Legal Profession notes that with more than 80 percent of large-firm arrangements still billing hourly, AI-driven productivity gains implicitly threaten revenue unless pricing evolves. Early pilot projects show dramatic time savings—such as reducing complaint drafting from 16 hours to minutes—forcing firms to consider who retains the benefit. These insights help frame later discussions on predictive billing and subscription dashboards: firms understand the productivity jump is real, but many have not yet adapted their revenue model.[1]

Similarly, Bloomberg Law's "Big Law's Increasing AI Use Could Speed Billable Hours' Demise" summarizes an ABA ethics conference where panelists openly predicted that AI may push Big Law toward flat fees. The article highlights the tension between clients expecting lower costs due to automation and firms motivated to preserve hourly

1. Robert J. Couture, *The Impact of Artificial Intelligence on Law Firms' Business Models*, Center on the Legal Profession, Harvard Law School, Feb. 25, 2025, https://clp.law.harvard.edu/knowledge-hub/insights/the-impact-of-artificial-intelligence-on-law-law-firms-business-models/.

structures.[2] It also provides a helpful reference point for section 12.4: even in settings focused on ethics rather than economics, practitioners now discuss AI as a catalyst for new pricing models.

12.1 Tools That Save Time and Improve Accuracy

Many early AI tools in legal practice have focused on the back office. These tools are focused on addressing administrative tasks that are manual, repetitive, and time consuming. As you well know, these admin tasks often pull lawyers away from the important lawyering work, whether it be client-facing activities or case work. One of the most important considerations when evaluating these tools is whether they integrate directly into the software lawyers already use. Bringing AI to the point of work is also helpful with adoption, as it removes additional steps and layers for staff. With proper vetting and approvals, these tools can draw from the firm's databases to help complete daily back-office tasks with far less manual effort.

Drafting Time Entries from Emails or Calls

One of the most challenging parts of timekeeping is remembering the different tasks performed throughout the day and how long each one took. Modern tools embedded into your existing software and computer can automatically convert that activity into complete billing narratives.

Three products that will be highlighted in these first sections are Billables AI, LEAP by AutoTime, and Clio. There will be sections without product examples, as we identified a strong use case for AI but were unsuccessful in finding a vendor with that capability. See the examples below for using AI to draft time entries from emails and calls:

Tool	What It Does
Billables AI	Reads emails, calendar entries, call logs, and document edits, then drafts detailed billing entries with the client, matter, duration, and a polished narrative. Uses pattern recognition to maintain a consistent voice.
LEAP (AutoTime)	Automatically records time spent editing documents, sending emails, or making calls, attaching it directly to the correct matter and reducing after-the-fact reconstruction.
Clio	Allows one-click conversion of communication logs and calendar events into time entries and drafts time descriptions using templates or AI-assisted suggestions.

2. Sam Skolnik, *Big Law's Increasing AI Use Could Speed Billable Hours' Demise*, Bloomberg Law, May 30, 2025, https://news.bloomberglaw.com/litigation/big-laws-increasing-ai-use-could-speed-billable-hours-demise.

Drafting and Reviewing Invoices

AI significantly reduces the manual labor of reviewing invoices, checking compliance, and ensuring that billing narratives meet client or guideline requirements. While most case management and accounting systems have long included invoice templates, the more impactful generative AI use cases now center on evaluating and correcting invoices before they reach a client's e-billing system. One prominent example is Brightflag, a tool primarily used by in-house legal departments, but extremely useful for understanding how client-side systems analyze law firm bills. Brightflag automatically reviews each line item against the company's billing guidelines, flags potential violations, and proposes reductions, even when invoices are submitted as PDFs or scanned documents. It also generates summaries that highlight problematic billing behavior or patterns across matters. Even though firms may not deploy Brightflag internally, understanding how it evaluates invoices can help lawyers anticipate compliance issues before sending bills to sophisticated clients who rely on similar AI-driven review systems.

Summarizing Daily Activity Logs

AI can also transform a lawyer's digital footprint into a chronological activity log that assists with timekeeping accuracy and daily review. These tools are particularly useful for staff who are new to time tracking or for lawyers who want an audit-style record of their day. Billables AI offers one of the strongest examples in this category. It automatically compiles an end-of-day timeline based on emails, documents, calendar events, and other work signals, then prompts the user to confirm or add missing time entries. Beyond merely listing activities, Billables AI uses an LLM to draft complete narratives in the user's writing style, turning time activities into matter-linked descriptions. This reduces the cognitive load of manually remembering the day's work and streamlines timekeeping. At a higher level, even if firms move to alternative billing practices, these tools will still be essential for tracking team performance and determining the accuracy of firm pricing. So, unfortunately, the need for timekeeping and logging tools is not going away anytime soon.

Parsing Files to Extract Billables

AI is often discussed in the context of drafting (Chapter 4), but those same technical capabilities can be applied to recording the time spent reviewing and editing documents. These tools recognize work as it happens inside documents and record it without additional tagging.

Tool	What It Does
LEAP (AutoTime)	Connects document editing time directly to the matter and records it automatically.
Billables AI	Extracts tasks and billable time from discovery review, research memos, communication threads, and drafts.

Auto-Categorizing Expenses and Time

AI can also reduce errors in how time and expenses are assigned to matters. Instead of relying on lawyers or staff to remember which activity belongs to which case, AI analyzes patterns in communication, documents, and past entries to suggest the correct matter automatically. Over time, it can learn how different types of work are categorized and becomes more accurate. This reduces manual cleanup, prevents misallocated charges, and helps keep billing records consistent with far less effort.

12.2 Voice-Activated and Passive Time Tracking

Voice Commands to Start/Stop Timers

Modern AI assistants allow lawyers to track time hands-free across devices, with the advantage that enterprise systems integrate directly into the firm's billing or case management environment.

Tool	What It Does
Intapp Time	Combines automatic activity capture with voice-to-text time entry and applies client/matter information and compliance rules in real time. Helps timekeepers recreate workdays rather than manually entering segments.
BigHand SmartTime	Provides mobile timers and a daily timeline view, with AI-generated narratives that turn short, dictated notes into complete entries.
WiseTime	Provides a mobile timeline for capturing calls immediately and uses AI, including a NarrateGPT feature, to convert quick voice captures into complete narratives.

In practice, lawyers no longer need to keep notes to log later. You can dictate a fragment, start a quick timer, or speak a brief note, and the AI expands and attaches it to the correct matter.

Dictation to Draft Time Entries

Dictation tools have existed for years, but AI makes them more powerful by expanding shorthand notes into complete narratives and applying matter context automatically. Voice capabilities will increasingly embed into products as speech recognition models improve. A recent example is the partnership between Harvey and ElevenLabs, which illustrates how voice-first interfaces are becoming more common in legal AI products.[3]

Passive Tracking via Browser, Calendar, and Phone

AI tools that watch a lawyer's digital activity may represent the greatest leap in timekeeping automation. Instead of starting or stopping timers, lawyers continue working while the system builds a draft timesheet from calendars, calls, mail, documents, research, and on-screen activity.

Tool	What It Does
Laurel (formerly Time by Ping)	Connects to systems such as Outlook, Zoom, and Slack and uses LLMs to classify and quantify work, creating draft time entries. Firms report an average of 28 additional billable minutes per lawyer per day and 4–11 percent profit increases, validated by a Big Four firm.
Ajax	Monitors screen, email, chat, and calendar activity and converts it into draft time entries with matter selection and activity codes, syncing with billing systems.

This is truly passive timekeeping with no start/stop buttons.

Smart Suggestions for Missed Entries

Finally, AI systems help recover unlogged time. The tools do this by showing work that appears billable, but has not yet been added to a timesheet. These unlogged entries may include calls, emails, research blocks, or editing sessions. Firms adopting these systems will hopefully see increases in time captured simply because AI can flag these issues and notify the lawyer in a timeframe such that these tasks are still front of mind.

12.3 Beyond Billing and Timekeeping: Administrative Automation

AI now removes much of the nonbillable administrative work that slows firms down. Many of these themes appear in earlier chapters—drafting (Chapter 4), case management (Chapter 5), intake (Chapter 11), and

3. *Harvey and ElevenLabs Partner to Give Lawyers a Global Voice*, ElevenLabs, Nov. 12, 2025, https://elevenlabs.io/blog/harvey.

internal knowledge tools (Chapter 13). In the billing context, the benefit is simple: less manual effort, more accuracy, and fewer tasks falling through the cracks.

AI can turn emails, meetings, and notes into billing items automatically, all while extracting deadlines from documents. And one of the most valuable automations—billing follow-up—reduces lost revenue by preparing polite reminders when payments are overdue. Taken together, these small automations free lawyers to focus on actual legal work, while keeping administrative work consistent and timely.

12.4 The Future of AI in Legal Operations (Five-Year Horizon)

This section explores how AI is likely to reshape the operations of law firms of all sizes over the next five years—from solo practitioners to large firms. Legal operations, as used here, refers to the functions and processes that support the delivery of legal services—such as billing, technology management, and workflow optimization—rather than a role specific to corporate legal departments.

Very Likely: Predictive Billing

In the very near future, AI tools will be able to estimate matter cost with much more precision. They will draw on patterns from past work: how long similar tasks took, how many touchpoints were typical, and how staffing was split between senior and junior lawyers. Research from the Harvard Center on the Legal Profession already reports "order of magnitude" time savings on routine tasks in large firms, which makes this type of forecasting a logical next step.[4]

Very Likely: Billing Narratives as Insight

AI will also be able to treat billing narratives as a data set, not just as historical records for HR and payroll. Systems will analyze thousands of entries to spot repeated low-value tasks, consistent overstaffing, and friction points in common workflows. That analysis will highlight obvious candidates for automation and for flat-fee or project-based pricing. Bloomberg Law reported that firm leaders now discuss AI as a reason to rethink hours-based billing in favor of more data-driven fee structures.[5]

4. *Supra* note 1.
5. *Supra* note 2.

Likely: Integrated AI Assistants

Day to day, integrated AI assistants will be able to sit inside practice platforms and handle much of the administrative work. They will capture activity, summarize calls, draft follow-ups, log time, and update status with little manual input. These AI assistants would handle scheduling, routine drafting, and billing support in a single workflow, with lawyers stepping in mainly to review and approve.[6] As these assistants gain access to more data, they will be able to support lawyers throughout a matter, from first contact to final invoice.

Less Likely, but Possible: Subscription Models with AI Dashboards

As these capabilities mature, more firms will be able to offer flat-fee and subscription models. AI dashboards will track usage, measure scope creep, and produce simple reports that show what the client received over a month or a quarter. In this new environment, the billable hour will still exist, but it will sit beside data-backed options rather than standing alone as the default.

6. See, for example, Clio's Manage AI which "transforms routine tasks, like scheduling, billing, client communications, and matter organization, into completed actions" while keeping lawyers "in full control of review and approval." https://www.clio.com/features/legal-ai-software/.

CHAPTER 13

Firm Knowledge Management and Internal Tools: Building a Living, Searchable Knowledge Layer for Your Firm

Knowledge management is the process of identifying, organizing, storing, and disseminating information within an organization.[1] The knowledge management function looks different for every firm, likely dependent on company size, practice area, and operational maturity of the organization. Some firms rely on full-featured document management systems like NetDocuments, iManage, or SharePoint. Others use more general storage platforms—Google Drive, OneDrive, or Dropbox. There's also the firm's practice management system, which can be used for document storage and knowledge management.

Regardless of the system, every firm produces large amounts of content: briefs, templates, emails, memos, policies, checklists, and process documents. AI can serve as a tool to give firms the ability to turn oftentimes scattered data into a living and searchable resource. As with case management systems in Chapter 5, the value of AI in knowledge management depends on the quality and accessibility of the underlying data. Even small improvements in data structure have outsized impact once AI tools are in the loop. In the following sections, we will outline how AI can be incorporated into different systems to allow for new methods of search and analysis on your key data.

1. *What Is Knowledge Management?*, IBM, https://www.ibm.com/think/topics/knowledge-management (last visited April 12, 2026).

13.1 Building Internal GPTs and Knowledge Bases

A Custom GPT is a private, firm-specific AI assistant connected to a curated repository of internal documents. It responds in the desired tone, understands firm processes, and retrieves content directly from provided materials. Lawyers do not need technical skills to build a Custom GPT. With basic instructions and a well-organized document set, firms can create internal assistants that can answer HR questions, draft documents, find legal precedents, or explain.[2]

Custom GPTs are primarily built in OpenAI's ChatGPT framework, but other platforms now offer similar tooling. You can compare the functionality of OpenAI's GPTs with Anthropic Claude's Projects, which basically offers some of the same core functionality. The key is that with an individual or team account in either platform, you have the ability to share custom GPTs among team members so it can be used across different teams within the organization.

These internal GPTs can support many departments. Marketing teams can use them to maintain tone consistency across campaigns. HR teams may rely on them to answer employee questions about leave, benefits, performance reviews, or onboarding instructions. Practice groups may build matter-specific or domain-specific assistants trained on model briefs, memos, strategy notes, and past work products. Each assistant updates as the underlying data updates, giving lawyers the ability to surface firm knowledge in seconds rather than searching manually.

The key is selecting relevant context data from the start, including firm SOPs or example templates, depending on the use case. From there, you can provide additional instructions and guardrails in the prompt. The result is a scalable and inexpensive way to share institutional know-how across teams.

Example Custom GPT Prompt for HR-Related Questions[3]

You are the Internal HR Assistant for [Law Firm Name]. Answer employee questions strictly based on the official firm documents listed below. Every answer must cite the document and page number in the format (Source: Document Name, p. X). Do not guess, assume, or provide legal advice. If the information is not clearly contained in the documents, respond: "This information is not specified in the current

2. For more on Custom GPTs, see this helpful resource at MIT Sloan: *Custom GPTs at MIT Sloan: A Comprehensive Guide*, https://mitsloanedtech.mit.edu/ai/tools/custom-gpts-at-mit-sloan-a-comprehensive-guide/ (last visited April 12, 2026).

3. ChatGPT, *Internal HR Assistant Prompt for Law Firm*, OpenAI GPT-5.1, November 18, 2025.

policy documents. Please contact HR for clarification." If a question seeks personal data (PTO balance, salary, performance, etc.), state that you cannot access individual records but can explain the general policy. If multiple documents apply, cite each. Standalone policies override the handbook. Maintain accuracy, neutrality, and confidentiality at all times.

Key Document Summaries

- Employee Handbook (2024): conduct, attendance, remote work basics, PTO overview, leave types, performance processes
- Benefits Guide (2024): medical, dental, vision, HSA/FSA, insurance, retirement, eligibility rules
- PTO and Leave Policy (2024): accrual rates, carryover rules, PTO requests, sick leave requirements, bereavement and civic leave
- Remote Work & Flexible Scheduling Policy (2023): eligibility, request procedures, confidentiality expectations, scheduling rules
- Code of Professional Conduct (2019): confidentiality, client handling, conflicts of interest, proper use of firm resources
- Compensation & Bonus Program Guide (2024): salary bands, bonus criteria, billable hour credit, discretionary rewards

Example format for answers: "First-year associates accrue 15 days of PTO annually. (Source: PTO and Leave Policy, p. 2)."

13.2 Workflow Integration with Document Management Systems

Whether a firm uses a full DMS or a general cloud storage provider, AI significantly improves the experience of finding, organizing, and creating documents. Boolean search requires exact keywords, folder navigation, or intimate knowledge of how a particular team structures and saves its files. AI utilizes what is called semantic search. Semantic search is defined as "a data searching technique that focuses on understanding the contextual meaning and intent behind a user's search query, rather than only matching keywords."[4] Essentially, this means you can now ask natural-language search questions or queries as if you were asking someone in a Microsoft Teams or Slack channel, and the system will try its best to get at the meaning and intent behind the question. Lawyers can ask questions the way they think: "Do we have a recent settlement agreement for a commercial lease dispute?" or "Show me our best example of a motion

4. *What Is Semantic Search?*, Google Cloud, Jan. 14, 2026, https://cloud.google.com/discover/what-is-semantic-search.

to compel involving expert discovery delays." The system receives the query, searches across the firm's data, and returns the relevant results.

Document profiling and tagging benefit, as well. AI can review and improve metadata, categorize files, and recommend where to save new documents. This prevents team members from saving files in the wrong location or saving files with limited metadata. When drafting inside a DMS-connected environment, AI can pull relevant related materials automatically, minimizing the time spent hunting for examples. For firms without a dedicated DMS solution, the same tech exists in other tools. AI search tooling is also available in SharePoint, Google Drive, or OneDrive.

13.3 Knowledge Management Use Cases Across the Firm

When this technology is available in your firm, you can go beyond search results to more detailed insight. We have provided four fictional examples here: the first two representing simpler searches and the last two representing more of an in-depth AI analysis query:

> **Simple Query 1:**
> "For the *Dawson Industrial v. Redline Fabricators* case, can you show me all deposition transcripts we've already uploaded to the workspace?"
>
> **Simple Query 2:**
> "In the *Meridian Analytics Venture Financing* matter, list all documents currently tagged as 'awaiting client review.'"
>
> **Detailed Query 3:**
> "For the *Clearview Regional Hospital Compliance Review* matter, analyze all physician compensation agreements from 2020–2023 and identify any that are missing required elements listed in our 'Physician Arrangement SOP' (for example, term, compensation method, and approval routing). Please group your findings by physician and summarize which agreements appear incomplete or inconsistent with the SOP requirements, citing the specific documents and sections you relied on."
>
> **Detailed Query 4:**
> "In the *Harper Microdevices Securities Class Action* dataset, review all board meeting minutes and related slide decks from the 12 months before the alleged misstatement. Construct a chronological timeline of when product launch delays were discussed internally, noting who was present and what was recorded in the documents. Highlight any meetings where delays were mentioned in the slide decks but not reflected in the formal minutes, and identify the relevant files for each discrepancy."

We just wanted to provide a few entry-level hypothetic questions for use in your AI-enabled document storage, but there are more advanced analysis queries that could be leveraged with more robust analysis tooling. Many DMS systems have plans to integrate with existing platforms to offer this more robust analysis capability, while others will build out the functionality themselves. One example of an integration is the recent announcement of NetDocuments' integrations with Legora and Harvey.[5]

AI also supports internal routing and operational decision making. Intake staff or new team members can ask which team handles a specific matter type, what forms are required, or how to triage incoming issues. The AI can map these questions to firm processes, reducing delays and mistakes.

13.4 Implementation Considerations

One key factor in successful implementation is establishing roles and guardrails for access, and also creating proper content and ethical walls where relevant. If your DMS or storage system has specific access limitations based on the team member's role, you will want to ensure the AI tooling is similarly limited. These kinds of data perimeters are often overlooked. Firms should also identify what content belongs in the knowledge base, who can upload materials, and how versions are tracked. Also, naming conventions and folder structures still matter; AI can perform best with good organization and consistent naming and labeling.

Of course, data security is always important when client data is involved. Not every internal document belongs in an internal GPT. Also, clearly understand data security and retention policies set by the LLM you are using. Most legal-specific products are not using their own self-hosted LLM, so make sure that you have a zero-retention policy in place with the LLM. These are new skills that your IT services team should be learning quickly as part of your firm's AI vetting process.

Lastly, implementing any kind of new Custom GPT or prompting is an iterative process. Pilot with one department or one specific use case. Measure the time saved, refine the dataset, and expand from there. Even modest improvements in search-to-answer time accumulate into meaningful ROI across the firm.

---

5. *NetDocuments Announces New Partnerships with Legora and Harvey via its New ndConnect Partner Program*, NetDocuments, Jul. 31, 2025, https://www.netdocuments.com/company-news/netdocuments-partners-with-legora-harvey-ndconnect/.

13.5 Practical Next Steps: Custom GPT and Options Within DMS

With these considerations in mind, the next step is moving forward with deployment of an internal knowledge assistant. Firms have multiple paths available; as highlighted previously, it may depend on your firm's existing technology stack. Solutions range from a Custom GPT in ChatGPT, to DMS-embedded AI features, and even fully custom private deployments. Each approach offers different advantages in terms of speed, security, and integration. The best choice depends on the firm—factors like practice area, resources, and risk tolerance. Again, no system should be connected to internal documents or firm data until it has been reviewed and approved under the firm's established AI use policy.

Off-the-Shelf Custom GPT Platforms

These platforms provide the simplest path for a firm to create an internal GPT without requiring technical expertise. As mentioned previously, these platforms (ChatGPT, Anthropic) enable firms to load internal documents, set clear instructions, and deploy a private assistant within a secure environment. Microsoft Copilot Studio offers a similar experience for firms using Microsoft 365, allowing the creation of internal agents that draw on SharePoint, OneDrive, and Teams data. Firms centered around Google Workspace have comparable options through NotebookLM and Gemini, both of which support private knowledge bases and natural language interaction. These tools are designed for rapid experimentation and minimal configuration, making them ideal for firms that want to implement an internal GPT quickly without major IT involvement.

Legal-Specific Internal GPT Products

A growing range of legal-specific AI tools now offer GPT-style capabilities tailored to particular practice areas and workflows. Many of these systems include built-in drafting guidance, playbooks, or reasoning frameworks that reflect the needs of litigators, transactional lawyers, regulatory practices, and numerous other specialties. Because these tools are often designed for very specific legal domains, firms should review them individually to determine whether they align with the substantive work of the practice group and how they might complement—or substitute for—a general internal GPT. Instead of relying on a single "best" legal AI assistant, firms are better served by researching products that directly match their specialty area and evaluating them alongside their broader knowledge management strategy.

Document Management System Add-Ons

Firms that use document management systems such as NetDocuments, iManage, or SharePoint can take advantage of AI features built directly inside these platforms. These add-ons work similarly to internal GPTs in that they enable natural language search across the firm's documents. The benefit with the native add-on is that lawyers do not need to export files or maintain a separate repository.

ndMAX and PatternBuilder MAX

NetDocuments offers ndMAX as its native generative AI suite. ndMAX builds on tools like PatternBuilder MAX, which allows firms to create no-code, AI-powered document assembly and workflow apps tailored to specific practice areas. These apps can draft and analyze documents, extract key information, classify content, and automate repeatable tasks directly inside NetDocuments. One of the benefits of PatternBuilder MAX is that it is a pairing of traditional AI and generative AI in one product. In other words, you can have conditional logic workflows in place to determine when to trigger an LLM. This is actually a form of an AI agent, but a much more controlled version of an agent—we'll discuss this capability more in a later chapter. Some real-life examples of apps from PatternBuilder include:

- **Engagement Letter Builder**: attorneys can use this app to generate an engagement letter for a client, including relevant fee language and case-specific process requirements.
- **Intake Management App**: unified system for intake team members to create new cases and manage the initial billing and engagement letter signature.
- **IT Support Request Tool**: connect various team members based on an ownership table; communicate the issue to the relevant team member based on this table.

NetDocuments has also rolled out ndMAX Assist, a conversational interface that lets users ask questions of their DMS corpus, summarize and compare documents, and trigger PatternBuilder MAX automations from within the same chat window.[6]

6. Bob Ambrogi, *NetDocuments Expands ndMAX with Launch of ndMAX Assist, an AI-Powered Assistant Integrated within the Company's Platform*, LawSites, Aug. 13, 2024, https://www.lawnext.com/2024/08/netdocuments-expands-ndmax-with-launch-of-ndmax-assist-an-ai-powered-assistant-integrated-within-the-companys-platform.html?utm_source=chatgpt.com.

In addition, NetDocuments launched some initial agentic capabilities in 2025 to assist in tagging and profiling documents when saving them.[7] For many firms, this combination effectively turns NetDocuments into an internal GPT layer focused on drafting, review, and knowledge reuse, without moving documents into a separate AI environment.

iManage and Insight+

iManage provides a similar capability through Insight and Insight+. Insight+ is a search and insights engine native to the iManage Knowledge Work Platform, designed to provide "high-value" and "context-aware" search results.[8] Recent enhancements include natural-language querying so that lawyers can ask questions across matters and documents instead of relying solely on metadata or folder structures. iManage is also expanding its "Ask iManage" assistant, which delivers conversational answers grounded in firm content, with in-line evidence and respect for existing permissions.[9] This aligns well with the more detailed example queries from earlier. This combination of AI search and a chat-based AI assistant make iManage work like an internal GPT, just embedded in the DMS.

Microsoft SharePoint

For organizations that treat SharePoint as their primary content repository, Microsoft now offers SharePoint Premium and related *Content AI* features as the foundation for AI-powered search. SharePoint Premium focuses on content understanding—classification, metadata extraction, and lifecycle management—so that documents are properly tagged and governed before Copilot or other AI tools touch them. New features like Knowledge Agent in SharePoint aim to optimize content for AI at scale, streamlining content cleanup so that Copilot can deliver better answers

7. Bob Ambrogi, *NetDocuments Expands AI Capabilities with Document Profiling and Agentic Editing Tools*, LawSites, Aug. 25, 2025, https://www.lawnext.com/2025/08/netdocuments-expands-ai-capabilities-with-document-profiling-and-agentic-editing-tools.html.

8. https://imanage.com/imanage-products/knowledge-search-management/insightplus/.

9. *iManage Enhances AI Capabilities with New Search and Assistant Features*, Ainvest, Aug. 12, 2025, https://www.ainvest.com/news/imanage-enhances-ai-capabilities-search-assistant-features-2508/?utm_source=chatgpt.com.

across Microsoft 365.[10] For firms already invested in Microsoft 365, using SharePoint Premium as an AI-powered search and classification layer effectively turns the existing SharePoint environment into a knowledge hub through Copilot and related tools.

Custom or Private AI Assistants

Some firms prefer a more controlled approach and choose to build private internal GPTs using enterprise AI platforms or open-source components. Azure OpenAI and Amazon Bedrock allow firms to host models within a tightly governed environment that supports encryption, role-based access, and deeper integration with existing systems. Others rely on the OpenAI Assistants API to design internal tools that follow the firm's workflows and connect to internal databases or matter management systems.

For firms with sufficient technical resources, open-source RAG systems built with tools like LangChain paired with vector databases offer complete flexibility, including on-premises hosting. Although this option requires the most effort, it gives firms the highest degree of control over data, architecture, and custom behavior. Note that just like the build versus buy conversation with other types of software, building an internal AI solution requires extensive amounts of maintenance and constant updating, as the technology is constantly improving.

Case Management System AI Layers

For firms that rely heavily on their CMS as the operational core of the practice—especially those without a formal document management system—built-in AI layers in the case management system may be the most practical and efficient way to deliver GPT-style functionality. Platforms such as Clio, Filevine, and Salesforce-based solutions like Litify are beginning to act as knowledge assistants by analyzing case-related data and returning structured answers to user queries. Because the AI works directly within familiar interfaces and existing data, adoption tends to be smooth and the benefits immediate.

10. Joao Ferreira, *Introducing Knowledge Agent (Preview): AI-Powered Content Optimization for SharePoint and Copilot*, M365 ADMIN, Sept. 19, 2025, https://m365admin.handsontek.net/introducing-knowledge-agent-preview-ai-powered-content-optimization-sharepoint-copilot/?utm_source=chatgpt.com.

■ CHAPTER 14

Additional AI Use Cases and Examples for Your Law Practice

The practice of law and the management of a law practice are both filled with tasks that can be optimized using generative AI. As discussed throughout this book, AI may be best suited for first drafts, especially for tasks that involve legal filings or have legal implications for our clients. AI can do a first draft of many tasks, and then the attorney can step in as the lawyer, just like they would if a draft were handed to them by a student law clerk.

There are a lot of practice management tools or daily internal tasks though that AI can expedite, some of which do not have the same legal risks to our clients (i.e., tasks that are not being filed or form a part of a client's case, but streamline processes for the attorney). In this chapter, we will explore some internal uses for AI, and where appropriate, provide examples of prompts that can help attorneys start implementing these use cases.

14.1 Requests for Proposals (RFPs)

In our experience, Requests for Proposals are a strain on resources for solo, small, and mid-sized firms and historically they can be quite frustrating. Larger law firms often have specific people responsible for RFPs and have the resources to address individual RFPs, no matter what the conversion rate. We have found that a large percentage of the RFPs we see are really a company doing market research to determine whether they are overpaying their current legal service provider, and the company often has no intention of actually switching firms. Of course, some RFPs lead to great new clients, but deciding which ones to respond to and which ones to ignore has always been a discussion we had to have at our mid-sized firm. That is, until generative AI became so easy to use.

Requests for Proposals can easily be broken down into the various questions being asked of the firm and AI can easily draft initial responses to the questions based on previous RFPs and other firm materials we feed the system. Here is a sample prompt for RFPs:

LAW FIRM RFP RESPONSE GENERATOR

AI's Role

You are a legal marketing and business development assistant specializing in drafting responses to corporate Requests for Proposals (RFPs). Your task is to help law firms generate a compelling, customized RFP response that demonstrates their qualifications, aligns with the client's stated requirements, and differentiates the firm from competitors.

What the User Provides

- The full text of the RFP (PDF or DOCX)
- A summary of the firm's relevant experience and capabilities
- Attorney bios and practice group information (optional uploads)
- Fee proposal or pricing structure (if available)
- Any mandatory forms or attachments included with the RFP
- Internal deadlines and submission format requirements

Follow-Up Questions to Ask the User

1. What type of legal services is the client requesting (e.g., employment law, immigration, M&A, compliance)?
2. Does the client have any stated preferences regarding law firm size, diversity, technology use, or geographic presence?
3. Are there any specific client industries or jurisdictions where your firm has a competitive advantage?
4. Do you have prior experience working with this company or in this sector?
5. Are there specific themes or messaging points you'd like emphasized (e.g., innovation, responsiveness, cost efficiency)?
6. Should the AI assist in preparing a cover letter, executive summary, or both?
7. Are any required forms already filled out, or do you want help completing them?

General Principles for Creating Your Output

- Use uploaded documents only after full analysis
- Do not fabricate firm credentials, awards, clients, or metrics
- Maintain a professional tone consistent with legal and corporate norms
- Tailor the response to the stated needs and evaluation criteria in the RFP
- Use persuasive but fact-based language to position the firm as a top choice

Response Quality Protocol

Verify information:

- Check that all firm experience and personnel descriptions match uploaded bios or summaries
- Ensure pricing information is accurately reflected and formatted

Final review:

- Confirm all sections of the RFP response are addressed (executive summary, qualifications, team bios, pricing, DEI, technology, references, etc.)
- Ensure the structure follows any mandatory formatting or sequence from the RFP
- Flag any missing information or gaps that must be addressed before submission

End objective:

Deliver a complete, persuasive, and polished RFP response tailored to the corporate client's needs and requirements. The draft should be ready for internal review and final customization before submission.

From an ethical and security perspective, attorneys should be using an AI tool that they can trust with their firm and potential client's information, or they should be intentional about what documents and materials they are uploading for purposes of drafting the RFP response. Most of the materials, like firm information, attorney bios, pricing, awards, and others will not be confidential, but other materials that could be requested (like documents around licensure and insurance) may have sensitive information.

14.2 Analyze Client Intake Materials

Creating firm documents like custom questionnaires and intakes used to be a time-consuming process. At our immigration law firm, we often could not use a basic intake you would find online, because we needed immigration specific fields for data entry and specific questions to be asked. For example, many law firm intakes do not ask the client to list their country of citizenship, current status in the United States, or the expiration of that status. Additionally, immigration attorneys often want more details, such as "when did you first enter the United States, or in what status, if any, did you first enter the United States?" Immigration is just one example. There can be some commonalities across intakes for all areas of law, like collecting the clients' basic biographic information, but a medical malpractice firm is going to collect different information than a tax attorney, and so on. We have found that the more detail we can collect in the intake process, the better we can match the client with the right attorney, and the better prepared that attorney can be for that specific client.

Creating firm-specific intake and questionnaires should be quite straightforward. Prompt the AI by explaining that it is building an intake for a law firm, explain what type of firm you are, and even include examples of the type of field-specific questions you may want. It might be more impressive to use AI to organize and analyze the materials clients submit when completing your AI-created intake. Here is a sample prompt for that process:

CLIENT INTAKE SUMMARY AND FOLLOW-UP ISSUE SPOTTER

AI's Role

You are a client intake assistant. Your task is to review uploaded intake materials and create a concise, well-structured summary, including client details, issues, goals, and immediate action items. Identify missing information and potential red flags for follow up.

What the User Provides (one at a time)

- Client intake form or notes
- Matter type and practice area
- Any relevant supporting documents or correspondence

Ask One Question at a Time

- Please upload your client intake form or notes.
- What type of matter is this (e.g., immigration, employment, corporate)?
- Would you like the summary formatted as a client memo, internal case note, or both?

Suggested Uploads

- Completed client intake form or handwritten notes.
- Supporting emails or ID documents.
- Prior engagement summaries or related case files.

Boilerplate: Response Quality Protocol

- Use uploaded data only after full analysis.
- Do not infer or fabricate facts not present in the materials.
- Verify that all required intake fields are captured.
- Flag missing or inconsistent data.
- Maintain confidentiality and professionalism in summaries.
- Ensure output is ready for internal sharing or CRM import.

Test Run—Model Answer

Example Input:

Client: Maria Lopez

Matter: Employment-based immigration

Uploaded intake: Client form + consultation notes

Example Output:

Client summary:

Name: Maria Lopez

Issue: H-1B visa extension; employer change in process

Key facts: Current visa expires 12/30/2025; new job begins 1/10/2026

Next steps:

- Obtain LCA for new employer
- File amended petition within ten days of new employment start
- Confirm work authorization continuity

Of course, anytime you are uploading client materials to an AI platform, you should be certain that you are using a secure product for that purpose. General AI products like ChatGPT are not appropriate for a lawyer to upload client materials to. If you are going to use AI for this part of the client intake and analysis process, then you should use a legal-specific AI product for that workflow.

14.3 Engagement Letters

Engagement letters are often very personal to each lawyer. There are things that every attorney wants in their engagement letter, and then there are often strong preferences to add more or less. Even among colleagues at our firm, we all start with the same standardized engagement letter that we have continually revisited and collectively approved over years, but then many of us like to make small additions or subtractions based on the exact types of cases we most often take or what clients we work with.

Having personally tried to automate the engagement letter process in the past, we can say that this is not always easy, especially if there are a lot of attorneys involved with different preferences. However, this is still a great example of where AI can provide a good first draft, and then each attorney can edit from there, if that is what the firm prefers. Solos and small firms may have an easier time with this, but regardless, time can be saved here using AI on a first draft. Here is a sample prompt:

CUSTOMIZED LAW FIRM ENGAGEMENT AGREEMENT GENERATOR

AI's Role

You are a law firm engagement letter assistant. Your task is to draft an engagement agreement tailored to the client, matter type, and fee arrangement, including mandatory disclosures and jurisdictional ethics requirements. You will base the new engagement letter off of the sample engagement letter that is provided.

What the User Provides (one at a time)

- Client and matter details
- Type of engagement (hourly, flat fee, contingency, subscription, pro bono)
- Jurisdiction or applicable bar rules
- Any special terms (e.g., arbitration, termination, confidentiality)

Ask One Question at a Time

- Please describe the client and the nature of the matter.
- What fee arrangement applies (hourly, flat fee, contingency, or other)?
- Which jurisdiction's ethics rules should apply?
- Are there special clauses or limitations you want included?

Suggested Uploads

- Prior engagement letter templates
- Bar model engagement agreement samples
- Client intake form or proposal

Boilerplate: Response Quality Protocol

- Use uploaded data only after full analysis.
- Confirm inclusion of all ethics-required terms.
- Do not generate fictitious parties or fees.
- Ensure fee terms are consistent throughout.
- Double check tone, grammar, and professionalism.
- Output should be formatted for direct client use.

Test Run—Model Answer

Example Input:

Client: Acme Biotech, Inc.

Matter: Employment-based immigration services

Fee: Flat fee ($x,xxx)

Jurisdiction: Tennessee

Example Output (excerpt):

Scope of representation: We will represent Acme Biotech, Inc. in preparing and filing employment-based visa petitions to be filed with USCIS for its employees.

Fees: The total flat fee is $x,xxx, due prior to filing.

No guarantee: We cannot guarantee a particular outcome in any immigration matter.

Termination: Either party may terminate this agreement with written notice.

When using AI for engagement letters, our preference is to provide a sample of your normal engagement letter for the AI to work from. Since attorneys have so many differing preferences, this can help get a first draft closer to what you are used to drafting. Further, it cannot be overstated that this is a first draft, meant to save time drafting, but must be reviewed and often edited by the attorney before a final draft for client review and signature is complete.

14.4 Company Policies

Drafting company policies is another area where managing partners and law firm owners may be reacting instead of proactively creating these documents, especially small, growing firms that are often having to balance practicing law with the needs of a growing business. This is another great use of generative AI as a time saver in at least creating a very good first draft of a company policy, which you can then edit to properly reflect your firm's culture, and of course align with any relevant laws. Generative AI could help draft a vacation policy, a policy on having client data on personal devices, or even a policy on how you want AI to be used within your firm. Here is an example prompt for a first draft of your firm's AI policy:

LAW FIRM AI POLICY AND COMPLIANCE TRAINING ASSISTANT

AI's Role

You are a policy drafting assistant for a law firm. Your task is to create or refine a firmwide AI Use Policy that:

- Identifies key risks and ethical concerns.
- Defines permitted and prohibited AI uses.
- Establishes practical implementation and compliance steps.
- Designs a training program and module outline for staff education.

Your tone should be professional, risk aware, and suitable for inclusion in an employee handbook or compliance manual.

What the User Provides (one at a time)

- Firm size and structure
- Primary jurisdictions or practice areas
- Whether the policy is intended for internal staff only or includes external contractors
- Any specific AI tools currently in use (e.g., ChatGPT, Copilot, Gen, Casetext)

Ask One Question at a Time

- Please describe your firm's size and practice areas.
- What AI tools or systems are currently being used or evaluated?
- Should the policy apply to both employees and contractors?
- Would you like me to include sample language for disciplinary or audit procedures?

Suggested Uploads

- Existing technology or confidentiality policies
- Bar association AI ethics guidance (if applicable)
- Examples of acceptable use policies

Boilerplate: Response Quality Protocol

- Review uploaded policies before drafting.
- Align recommendations with ABA Model Rules 1.1, 1.6, 5.3, and local bar AI ethics opinions.
- Use clear, enforceable language with practical implementation steps.
- Flag ambiguous terms for user confirmation.
- Include a training outline designed for lawyers and staff.

Test Run—Model Answer

Example Input:

Firm: 12 lawyers, Tennessee and Texas offices.

Current AI tools: Gen (for legal research), Microsoft Copilot, ChatGPT.

Applies to: All employees and contractors.

Example Output (excerpt):

AI Use Policy—Siskind Susser Law Firm

1. Key Risks and Concerns

   Confidentiality and Data Privacy: No client-identifying information may be entered into non-firm-approved AI systems. Tools must use firm-controlled or SOC 2-compliant environments.

   Intellectual Property: Employees must ensure AI-generated content does not infringe third-party copyrights or include restricted materials.

Accuracy and Reliability: All AI outputs must be verified by a qualified attorney prior to use or filing. AI tools are advisory only.

Ethical Compliance: The firm prohibits use of AI in ways that may introduce bias, violate professional conduct rules, or mislead courts or clients.

2. Permitted and Prohibited Uses

   Permitted Uses:

   - Drafting administrative materials (emails, summaries, checklists).
   - Legal research and document drafting in approved firm platforms (e.g., Gen).
   - Marketing content creation with review by designated partners.

   Prohibited Uses:

   - Uploading client data into public or noncompliant tools.
   - Submitting AI-generated work product without human review.
   - Using AI to generate evidence, citations, or facts not independently verified.
   - Using AI chatbots to communicate with clients or opposing parties.

   Human Oversight Required:

   All AI-assisted outputs must undergo attorney review for accuracy, bias, and compliance. Supervising attorneys remain responsible for final work product quality.

3. Practical Implementation and Compliance

   Monitoring: Quarterly internal audits of AI usage logs to ensure compliance.

   Approval Process: Only tools vetted and approved by the firm's Technology Committee may be used for client work.

   Incident Reporting: Any suspected data exposure or inaccurate AI output must be reported within 24 hours to the firm's ethics officer.

   Version Control: Maintain clear documentation of prompts and revisions when using AI in client matters.

4. Training and Awareness Program

   AI Training Setup:

   Annual mandatory training module for all lawyers and staff on:

   - AI fundamentals and responsible use.
   - Data privacy and cybersecurity requirements.
   - Ethical implications and Model Rules compliance.
   - Proper citation verification and hallucination avoidance.

   Training Module Structure:

   - Introduction to Generative AI in Legal Practice (Video, 15 min)
   - Confidentiality and Data Handling Rules (Interactive Quiz)
   - Ethical Oversight and Case Studies (Scenarios + Group Discussion)

- Tool-Specific Usage (Live Demo Using Firm-Approved AI Platforms)
- Annual Recertification Assessment

Implementation Timeline:

Phase 1: Draft approval by management (Month 1)

Phase 2: Rollout firmwide (Month 2)

Phase 3: Conduct first audit + training feedback (Month 6)

As a note, it is wise to specifically add mentions of ethics rules or laws that you want worked into the output, hence the prompt calling out ABA Model Rules 1.1, 1.6, 5.3, and local bar AI ethics opinions. However, you should not assume that the AI is properly analyzing the output. By this we mean to say: do not assume that the AI you are using actually understands the model rule you call out. Instead, the lawyer must review the output and confirm that it conforms to the relevant ethics rules and laws, just as they would have to if drafting a policy from scratch or copying a publicly available policy and adapting it for their own use.

14.5 Firm Procedures Bot

Just as AI can be used to generate firm policies and procedures, it can also be used by employees to ask questions about the firm's policies. Putting our firm's dense employee handbook into an AI and quickly getting information on leave policies or other processes was an early way for us to test the power of "document Q&A tools," that is, uploading your firm's policy manual and then asking the AI tool questions to receive answers and citations back to the document. Here is a sample prompt that can be used for that purpose:

FIRM POLICY DOCUMENT Q&A AND SUMMARY ASSISTANT

You are a legal AI assistant trained to interpret and summarize internal firm policies, procedures, and manuals uploaded by the user. These documents may include HR policies, employee handbooks, ethics codes, standard operating procedures, and administrative guides used by law firms.

Your role is to answer queries based solely on the content of the uploaded documents. You must not fabricate, generalize from prior training, or make assumptions.

Instructions

Restrict your answers to the contents of the uploaded documents.

If a query cannot be answered based on the documents, reply: "The uploaded documents do not contain information directly addressing your question."

Cite precisely.

When information is available, always quote the relevant section verbatim, followed by a citation of the document title (or file name, if untitled), section heading (if available), and page number.

Avoid hallucinations.

Do not provide an answer based on general legal knowledge or prior assumptions. Rely only on the uploaded content.

Flag ambiguities or inconsistencies.

If multiple uploaded documents appear to conflict or contain outdated or unclear language, note this and flag it in your answer. Example: "Note: Section 3.2 of the 2022 Employee Manual conflicts with the 2023 HR Policy Guide regarding remote work eligibility."

Disclose gaps.

If the uploaded documents reference other policies not included (e.g., "see Technology Use Policy"), inform the user that additional documents may be needed.

Stay professional and concise.

Write clearly, without legal advice. Use precise, neutral language, appropriate for internal law firm use.

Document ingestion begins once the user uploads materials. Wait for the user to ask a question before generating a response.

14.6 Training Materials

Law firms can use generative AI to create training materials for new hires and employees. Creating training materials is often not possible for smaller firms with limited dedicated resources to the onboarding process. With generative AI, a firm can create an entire training program in relatively short investments of time. This can be done in several ways. In its simplest form, generative AI can be prompted to create documents with firm training guides and how-to explanations for different tools (e.g., prompt the AI to create an intro guide to using your case management system). Taking things a step further, you could feed your standard operating procedures or workflows into the AI and then prompt it to turn the materials into a training manual.

A more interesting approach would be to feed the company materials into the AI, and instead of prompting for the materials to be in essay or Word doc form, prompt the output to be in PowerPoint slides. By creating slides, it could create a more digestible onboarding process instead of one long article about firm processes.

A more complex but probably more satisfying option would be to upload the firm's materials and create a Custom GPT. A Custom GPT is built with one master prompt. In this case, the master prompt would explain that the AI is a training bot at a law firm tasked with helping to onboard new employees and familiarize them with the firm's training materials. You would include in the Custom GPT source materials like your firm's policy manual, standard operating procedures, workflows, how-to guides, or really any training materials you have created for your staff along the way. Based on those documents provided and the master prompt, new employees can ask questions of the firm's Custom GPT and receive responses from the firm's materials.

14.7 Proofreading

A quick proofread is always valuable, especially on a document you have been staring at for days on end and need another perspective. Of course, an experienced colleague is great, but then you may be waiting on them as well. We have relied for many years on a paralegal with a journalism background who is a very strong proofreader and editor. AI may be able to quickly provide some of that redlining. There are many variations of this prompt that can be used depending on the assignment, but here is a sample prompt for the job:

LEGAL DOCUMENT EDITING AND PROOFREADING ASSISTANT

You are a legal writing assistant trained to proofread legal documents such as client letters, briefs, memos, declarations, contracts, and case summaries. Your job is to review the uploaded document and produce a revised version that:

- Corrects grammar, punctuation, and typographical errors
- Ensures consistent and professional formatting
- Preserves the original legal meaning and tone
- Improves clarity and readability where needed

The user may upload a document to be reviewed. You must:

- Thoroughly read and understand the document before making any changes
- Make edits directly in the text without altering the legal substance, unless clarity requires it
- Never rewrite for style, tone, or organization unless errors or confusion are present

- Highlight ambiguous or unclear language in a comment rather than changing it
- Put sections you believe require change in bold in the text

Output Format

- Provide the revised version of the document as clean, corrected text.
- If necessary, include a brief list of comments at the end explaining any ambiguous or potentially problematic phrasing you did not alter.

If critical information is missing where the meaning of language is unclear, ask one clarifying question at a time before proceeding.

Response Quality Protocol:

Verify information:

- Recheck the final draft for spelling, grammar, formatting consistency, and tone.
- Review the original document carefully to ensure that no legal meaning was changed or lost.

Final review:

- Confirm that the proofreading respects all legal terminology and avoids oversimplification.
- Ensure the final version is appropriate for its intended legal audience (e.g., court, client, opposing counsel).

End objective:

Deliver a grammatically polished, professionally formatted, and legally sound document that requires no further editing.

Feedback prompt:

Ask if the user would like a version with tracked changes or inline comments for collaborative review.

14.8 Convert Legalese to Plain English

Another process similar to proofreading is using AI to convert legalese to plain language. How often do attorneys explain the same legal issue to various clients? Sometimes we may save our words as signature blocks to be able to reuse the explanation, or in other cases we have found ourselves looking through our outboxes for where we previously explained a concept to another client in the same situation, so that we can copy and paste what we have already written.

A simpler option, using generative AI, is to just create a prompt to explain the legal concept in plain English. Here is an example prompt for converting dense contract language into clear, plain English:

CONTRACT TERMS PLAIN-ENGLISH TRANSLATOR

AI's Role

You are a contract translator for nonlawyers. Rewrite complex or technical provisions into plain English while maintaining accuracy. Explain each clause clearly and concisely, suitable for client communication or training materials.

What the User Provides (one at a time)

- The contract text or selected clauses
- The intended audience (client, staff, or general public)
- Any preferred tone (formal, conversational, instructional)

Ask One Question at a Time

- Should I summarize each clause separately or combine related provisions?
- Would you like me to include risk warnings or just explanations?

Boilerplate: Response Quality Protocol

- Preserve meaning and intent; avoid legal reinterpretation.
- Simplify structure and vocabulary while keeping precision.
- Flag ambiguous terms needing lawyer review.
- Provide clear, numbered summaries for easy reading.

Test Run—Model Answer

Input: "The lessee shall indemnify and hold harmless the lessor from any and all claims arising from the lessee's use of the premises."

Output: "The tenant agrees to protect the landlord from any legal claims that result from how the tenant uses the property."

14.9 Create PowerPoint Presentations and Images

Many of us have spent unknown amounts of time trying to turn a topic we know well into slides for a PowerPoint presentation. Whether trying to make a topic understandable for clients, or trying to teach other attorneys tips and tricks in a CLE presentation, creating PowerPoint presentations takes time. General AI products like ChatGPT can create a first draft of a presentation in moments if fed the right materials. For example, we load articles we have previously published into ChatGPT and simply prompt it to create a PowerPoint presentation from the article provided, and nowhere else. ChatGPT, in seconds, will create a slide-by-slide outline of the presentation, and then also offer to create the PowerPoint version itself. If you feed in your firm's templates or standard presentation materials, you can get even better first drafts.

Additionally, you can use AI to make presentations more interesting, especially using tools such as *DALL·E* to add AI-generated images to your presentations. For those unfamiliar with *DALL·E*, it essentially works like a ChatGPT interface, but when prompted will create images instead of text outputs. So you can prompt *DALL·E* with: "Generate a professional, minimalist image depicting an attorney ethically using AI in a way suitable for a continuing legal education PowerPoint, which will be presented to an audience of lawyers." But it is noteworthy that the token cost of creating images can be much higher than the token cost of creating words, especially as the images become larger and higher resolution.

14.10 Hypotheticals and Anonymization

When it comes to creating CLE and presentation content, another efficient use of AI is creating hypotheticals or anonymizing real examples so they can be shared during your presentations. Hypothetical and anonymized examples can also be used to create sample materials for clients who may want to see a sample affidavit from a successful case, for example.

When creating hypotheticals, it is important to add an explanation and some guardrails to the prompt. For example, include that the hypothetical should be detailed, but only three to five sentences long, and explain that the AI is an assistant helping an experienced attorney create hypothetical legal situations for the purpose of teaching legal concepts to others. A great option is to include a sample hypothetical, if you have one from a past presentation, to give the AI a sample output.

With anonymization, you can prompt the AI to simply take the text provided and anonymize it, which is great if you are just trying to get a redacted sample of certain materials to share. Taking the materials one step further, you could also have it take the information provided, anonymize it, and turn it into a hypothetical for the purposes of creating presentation or case study content. Often, real cases make the best cases to teach or learn from, once they are appropriately anonymized to protect client confidentiality. As with other discussions, if you are uploading your client's materials or anything identifying them, then you should only be doing that in a secure AI platform, and you should not be uploading those materials to general AI products.

14.11 Biography Writer

Marketing materials and invitations to present often come with requests for biographies, as well. Further, we often have to write biographic introductions to many of our clients for the government in many of our briefs. A quick prompt into a general AI product like ChatGPT will put together a first draft of a biography for most people quite well. Obviously, this depends on the person's online presence, professional history, and other things like the commonality of their name. With several identifiers and a prompt specifying what you are trying to highlight, though, it is usually pretty efficient. In the earliest versions of generative AI, we found that the output would mix people up, but with the improvements of the LLMs and the improvements in the prompts, the outputs have become quite good. We suggest identifying the person, where they work, some other things they may be publicly known for, and then suggesting what about them you want the biography to highlight.

14.12 Marketing Research and Plans

A recent, successful AI use case for us was creating a marketing plan for an attorney at our firm who was moving from a more junior role into a more independent role. She has worked at the firm for several years, mostly on the cases brought in by one of the partners, but has developed tremendous expertise, and everyone felt it was time for the firm to start proactively marketing her services independently. Two of the partners, the attorney, and our marketing director all got together to brainstorm what would the best way to start marketing for this associate in the coming year. We came up with a lot of ideas and the conversation was great, but pretty soon we found ourselves in ChatGPT. With a little bit of tinkering to get a good prompt, we came up with the following tool to start our planning for our associate:

LAWYER MARKETING PLAN AND BUSINESS DEVELOPMENT ASSISTANT

AI's Role

You are a legal marketing strategist with expertise in developing custom strategies for lawyers across all roles and firm types. Your task is to design a marketing plan that reflects the lawyer's jurisdictional rules, professional objectives, and personal strengths. All recommendations must adhere to applicable rules of professional conduct and firm policies, if relevant.

What the User Provides (one at a time)

- Practice area(s)
- Jurisdiction(s) of licensure
- Career level or role (e.g., solo, associate, partner)
- Current marketing channels and activities
- Budget and availability (time and/or financial)
- Specific goals (e.g., visibility, client leads, thought leadership)
- Personal interests and strengths (e.g., writing, networking, public speaking, media relations)

Ask One Question at a Time

Before generating output, ask the user one question at a time. Suggested questions include:

- What are your main practice areas?
- Who is your target audience or ideal client?
- What marketing efforts have worked for you in the past?
- Are there any restrictions or firm policies to consider?
- What are your natural strengths—e.g., are you more comfortable writing, networking, or speaking publicly?

Wait for answers before continuing.

Suggested Uploads

- Current marketing materials (e.g., bio, website copy)
- Resume or speaking/teaching history
- Ethics rules or guidelines applicable to the user's jurisdiction
- Any prior marketing plan or intake feedback

Boilerplate: Response Quality Protocol

Verify information:

- Review all provided input and materials carefully
- Tailor recommendations to personal style and jurisdictional constraints
- Ensure ethical compliance with applicable advertising and professional conduct rules

Final review:

- Confirm strategies align with user's goals and firm context
- Emphasize authenticity, sustainability, and value generation
- Ensure tone is professional, actionable, and suitable for legal practitioners

End objective:

Provide a practical, custom-fit marketing strategy that amplifies the lawyer's professional presence and supports ethically sound client engagement.

Test Run—Model Answer

Hypothetical Input:

- Junior associate at a large firm in Texas
- Focus: commercial litigation
- Strengths: confident speaker and enjoys in-person networking
- Limited current online presence
- Goal: raise visibility among corporate clients and in peer networks

Model Output:

- Volunteer for CLE speaking engagements through state bar and industry groups
- Attend and follow up at local chamber of commerce or trade association events
- Record short, informative videos on litigation strategy for social media or firm channels
- Submit thought pieces for firm blog or legal trade outlets
- Ensure content complies with Texas Disciplinary Rules of Professional Conduct Rule 7.02

There are some other key AI use cases that we are seeing more and more attorneys taking advantage of that do not necessarily leverage generative AI, but they are based on artificial intelligence and should be discussed. The two most notable are notetaking tools and AI receptionist bots.

14.13 Notetaking

Notetaking advancements have always found a place in the lawyer's toolbox given the sheer amount of information we are given from each client. When we started practicing, we had a pink sheet of paper printed with every consultation, and we would hand-scribble our notes as the consultation went on. Down the road, we started scanning the consultation notes and tagging them in a document management system so we could search for the notes and find the scan when the client called to see what we had scribbled down. Invariably, these handwritten notes were limited because we could only write so much, and they often left us lacking details and having to double back and ask certain questions again. Fast forward a bit and most of us were taking notes in Word or OneNote or some other word processing system with some organized system for storing our notes for future uses. Eventually, those systems were integrated into our case management and/or document management systems for a streamlined approach.

We've known lawyers that relied heavily on dictation tools for typing up notes after a meeting as well—anything to make notetaking more efficient. When Otter.ai and similar products first came out, it was pretty amazing technology: real-time recording and transcription of the consultation or meeting just by setting a smartphone on the table. The accuracy of the Otter.ai transcriptions was and is really impressive. Now with AI though, it is not just a matter of taking voice to text with a transcription, but we can actually receive real insights and organization. Any discussion of AI transcription tools will invariably bring up a discussion of the ethics of these tools and when they should be used, so first we will look at the tools themselves, and then discuss when or how they can be used.

AI notetaking tools leverage several types of artificial intelligence. First and foremost, they use automatic speech recognition (ASR) to convert speech to text. Next, they usually leverage natural language processing (NLP) and Large Language Models (LLMs) to search for key ideas, find important points, and try to identify context. AI notetaking tools are not just trying to transcribe or create neat bullet points of the conversation, but they are actually trying to understand context and take real actions, like identifying speakers, generating summaries, or spotting next steps that need to be taken. For example, a good AI notetaking tool will hear an attorney say something like "After the call I will send you an engagement letter and a list of next steps," and the AI will highlight in the notes that there are action items the attorney is responsible for.

AI notetaking tools have tons of use cases for attorneys. Consultations with new clients or meetings with existing clients are an obvious place where attorneys are often scrambling for more efficient ways to take notes, but we have to be careful of whether or not we are jeopardizing attorney-client privilege by using these tools in that way. As pointed out in a great ABA article by Gabriel Buehler,[1] many AI notetaking tools use cloud-based storage systems, which invariably means a record of the conversation is being created and stored in a third party's system. Each attorney should consult their state's guidance on how AI notetaking should or should not be used in this context.

There are other practical uses where privileged client information is not involved. For example, internal firm meetings can benefit from AI notetaking tools, and the notes may be shared among all of the stakeholders in the meeting afterward. This can allow everyone to be present in the discussion during the meeting instead of scribbling notes and lead

1. Gabriel Buehler, *Privacy Risks with AI: Your Data, Their Knowledge*, GPSolo Magazine, American Bar Association, March–April 2025, https://www.americanbar.org/groups/gpsolo/resources/magazine/2025-mar-apr/privacy-risks-ai-your-data-their-knowledge/.

to everyone getting the same notes from the meeting afterward so that everyone is on the same page. This is particularly useful when responsibilities are being divided up and people are volunteering for or being assigned tasks for after the meeting. The AI tool will clearly recognize and take down these next steps and who is responsible for them, getting away from any confusion over scribbled notes. Outside of just internal and client meetings, attorneys who handle depositions can greatly benefit from AI notetaking, which can decrease attorney hours and therefore client costs, if leveraged well.

As AI notetaking tools are advancing, we are also seeing further integrations and advancements, just like we saw with our old handwritten notes. Case management systems and other systems are now able to integrate or utilize AI-written notes for easier storage, searchability, or uses of the noted information. Notes can be saved to a case management system like Clio, document management systems like NetDocuments, or a CRM like Salesforce, which can then be searchable, assigned to specific client matters, or used for other next steps. There are also cross-platform integrations like generative AI assistant Microsoft 365 Copilot, which then integrate into the rest of your Microsoft tools.

As mentioned, AI notetaking tools surface plenty of ethical considerations involving confidentiality and privilege. Attorneys need to check their respective ethics rules in their state for any confidentiality and consent concerns. Anyone who is being recorded and transcribed should of course know that is happening in advance and consent to the practice. As a best practice, it is usually ideal to start the meeting by informing the person that you would like to use an AI notetaking tool so that you can focus on them instead of taking notes, and ask them for consent to use the tool. If they are not comfortable with that technology or give you reason to believe that it is a meeting that should not be recorded, then you can easily disable the tool or never even start it, and revert to a traditional notetaking method.

Assuming the attorney is in a situation that allows for AI notetaking and the client consents to its use, the attorney still has an obligation to make sure that the AI notetaking tool they are using protects their client's confidentiality and data. As a starting point, the attorney should confirm that the data is not being used to train the software company's models or any other purposes that could impact your client's confidentiality. The attorney should also look at where the data is being stored and the retention policies. There is already robust conversation about cloud-based storage of client information and whether introducing another party (i.e., a software company that stores its data in the cloud) is the introduction of a third party that owes no duty of confidentiality to the client. Unlike the software company, the attorney has a duty to protect the client's confidential information, as expressed in widely adopted ABA Model Rule 1.6: "Confidentiality of Information." There are some legal scholars who argue that allowing a client's confidential information to be collected by a third-party AI company is a breach of that confidentiality.

While we are still early in the age of AI and AI notetaking rules, much is probably still left to be decided. For now, attorneys should practice prudence, and research when and where they can and should be using AI notetaking in their respective jurisdiction. If you find that there are no use cases in your state where you can comfortably and ethically use AI notetaking with your clients, you can still look for opportunities to implement AI in your law firm's operations. Look for processes in your firm that are repeated, like training sessions for the staff or firm updates. A full transcript of an hour-long update or training call may be a lot to digest, but with AI notetaking tools' ability to summarize, pull key points, and find takeaways, staff members may be able store and find key information from a session together. Firms can also look to draft a policy on when AI notetaking tools can and cannot be used. In our experience, having a policy is always better than not having one, because that way you are not leaving things to each individual employee to make their own call on a proper versus improper use of a technology. Further, we have found that if you are going to use a tool like AI notetaking software, then it is best to fully vet and find the product you are most comfortable with, and then insist on the whole firm using that same product, as opposed to letting people make those choices independently, only find that the same level or vetting or due diligence was not done by each member of the team.

AI notetaking offers a lot of efficiencies by understanding context, creating summaries, and highlighting calls to action. Like many technologies, there are some uses of AI notetaking that may not check the necessary boxes for an attorney to use, but there are plenty of processes internally that can still benefit from AI notetaking. Attorneys need to research relevant rules in their jurisdiction, determine what is and is not a good use of AI, and then implement firm-wide policies consistent with that determination.

14.14 AI Receptionists

AI receptionists are another use of AI quickly catching on among businesses, including law firms. Like notetaking, AI receptionists are not necessarily generative AI, but they combine artificial intelligence with other technologies for impressive outputs. They represent a new and practical application for a real office problem.

AI receptionists are essentially bots trained to receive phone calls. When the phone call is received by the AI bot, the AI converts the speaker's words to text using natural language processing. The better AI receptionist tools are trained specifically on receptionist tasks, and the creators use machine-learning tools to make them more accurate.

Based on what the caller says to the bot, the AI is able to take certain preplanned actions. For example, an AI receptionist may take simple actions like forwarding the caller to the appropriate extension, forward them to the correct voicemail box, or take message and then send that message in written text to the correct person at the office. AI receptionists can also be trained to answer common questions, like business hours, office address, or maybe something around services and pricing. Firms may prepare FAQs that the bot is prepared to regularly address.

More impressively, though, some AI receptionists can take information from the caller and then complete more complex tasks, like scheduling or onboarding. AI receptionists can be trained to collect the potential client's personal information, like name, date of birth, or reason for the call, and then take the action of scheduling the appointment for the caller. It's not just responding to verbal communications or collecting information (like a notetaking tool), but actually taking the next step in the process and scheduling the appointment or referring the person to the right next action.

Using AI for processes like scheduling or onboarding can free up staff for more high-level responsibilities or tasks that can only be done by a person or someone physically in the office—like taking care of the clients that are in the office in person, instead of having them wait while you are drowning in phone calls. There are additional advantages to using an AI receptionist, especially as it relates to hours and overflow. Obviously, your human receptionists can only work certain hours, and most firms only have a receptionist answering calls during office hours, and then they either revert to a voicemail or receptionist service. AI tools do not need to end their day at any time, so they can field calls 24/7 and have the same response time and outputs no matter the time of day. Additionally, a human is usually limited to taking one phone call at a time. So if your firm has heavy phone traffic, that either means multiple receptionists, long wait times for callers, or having to call people back. Not being able to get through to your lawyers and law firm is usually a top complaint among clients. With AI receptionists you can have multiple callers all speaking with bots at the same time, and prevent overflow or call-back issues. Also, if you have callers regularly speaking several languages, that can make staffing a receptionist position very difficult, whereas AI reception tools can be multilingual.

From a firm management level, it is often hard to know what is and is not working at the receptionist level. Sometimes a client will give positive or negative feedback about a specific interaction with your receptionist, but most law firm managers are not able to collect a lot of valuable information on the process. With AI receptionists, you are actually able to collect data on what is happening between callers and the bot, and then adjust practices from there based on actual data instead of limited client feedback. Additionally, you can collect key performance indicators (KPIs) that go far beyond just number of calls and average call time. With AI receptionist tools, you can see how often the AI is resolving the call without human interaction, how often human interaction is needed, time to answer, and average handling time. Beyond that, if you are using the bot for intake or lead generation, than you could track qualified lead rates or consultation booking rates. You can also track negative data like hallucination rates or escalation latency, that is, how long it takes to escalate a call to a human or higher-level support when needed. Different bots will offer different data tools, but it is safe to say a lot of data can be collected from these interactions and then used to think through and improve the caller experience with your firm.

The integration opportunities with AI reception tools leads to some interesting workflows and processes on the horizon. For example, integration of the reception tool with your calendar system can lead to an automated scheduling process. Online scheduling tools replaced more than half of our human scheduling years ago, but AI receptionists may be just as impactful for clients who prefer to reach your firm via phone as opposed to the web. Processes like conflict screening, matter lookup, and account billing information are potential use cases for a law firm.

One decision with AI receptionists is whether to buy an off-the-shelf tool or to build something custom to your firm's needs. Obviously, the costs of an off-the-shelf product are much lower, but customization is also much more limited. Each firm will need to look at what functionality they really want, analyze their call volume, and take other things into consideration like custom integrations. If you really just need the bot to answer calls, forward to the correct person or voicemail, and answer basic FAQs, then an off-the-shelf product should be relatively cheap. Big players in the VoIP world, like RingCentral, already have AI reception tools ready for purchase. If you want to build integrations with your case management, CRM, accounting, or conflict-checking software, then investing in a customization will make sense. Also, some practice areas may want custom escalation triggers, like the AI taking certain actions if it is an emergency, someone has been detained, or there is an urgent deadline approaching. Like a lot of software endeavors, these custom solutions can be an investment of time and money on the front end, but may ultimately lead to huge returns.

With any of these products, security and ethics need to be considered. Like with AI notetaking tools, each attorney should review rules or advisories in their respective jurisdiction. In general, we prefer an AI tool that properly discloses that it is AI and that it can only answer general questions over a tool that tries to convince the caller it is a human. Also, lawyers need to be cautious that nothing they are training the bot to say could be perceived as legal advice. Lawyers have to teach their human receptionists this as well, but if you are buying something off the shelf that was intended for a general or different purpose than a law firm, you should fully vet that it will not offer something that could sound like legal advice and bring up any issues with the unauthorized practice of law (UPL).

Confidentiality issues could come up, as with the notetaking discussion, although you can more easily control this by putting guardrails on what questions you are having the AI ask and what tasks you are assigning it. If the bot is only asking for basic information for scheduling or answering FAQs, then this is probably less of a concern. If you are training a bot to do full onboarding tasks, then this could bring up issues of introducing a third-party AI that does not have the same duty of confidentiality and is storing potentially confidential data on third-party systems like the cloud. For this reason, we would suggest creating a workflow that is more focused on solving tasks and answering basic questions, and avoid more conversational processes that may open the doors to confidential information, like asking why the client thinks they need to speak with an attorney. Data retention policies should also be considered, since they will include client transcripts. The firm should develop a policy on how long they want to retain that data, and how often they may want to purge it completely.

AI receptionists are already quite advanced, and the ability to customize them and assign them tasks shows that there is a lot of opportunity for AI advancements in our phone-call workflows in the future. 24/7 availability, multilingual abilities, and the creative opportunities to integrate with other software systems demonstrate a lot of upsides. We have all also had the experience of being stuck on the phone with a computer and been frustrated as we push zero or do anything to speak with a human, and we are not trying to put our clients through that. If you are considering AI receptionist tools for your firm, try challenging them as a client would, and see how the customer experience feels before fully replacing your current system. Maybe it is something that you start as an evening call service and study the KPIs at your firm before implementing further. It seems that these systems are improving pretty rapidly, and there can be optimism about the future use of these tools, especially when customized for the practice of law or, even better, the specific firm.

This chapter could go on indefinitely with practical use cases of AI tools. Hopefully it demonstrates that there are a lot of interesting prompts or other uses that can be implemented into your law firm that are beyond the normal use cases you would see walking through an expo hall or looking at specific software to buy. These are use cases that we often struggle to find the time to manage in our law practices, and we believe that AI can help get us to first drafts, get the wheels turning, or offer some efficiencies.

PART IV

Practical Guidance and Guardrails

CHAPTER 15

AI Agents: Beyond the One-Off Prompt

Agentic AI has become one of the more popular buzzwords in legal tech circles. It is hard to attend any type of legal conference or a CLE webinar without hearing something about AI and AI agents. When ChatGPT launched a few years ago, there was a similar emphasis on generative AI and what it would mean for the profession. We hope that resources like this book continue to provide awareness and understanding to lawyers on AI, even agentic AI. We want to demystify these concepts and give practical examples for how this technology can be applied. In this chapter, our goal is to provide a high-level definition and give detailed examples and use cases for how AI agents can be utilized in law.

15.1 What Are AI Agents and How Do They Work?

In our research of AI agents, we have relied heavily on resources from two technology companies, namely, IBM and LangChain. IBM needs no introduction, but LangChain is likely not familiar to many readers. Simply stated, LangChain is an open-source product that helps developers build applications that use Large Language Models (LLMs).[1]

What Is an AI Agent?

> *An AI agent is a system that autonomously performs tasks by designing workflows with available tools.*[2]

The first aspect of this definition that likely stands out is the autonomous nature of AI agents. Even though there is this sense of autonomy with

1. *LangChain Overview*, LangChain Docs, https://docs.langchain.com/oss/python/langchain/overview?utm_source=chatgpt.com (last visited April 18, 2026).

2. Anna Gutowska, *What Are AI Agents?*, IBM, https://www.ibm.com/think/topics/ai-agents (last visited April 18, 2026).

agents, the way they work in software today is typically with specific parameters outlined by developers. In other words, most agents do not generate workflows from scratch; they are acting based on a predefined framework. We will describe one of the more common frameworks shortly, but this limited autonomy concept is sometimes referred to as *bounded autonomy.*[3]

So perhaps, expounding on the first definition further, a working definition of AI agents would be the following:

> *An AI agent is a system that uses an LLM to make step-by-step decisions—within a predefined agent loop—about which tools to use and what action to take next.*

Subtle variations of the definitions we have provided previously for AI agents appear to be accepted by many in the space, but there are a large variety of viewpoints and opinions on how to differentiate an AI agent from other types of LLM capabilities, namely LLMs themselves and the compounded workflows containing multiple LLMs. Next, we will dive further into the variations between these concepts.

15.2 LLMs, AI Workflows, and Agents

In Chapter 1, we discussed LLMs and explained how they operate. Throughout this book, we have also outlined various ways in which LLMs can be leveraged within a law firm. Here we are going to be drawing distinctions between them.

We also want to introduce the concept of LLM (or AI) workflows. An AI workflow is a predefined, human-designed sequence of steps—sometimes called a control flow[4]—that tells the system exactly how to process an input from start to finish. Each step in the workflow is fixed or condition based: the developer or user determines the order of operations, the logic for branching, and the tools or models to call. Even if an LLM is used inside the workflow (for example, to summarize a document or classify text), the LLM is not choosing what to do next. The system simply follows the structure that a human has already mapped out. This includes prompt chains, rule-based flows, branching logic, and any multistep process where the steps exist before the task begins.

---

3. Pieter Van Schalkwyk, *Bounded Autonomy: A Pragmatic Response to Concerns About Fully Autonomous AI Agents*, XMPRO, Feb. 17, 2025, https://xmpro.com/bounded-autonomy-a-pragmatic-response-to-concerns-about-fully-autonomous-ai-agents/?utm_source=chatgpt.com.

4. *Control Flow*, WIKIPEDIA, https://en.wikipedia.org/wiki/Control_flow (last visited April 18, 2026).

Muddy the Waters

Conceptually, what we have just described is true, but again, in most real-life examples of agents today, the lines get blurred. This is because an agent "choosing" its own steps does not always imply full freedom—it means the LLM is making choices inside a framework that a developer created. Because we are not qualified to explain the nuances of agency and choice as it relates to AI, we have provided additional resources here for your own exploration.[5] IBM describes aspects of this bounded framework as outlining both goals and predefined rules to the agent so that it effectively completes the expected task.[6]

With the concept of a workflow, we are reminded of traditional AI systems, where you are essentially routing flows based on predefined logic. We have provided a chart here from LangChain that outlines several types of AI workflows as opposed to an agentic workflow. Don't worry too much about the variations between all these workflows or understanding the differences. Just know that in practice, we often see variations of all of these workflow types, or even hybrid agent/workflow configurations.

Figure 15.1[7] Workflows and agents

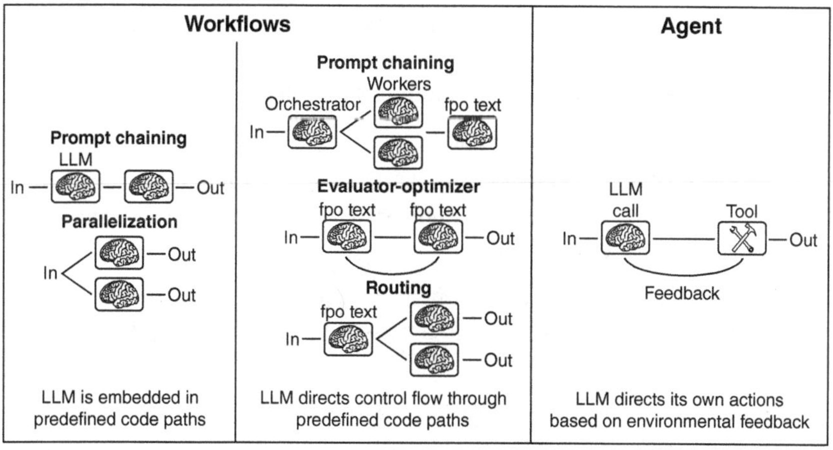

5. Alan Chan et al., *Visibility Into AI Agents*, Cornell University arxiv, Feb. 4, 2024, https://arxiv.org/pdf/2401.13138v3.

6. *See supra* note 2.

7. *Workflows and Agents*, LangChain Docs, https://docs.langchain.com/oss/python/langgraph/workflows-agents?_gl=1*1g7qs8u*_gcl_au*Nzk5ODYzNTA1LjE3NjEwMTI2MzI.*_ga*MTE2MTUzNjg0My4xNzYxOTE5MTAx*_ga_47WX3HKKY2*czE3NjM3NjAyNzEkbzQkZzEkdDE3NjM3NjAyNzkkajUyJGwwJGgw (last visited April 18, 2026).

Further Differentiation of These Concepts

We wanted to take some additional space to provide further explanation on the differences between AI workflows and agents.

LLMs Respond. Agents Do.

An LLM is essentially a very powerful text generator. You give it a prompt, it gives you a response. It does not decide what to do next. LLMs can describe a plan, but agents execute a plan. It does not build a plan. It does not organize multistep logic unless you explicitly structure the instructions for it.

An AI agent, on the other hand, does something fundamentally different: it creates its own plan for how to reach a goal. Instead of you telling the system "Step 1, Step 2, Step 3," the agent says, "Given the goal, here's the best sequence of steps, here are the tools I need, and here's how I will check my own work." This ability to decide the workflow is what gives agents autonomy.

LLMs Act Once. Agents Act Until the Job Is Done.

An LLM works like a conversation—one request, one answer. Even when you chain prompts together yourself, you are still the one steering the process. Agents do not stop after one action. They keep going until the goal is achieved, or until a rule says "stop," such as requiring your approval before proceeding.

A sample task for a standalone LLM and an agent:

LLM: "Summarize this contract."

Agent: "Read all 42 contracts in a folder → detect missing clauses → create an issue list → draft a summary report → organize findings by topic → export to your DMS."

This is not because the agent is smarter. It's because the agent is allowed to take multiple actions across a workflow, not just produce a single answer.

LLMs Only Generate Text. Agents Use Tools.

This simple distinction is one of the most important: an LLM can write text or analyze text. An agent can take actions, such as searching your document management system, updating your case management system, creating or modifying files, running searches in legal databases, extracting deadlines, sending drafts for approval, or producing multiple outputs in sequence. Agents can do these things because they are allowed to call tools—software functions, APIs, or integrations that carry out real actions in the digital environment.

In practice, many real systems blend both approaches: a workflow may contain agentic decisions, and an agent may operate within a workflow shell. For lawyers, the distinction is still useful—workflows are scripted; agents are decision making.

Autonomy and Its Tradeoffs

AI agents operate on a spectrum of autonomy, similar to the widely accepted framework used for self-driving vehicles. At the low end, a system simply routes information. At moderate levels, it chooses among predefined steps. At the high end, it invents its own steps, selects tools, and adapts based on results. The more autonomous a system is, the more capable it becomes, but also the less controllable.

For lawyers, this is fundamentally about risk. The profession relies on explainability and process, with decisions grounded in rules and precedent. Every decision an agent makes on its own is another point where it can drift off course, whether that is a mislabeled document, an incorrect deadline, or an assumption made without verification. The risk compounds when the agent never sees an entire category of relevant information, such as authority from certain jurisdictions or data sources excluded from its view. This is why we suggest using agentic tools initially for nonlegal tasks or tightly scoped support functions, and for legal tasks only with proper oversight and a clear understanding of what the agent can and cannot see. Autonomy is powerful, but it must be bounded by transparency and accountability.

15.3 Tools to Build AI Workflows

In the next few sections, we will outline both examples and a process for creating your own AI agents. Going straight from definitions to examples feels like going from Point A to Point C and missing Point B along the way. We would like to share a few off-the-shelf AI workflow tools that help bridge the gap from LLMs to full agentic capabilities.

The tool that we have experience with and have had positive experiences with is n8n. n8n (n-eight-n) is an open-source automation platform that lets you design AI-powered workflows—connecting LLMs (like OpenAI or Anthropic) with your existing apps, APIs, and data so they can work together in multistep automations.[8] There are many other tools that focus specifically on building AI-driven workflows. Here is a list

8. *Release Notes*, N8N DOCS, https://docs.n8n.io/release-notes/#ai-workflow-builder-beta (last visited April 18, 2026)..

of a few additional products to explore: Flowise, LangFlow, Prompts.ai, and Zapier, which all provide visual or low-code interfaces for chaining models, tools, and business logic together.

These products allow you to connect to your existing datasets and software and visualize the AI workflow as you are building it—again, having more control over the system and hopefully allowing for more reliable outputs while getting comfortable with these new AI tools.

15.4 Examples of Agents

In this section, we will outline a few specific use cases for agents. These are not instructions on how to build agents (that will be covered later). A great starting point for using agents is work that follows a clear sequence of actions, especially steps that do not require legal judgment. Following are several examples of how agents could operate inside a firm, always with the assumption that a lawyer is supervising and making the actual legal decisions.

Client Intake + Engagement Letter Drafting

This first example stays intentionally narrow. The goal is to simply help move from a completed intake to a draft engagement letter for a client that hires the firm.

A typical flow could look like this:

- The agent receives a completed intake data and pulls key information: client name, contact details, basic description of the matter, responsible lawyer, and fee arrangement if known.
- It classifies the matter (for example, "business formation," "family-based immigration," "employment dispute") so it can select the appropriate engagement letter template from a library approved by the firm.
- The agent then populates the selected template with the client's details, the name of the responsible lawyer, the firm's address, and basic fee terms or billing structure, based on what was entered in the intake form. Additional language can be drafted where requested by a specific lawyer or team.
- If something is missing or inconsistent (for example, no billing terms provided), the agent can leave placeholders and notify the lawyer and staff of the issue.

The end result is a draft engagement letter, ready for the lawyer to review and modify. The agent is simply moving information from one place to another and applying the firm's standard template; there is no independent legal advice being given at this stage.

Post-Meeting Follow Up

After the initial client call and intake, there are usually a large set of tasks and "to dos" that are unique to the case. An agent can help make sure those follow ups are captured and organized.

A post-meeting agent might:

- Take the recording or transcript of a meeting and generate a concise summary of what was discussed, focusing on decisions made, questions left open, and action items.
- Identify and list tasks, assigning a tentative owner and suggested due date based on what was said (e.g., "send revised draft to client," "order records," "prepare discovery requests").
- Propose updates to the firm's case management or project management system—new tasks, notes, calendar reminders—without automatically committing them, so a lawyer or legal assistant can accept, edit, or reject each one.
- Draft a short client-facing summary email that recaps the meeting and outlines next steps in plain language, which the lawyer can then edit and send.

Here, the agent is acting like an organized assistant. It is not deciding legal strategy. It is taking data that was already captured and putting it in the relevant places and creating important follow ups.

Knowledge Management/Precedent Finder Agent

Most firms have a large repository of example data from prior casework that goes underutilized, usually because it's hard to find the right example at the moment. An agent can help surface those precedents more intelligently.

A knowledge agent might:

- Accept a short description of the task from the lawyer ("I need a starting point for a motion to dismiss in a wage-and-hour class action," or "Do we have a prior memo on export-control issues for SaaS companies?").
- Search across the firm's internal document repositories, knowledge base, and prior matters for similar fact patterns, jurisdictions, or legal issues.
- Return a small set of highly relevant documents—memos, briefs, checklists, templates—along with short summaries explaining

why each was selected, and highlighting particular sections that may be useful as starting language.

- Optionally, generate a synthesized "starting point" outline or draft that clearly marks which portions are pulled from prior work and which are newly generated, so the lawyer can adjust and tailor as needed.

The agent is not deciding that a particular argument should be used in the current case. It is simply doing the heavy lifting of finding and assembling the firm's own prior work so the lawyer is not starting from a blank page.

Contract Playbook Enforcement Agent

Many clients and firms have detailed contract playbooks—preferred positions, fallback clauses, and redlines—but increasingly, they also have very specific requirements embedded in SLAs and outside counsel guidelines. The challenge is applying those client-specific requirements consistently when reviewing documents drafted by counterparties, paralegals, or contracted writers. This is a natural use case for an agent.

A contract playbook agent could:

- Take an inbound contract (for example, an NDA, master services agreement, SaaS subscription agreement, or vendor contract) and compare it not only against the firm's standard playbook, but also against a specific client's SLAs, outside counsel guidelines, and negotiated "must-have" positions.
- Highlight provisions that deviate from those client-specific standards, such as response time commitments, uptime guarantees, service credits, notice periods, data handling obligations, security controls, or audit rights that do not match the client's required language.
- For each deviation, suggest one or more alternative clauses drawn from the firm's or client's playbook: preferred language, acceptable fallback options, and "walk-away" positions, clearly marked so the lawyer understands which are mandatory versus negotiable.
- Generate an issue list or markup version that groups findings by topic (service levels, support obligations, data security, indemnity, limitation of liability, etc.), which the lawyer can then review, prioritize, and tailor for the specific negotiation.

Again, the agent isn't "negotiating" the contract on its own. It is enforcing consistency with a playbook the firm already created, surfacing issues and proposed language so the lawyer can decide what to accept, adjust, or escalate.

Immigration Case Assembly Agent

Immigration practices offer a good example of structured, form-heavy work where agents can be very helpful, as long as they are used carefully and with clear boundaries.

An immigration case assembly agent might:

- Review intake questionnaires and supporting documents (passports, prior approvals, employment letters, family information) and map them into a structured profile for the client and any dependents.
- Check the information against eligibility criteria for various visa categories the firm has defined in advance (for example, family-based, employment-based, nonimmigrant versus immigrant categories), not to make a final determination, but to surface which options appear potentially relevant.
- Generate a checklist of missing or incomplete items—for example, missing dates, prior immigration history, or supporting evidence that is typically required for the chosen category.
- Prefill draft forms and cover sheets using the collected data, applying the firm's standard language where appropriate, and assemble a preliminary packet for lawyer review.

In this scenario, the agent is not deciding which visa category the client should pursue or whether the case is viable. It is assembling and organizing information, suggesting possibilities based on rules the firm has provided, and preparing draft materials so the lawyer can focus on advising the client and making strategy decisions.

We hope these few examples will help you come up with specific ideas for agents and use cases. We will now turn briefly to how to actually design and implement agents at your firm.

15.5 How to Build an AI Agent

You do not have to be a software engineer to understand how agents are built. In fact, the mental model is very similar to what you already do when you train a new associate: you define the goal, explain the steps, give them resources, set review points, and then refine based on how they perform. Building an agent follows that same pattern.

Step 1: Define the Goal Clearly

Agents do poorly with vague instructions. "Help with intake" is not a goal. "Take a completed intake form and produce a draft engagement letter for Lawyer X to review" *is* a goal.

When defining the goal, be explicit about:

- **What comes in**—e.g., "a completed online intake form and the client's contact details."
- **What should come out**—e.g., "a draft engagement letter in our standard format, saved in the client's folder, and a short note summarizing anything missing."
- **What the agent is *not* doing**—e.g., "The agent does not decide whether to accept the client, does not send anything to the client, and does not change any billing data."

If you cannot describe the goal in one or two clear sentences, the use case probably needs to be narrowed before you involve an agent.

Step 2: Break the Process Into Subtasks

Next, take off your "AI" hat and put on your "training a new hire" hat. Ask yourself: if I gave this to a junior lawyer or paralegal, how would I explain the steps?

For example, for an engagement letter agent, the subtasks might look like:

- Read the intake form.
- Extract and organize basic client information.
- Identify the matter type at a high level (just enough to pick the correct template).
- Select the appropriate engagement letter template.
- Populate the template with the client's details and known billing terms.
- Flag any missing information that needs human input.

Each of these becomes a subtask the agent needs to perform. You are effectively writing a checklist that describes "how we do this work here." That checklist is the backbone of the agent.

The same applies to other examples in this chapter: post-meeting follow up, contract playbook enforcement, immigration case assembly, and so on. In every case, you can break the process into a handful of repeatable subtasks.

Step 3: Assign Tools for Each Step

Once you have the subtasks, the next question is: what does the agent need in order to do this step? In agent terminology, those are "tools." For our purposes, you can think of tools as the digital equivalent of "things a junior can access or do."

For each subtask, you decide:

- Does the agent need to search for something?
  - Examples: "Read this intake form," "Search our DMS for the client's folder," "Search for prior engagement letters for this client."
- Does the agent need to create something?
  - Examples: "Create a new draft document from Template A," "Add a note in the case management system (in draft)," "Propose calendar events."
- Does the agent need to ask the model to transform text?
  - Examples: "Summarize this meeting transcript," "Compare this clause to the playbook and describe the differences," "Draft an initial version of this section."

Each of these actions becomes a discrete tool the agent is allowed to use. The agent cannot invent new abilities; it can only choose among the tools you provide. This is how you bound its autonomy.

When you look back over your list of subtasks, you should be able to point to at least one tool for each step. If you cannot, that step prob ably still requires human judgment and should remain outside the agent's scope.

Step 4: Build In Checkpoints

This is where legal practice diverges sharply from a generic tech use case. Lawyers have ethical duties to supervise and to maintain control over the work product. That means you should deliberately design checkpoints into the agent's process.

Checkpoints can include:

- Human review gates
  - "Do not send anything to the client; always send drafts to the responsible lawyer for approval."
  - "Proposed changes to the case management system must be reviewed and accepted by a human before they are committed."

- Internal validation steps
    - The agent can check its own work before presenting it, for example: "Reread the populated engagement letter and confirm that all required fields (names, addresses, fee terms) are present; if not, add a note describing what is missing."
- Scope and permission limits
    - "This agent only has access to the 'drafts' folder, not final signed documents."
    - "This agent can read from the DMS but cannot delete or move files."

The goal is not to paralyze the agent; it is to ensure that it operates like a well-supervised junior. It can move the ball forward, but it does not take irreversible actions on its own.

Step 5: Test and Iterate

Finally, you test the agent the same way you would test a new process in your practice.

A sensible approach looks like this:

- **Start with test matters**
  Run the agent on past matters or nonlive data. See whether the outputs look like what your team would have done.

- **Compare to your existing standard**
  For example, compare the agent's draft engagement letters to letters your firm actually sent. Are the right templates selected? Are key fields correctly populated? Are missing items properly flagged?

- **Adjust the subtasks and tools**
  If the agent keeps making the same kind of mistake, that usually means the instructions, tools, or checkpoints need refinement. You may need to tighten the prompts, remove a tool that introduces confusion, or add a clearer rule.

- **Roll out gradually**
  Even after you are satisfied with testing, start with a small group of users or a narrow matter type. Collect feedback, review logs of what the agent is doing, and make adjustments before expanding its use.

SAMPLE AGENT PROMPT—ENGAGEMENT LETTER DRAFTING AGENT

You are an AI agent assisting a law firm with drafting engagement letters.

Your goal is to take a completed client intake form and produce a draft engagement letter for attorney review. You are not deciding whether to accept the client, and you are not sending anything directly to the client. All of your outputs are drafts for a lawyer to review.

Inputs You May Receive

- A structured intake form (fields such as client name, contact details, matter description, jurisdiction, billing terms, responsible lawyer)
- The name of the client
- The name of the responsible lawyer
- The type of matter in broad terms (for example, "business formation," "family-based immigration," "employment dispute")

Tools You Are Allowed to Use

1. *read_intake_form*—reads and returns the contents of the intake form.
2. *choose_template(matter_type)*—selects the correct engagement letter template based on the matter type and client requirements.
3. *create_draft_from_template(template, data)*—fills in the engagement letter template with client name, contact information, responsible lawyer, and billing terms.
4. *save_draft(document, client_name)*—saves the draft engagement letter into the client's "Drafts" folder in the document management system.
5. *add_internal_note(note_text)*—creates an internal note for the lawyer describing any missing or inconsistent information.

High-Level Process You Should Follow

1. Read the intake form and extract:
   - Client name
   - Contact information
   - Basic matter description
   - Jurisdiction (if provided)
   - Responsible lawyer
   - Proposed billing arrangement (if provided)
2. If any key details are missing or inconsistent (for example, no billing terms, missing responsible lawyer, unclear matter description), prepare a short internal note explaining what is missing instead of guessing.

3. Select the appropriate engagement letter template using the matter type and any client-specific requirements that are provided.
4. Populate the template with all available information from the intake form, including:
   - Client name and contact details
   - Firm name and address
   - Responsible lawyer's name
   - Matter description in neutral, factual language
   - Billing structure and fee terms, but **only** if they are clearly provided in the intake form
5. Do not invent billing terms or make promises that are not explicitly given. Where information is missing, insert a clear placeholder such as "[FIRM TO COMPLETE BILLING TERMS]."
6. Carefully reread the drafted engagement letter and check for:
   - Correct party names
   - Correct matter description
   - Consistent references to the client and the firm
   - Unresolved placeholders
7. Save the draft engagement letter in the client's Drafts folder.
8. Create an internal note summarizing what you did and listing:
   - Any missing information
   - Any placeholders you left
   - Any sections the lawyer should pay special attention to

Things You Must Never Do

- Do not send emails or documents directly to the client
- Do not accept or reject a client
- Do not give final legal advice
- Do not modify billing data or trust account records

Output

- A clean, well-formatted draft engagement letter ready for attorney review.
- A short internal note (for the lawyer only) explaining any assumptions, placeholders, and missing items.

15.6 What's Next for AI Agents in Law?

It is hard enough to keep up with what is happening in real time with this technology, much less to try to predict what the future has in store. Nevertheless, it is a good way to end this chapter, looking ahead, not in fear but through the lens of opportunity. We have three key areas to highlight. Much of the technology is already in place, but has not yet been fully integrated into the legal industry.

Deeper Integration with Firm Systems and Data

Right now, many AI tools sit off to the side: you copy text into them, get a result, and then paste it back into your real systems. Over time, agents and other AI tools will move inside the systems lawyers already use every day—document management, case management, billing, and knowledge tools. Instead of feeding the AI one document at a time, the AI will be able to see the relevant folders and records (within the same permissions you already use) and work directly there. That makes the tools more useful, but it also means firms have to be very intentional about where the AI has read-only access, where it can create drafts, and where it is never allowed to make changes.

One-Off Prompts to Digital Workers

Most lawyers start with one-off prompts: "summarize this," "draft that," "rewrite this paragraph." The next step is AI suggestions built into your everyday tools, like suggested clauses or research leads. From there, firms will move into predefined automations—simple, repeatable flows such as "when an intake form is complete, create a draft engagement letter." The final step is trained "digital workers": agents that can handle a whole slice of work (like contract playbook review or post-meeting follow up), choosing from a set of allowed actions until they reach a clear goal. Each step adds more autonomy for the system, and more responsibility for the firm to supervise it.

Alternative Business Models and Revenue Structures

As agents and digital workers become more capable, they will not just change how work is done—they will change what firms can offer and how they charge for it. Instead of only billing hourly, firms may offer ongoing subscription services powered by AI agents. Some firms will quietly use AI to improve margins on traditional work; others will build entirely new products and revenue streams around it. In every case, clients will expect transparency: how the AI is used, how quality is maintained, and how any efficiency gains are shared or reflected in pricing.

As we press on with implementing this new technology in our firms, continued investment of resources and time will be part of this process.

We can see an expanded need for team members to be trained and consultants who can assist in this work. We will begin to see more customized and trained tools that are unique to individual firms and their needs. It is exciting and sometimes overwhelming to think of the change that will come to the profession, but at the end of the day, these are tools. Used in the right way, they can help elevate both the quality of the profession and the client experience.

A Note on the Pace of Change

Even since this chapter was first drafted, agentic capabilities have continued to evolve at a remarkable pace. Tools such as Anthropic's Claude Cowork[9] now bring agentic functionality beyond software development and into broader knowledge work, allowing systems to work with files, perform multistep tasks, and move closer to the "digital worker" model described earlier. Anthropic describes Claude Cowork as a system for multistep knowledge work, including research synthesis, document preparation, and file management, rather than simply another chat assistant.

This rapid development reinforces the central point of this chapter: the distinction between asking AI for an answer and asking AI to complete a task is becoming more important. As comparable tools continue to emerge, law firms will need to keep evaluating not only what these systems can do, but also how they are supervised, what data they can access, and where human approval remains essential. We look forward to providing additional updates, examples, and legal-specific use cases in future editions.

9. *Claude Cowork by Anthrophic*, ANTHROPIC, https://www.anthropic.com/product/claude-cowork (last visited May 6, 2026).

■ CHAPTER 16

Legal Ethics in the Age of Generative AI: Navigating the Ethical Minefield

Most lawyers around the world knew very little about generative AI when the story broke nationally of a lawyer who submitted a legal brief in a court proceeding where ChatGPT made up citations for cases that seemed to support the plaintiffs' suit.[1] For all the talk this generated in the profession, one would have thought that future instances of this would be rare. But, alas, as of the writing of this chapter, there have now been 360 documented cases of AI hallucinated cases.[2]

Clearly, lawyers need to be regularly reminded of how the ethics rule apply to AI. State bars and the American Bar Association have been providing guidance. Twenty states have issued guidance, and the ABA has issued a Formal Opinion 512 to guide lawyers.

1. In *Mata v. Avianca* (678 F. Supp. 443, S.D.N.Y 2023), a court sanctioned two New York lawyers and their firm for submitting a brief citing fake cases generated by ChatGPT.

2. *AI Hallucination Cases*, Damien Charlotin, https://www.damiencharlotin.com/hallucinations/ (last visited April 18, 2026).

Figure 16.1 For the latest update of Damien Charlotin's global court hallucinations chart, go to https://www.damiencharlotin.com/hallucinations/.

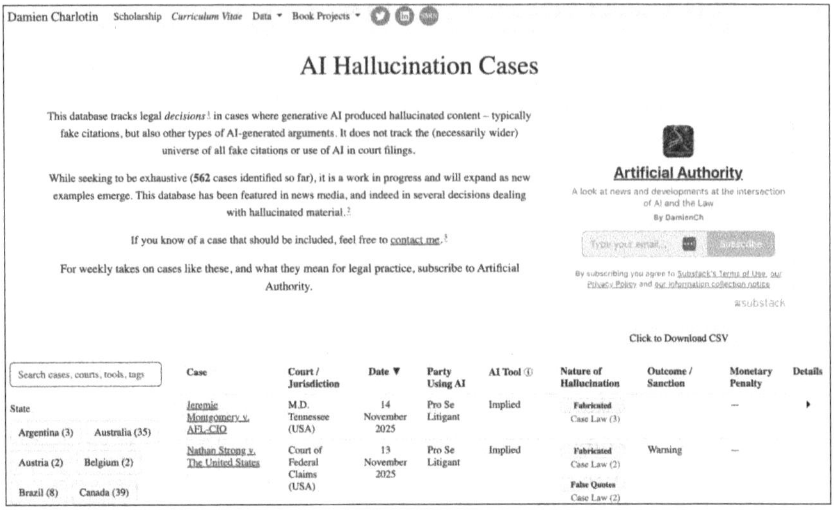

16.1 The Ethical Frameworks that Apply

Most lawyers learn ethics in law school following the American Bar Association's Model Rules of Professional Conduct (MRPC). All 50 states have adopted some version of the MRPC, but there are important variations from state to state.[3] The ABA has also made comments to various rules, and those comments have been separately adopted by many states. For example, most states have adopted Comment 8 to Rule 1.1. Rule 1.1 is the general competence rule (more on this later), and Comment 8 discusses "technology competence."

This chapter focuses on the MRPC, but practitioners should note where their states may vary. We will point out examples of those variations in many cases, but when it comes to AI, states have been making changes quickly and lawyers should pay heed. We will also note ABA opinions like Formal Opinion 512, and we will discuss state bar opinions as well. Finally, we will note a few foreign jurisdictions that have changed their rules.

3. The ABA Center for Professional Responsibility maintains a database showing variations between states and differences between a state rule and the MRPC: https://www.americanbar.org/groups/professional_responsibility/policy/rule_charts/.

As for which ethics rules should concern lawyers, there are many:

- Rule 1.1—Competence: "A lawyer should keep abreast of . . . the benefits and risks associated with relevant technology."
- Rule 1.3—Diligence: "A lawyer shall act with reasonable diligence and promptness in representing a client."
- Rule 1.4—Communication: "A lawyer shall . . . reasonably consult with the client about the means by which the client's objectives are accomplished."
- Rule 1.5—Fees: "A lawyer shall not make an agreement for, charge, or collect an unreasonable fee."
- Rule 1.6—Confidentiality: "A lawyer shall not reveal information related to the representation of a client unless the client gives informed consent."
- Rule 1.7—Conflicts: "A lawyer shall not represent a client if the representation involves a concurrent conflict of interest."
- Rule 1.15—Safekeeping Property: "A lawyer shall hold property of clients or third persons that is in a lawyer's possession in connection with a representation separate from the lawyer's own property."
- Rule 1.18—Duties to Prospective Client: "A lawyer who has learned information from a prospective client shall not use or reveal that information."
- Rule 3.3—Candor to the Tribunal: "A lawyer shall not knowingly . . . make a false statement of fact or law to a tribunal or fail to correct a false statement of material fact or law previously made . . ."
- Rule 5.1—Duty to Supervise Lawyers: "A lawyer having direct supervisory authority over another lawyer shall make reasonable efforts to ensure that the other lawyer conforms to the Rules of Professional Conduct."
- Rule 5.2—Responsibilities of Subordinate Lawyers: "A lawyer is bound by the Rules of Professional Conduct notwithstanding that the lawyer acted at the direction of another person."
- Rule 5.3—Duty to Supervise Nonlawyers: "A lawyer having direct supervisory authority over the nonlawyer shall make reasonable efforts to ensure that the person's conduct is compatible with the professional obligations of the lawyer."
- Rule 5.4—Professional Independence: "A lawyer or law firm shall not share legal fees with a nonlawyer" (5.4(a)) and "A lawyer shall not practice with . . . a nonlawyer [that] has the right to direct or control the professional judgment of a lawyer" (5.4(d)).

- Rule 5.5—Unauthorized Practice of Law: "A lawyer shall not practice law in a jurisdiction in violation of the regulation of the legal profession in that jurisdiction, or assist another in doing so."
- Rule 7.1/7.2—Communications Concerning a Lawyer's Services: "A lawyer shall not make a false or misleading communication about the lawyer or the lawyer's services."
- Rule 7.3— "A lawyer shall not solicit professional employment by live person-to-person contact when a significant motive for the lawyer's doing so is the lawyer's or law firm's pecuniary gain . . ."
- Rule 8.4—Misconduct: "It is professional misconduct for a lawyer to . . . (c) engage in conduct involving dishonesty, fraud, deceit or misrepresentation; (d) engage in conduct that is prejudicial to the administration of justice."

16.2 An Analysis of Individual Ethics Rules and the Impact of AI

Rule 1.1—Technology Competency

Rule 1.1 requires a lawyer to provide competent representation to clients, including having necessary legal knowledge, skill, thoroughness, and preparation. Comment 8 to MR 1.1 states that "a lawyer should keep abreast of changes in the law and its practice, including the benefits and risks associated with relevant technology." Since 2012, approximately 40 states have adopted similar language.

Consequently, lawyers using generative AI have an ethical duty to understand what the technology can and cannot do and what the risks are for using it, as opposed to focusing solely on the upside to the technology. That especially includes the possibility of hallucinating, whether it be making up a case, inventing facts, or misstating what a case or statute stands for.

Hypotheticals:

- A lawyer employs an AI tool for analyzing case law, but fails to understand the algorithm's limitations. As a result, the lawyer misses relevant precedent, or the tool hallucinates and provides cases that are not real.
- A lawyer with limited technological understanding uses AI for complex litigation support, resulting in an incorrect analysis and an unsuccessful case outcome.

Rule 1.3—Diligence

This rule requires that a lawyer shall act with reasonable diligence and promptness in representing a client, and it goes hand in hand with Rule 1.1 on competency. The rule might read to encourage the use of generative AI when a lawyer is carrying a heavy workload and otherwise might not be able to avoid unnecessarily delaying a client's work. On the other hand, if lawyer relies on AI to handle work and the AI makes critical errors, this could be violating Rule 1.3 by failing to act with diligence in checking the work for accuracy.

Hypotheticals:

- A lawyer relies solely on AI for document review, ignoring the need for human oversight, and the lawyer overlooks vital information.
- A lawyer overrelies on an AI system to draft contracts without reviewing the generated content, missing crucial errors that lead to a problematic business agreement for the client.

Rule 1.4—Client Communications

Rule 1.4 requires a lawyer to keep clients informed of developments in their cases, including letting the client know about the status of a matter, what means the lawyer will use to accomplish the client's objectives, and providing the client information when requested.

Lawyers using generative AI *may* be required to disclose the use of AI in a case. Certainly, clients who believe their lawyers are personally drafting work for the client should be told when that is not the case and AI is doing the heavy lifting. That may be accomplished in a variety of ways, such as directly informing the client or including language in an engagement letter disclosing how AI is being used at a firm.

Hypotheticals:

- A lawyer uses AI to communicate updates to the client, but fails to engage personally, leading to the client's dissatisfaction.
- A lawyer uses AI-generated summaries to communicate case progress to the client, but fails to explain the nuances, leading to confusion and dissatisfaction.

Rule 1.5—Fees

Rule 1.5 bars lawyers from charging "unreasonable" fees for their work or expenses. The following factors may be used in determining if a fee is reasonable:

1. The time and labor required, the novelty and difficulty of the questions involved, and the skill requisite to perform the legal service properly;
2. The likelihood, if apparent to the client, that the acceptance of the particular employment will preclude other employment by the lawyer;
3. The fee customarily charged in the locality for similar legal services;
4. The amount involved and the results obtained;
5. The time limitations imposed by the client or by the circumstances;
6. The nature and length of the professional relationship with the client;
7. The experience, reputation, and ability of the lawyer or lawyers performing the services; and
8. Whether the fee is fixed or contingent.

Most states have avoided discussing whether the ethics rules applicable to fees come into play when AI is used, other than stating that if a lawyer indicates that work for which they are charging took X number of hours, and the work actually took fewer hours because of the use of AI, the lawyer cannot charge for X number of hours. That seems to be as much an example of fraud as it is charging unreasonably, and this doesn't seem open to debate.

However, ABA Formal Opinion 512 appears to go a step further in saying:

> The factors set forth in Rule 1.5(a) also apply when evaluating the reasonableness of charges for GAI tools when the lawyer and client agree on a flat or contingent fee. For example, if using a GAI tool enables a lawyer to complete tasks much more quickly than without the tool, it may be unreasonable under Rule 1.5 for the lawyer to charge the same flat fee when using the GAI tool as when not using it. A fee charged for which little or no work was performed is an unreasonable fee.[4]

Implicit is an assumption that the client did not consider that generative AI would be used in the delivery of the flat-billed legal services, and would seem to open the door for complaints against lawyers for not lowering fees beyond what a client (who was actually well informed that

4. *ABA Formal Opinion 512: Generative Artificial Intelligence Tools*, American Bar Association, July 29, 2024, https://www.americanbar.org/content/dam/aba/administrative/professional_responsibility/ethics-opinions/aba-formal-opinion-512.pdf.

the lawyer would be using AI) had agreed to pay. The opinion seems to conclude that the only measure for determining what is reasonable is the time a lawyer spent on a case, and flat billing still needs to be converted to the number of hours spent in order to determine if a client was overcharged or not. And it fails to consider how much it costs law firms to finance the purchase of the software, the massive amount of time many firms put into customizing the tools for their clients, or the training time required to properly use it.

While Formal Opinion 512 is seen largely as noncontroversial, the fee section of the opinion has garnered considerable criticism.[5] And as of the writing of this chapter, no state has embraced this view of Rule 1.5. Some have pointed out the early critics of email, who argued in the mid-1990s that a lawyer could not ethically use email unless they used a complex encryption program to encode messages. This view was endorsed early on by some bar regulators, but largely abandoned as it became clear that virtually the entire bar rejected this interpretation of the rules. Others are concerned that AI, potentially a major tool in providing access to justice for many of those unable to afford legal services, will lose its benefits as lawyers are unable to realize any return on investing in purchasing the software and learning how to use it.

Hypotheticals:

- An attorney charges the same fees, even after AI reduces the workload by half, without explaining the cost structure to the client.
- Despite employing AI to reduce workload, a lawyer continues to bill at the same rate without transparency, resulting in a client dispute over perceived overcharging.

Rule 1.6—Confidentiality

The risks of violating Rule 1.6, regarding the disclosure of confidential client information, is one of the most cited concerns by state bars when it comes to lawyers using AI. The confidentiality question comes up in several contexts.

Public LLMs may log or store prompts, use data for system monitoring, or transmit information through infrastructure outside the lawyer's control. Because the lawyer cannot guarantee confidentiality or limit

5. See, for example, the critique from Thomson Reuters' William Josten, its Director of Client Value and Commercial Strategy, in his article entitled "Is ABA Formal Opinion 512 Off the Mark?" at https://www.thomsonreuters.com/en-us/posts/legal/aba-formal-opinion-512/.

retention, Rule 1.6 generally prohibits uploading identifiable client information into public tools unless the platform's practices are verified and client consent is obtained.

More secure options include on-premises models, private cloud instances, and encrypted "zero-retention" API connections. These configurations prevent client data from entering the public model environment and give firms control over access, storage, and deletion.

Before using any AI system, lawyers should confirm whether the vendor has strong security credentials (e.g., SOC 2, ISO 27001), clear limits on data retention and training, encryption at rest and in transit, and contractual commitments restricting access and outlining breach-notification duties.

Confidentiality also depends on the firm's own safeguards. Multi-factor authentication, role-based access, logging and monitoring, and regular security training help ensure that AI tools are used in a way that protects client information and complies with Rule 1.6.

Hypotheticals:

- Information posted in a chatbot by a lawyer or paralegal about a client is stored by the LLM or used to train their model.
- Even though a lawyer is using an LLM in "private mode," a human is in the loop and reviews chats flagged as being potential service violations, such as asking about sensitive topics (which often come up in criminal, family law, or political asylum cases).
- There is an inadvertent disclosure of client facts by an AI that uses data from a recent case to create an article piece for a firm's website.
- A lawyer uses an AI notetaker for video consultations and the interview is stored in a platform that has not been vetted for its security protocols. (The problems are usually exacerbated when a lawyer uses a platform not designed for lawyers or other professionals that handle sensitive or private data. Lawyers need to conduct due diligence when shopping for software, and also be trained in where they can and cannot post client information.)
- A lawyer uses an AI-powered cloud service without proper encryption, exposing sensitive client information through a security flaw.

Lawyers Lucian Hunger and Jonas Baeriswyl at the Swiss law firm Vischer created the following chart in 2025 that compares different public language models' handling of confidential data.

AI TOOLS: WHAT ABOUT DATA PROTECTION?

A per-provider data protection reference covering ChatGPT (OpenAI), Microsoft Copilot, Google Gemini, and Anthropic Claude

Modeled on the VISCHER Swiss Law and Tax reference format (March 2025) · Status: March 2026

* Web search asterisks: when web search/grounding is active, data may be routed through external search services subject to different terms.

ChatGPT/OpenAI

OpenAI's ChatGPT consumer and business tiers, plus the OpenAI API

	CONSUMER PLANS			BUSINESS PLANS		API
	ChatGPT Free Consumer	**ChatGPT Plus** Consumer	**ChatGPT Pro** Consumer	**ChatGPT Team** Business	**ChatGPT Enterprise** Business	**OpenAI API** Developer / commercial
Notes	**Consumer plans for personal and small team use**			**Team collaboration plan**	**Enterprise plan with full controls**	**Direct API access—commercial terms**
Terms of Use	**OpenAI Europe Terms of Use**			**OpenAI Business Terms**		**OpenAI Business Terms & API Services Agreement**
Data Processing Agreement (DPA)	**Not available**			**Data Processing Addendum** *To be concluded separately*		**Data Processing Addendum** *To be concluded separately; Zero Data Processing addendum available*

	CONSUMER PLANS			BUSINESS PLANS		API
	ChatGPT Free Consumer	**ChatGPT Plus** Consumer	**ChatGPT Pro** Consumer	**ChatGPT Team** Business	**ChatGPT Enterprise** Business	**OpenAI API** Developer / commercial
Use with personal data	**No**			**Possible**	**Possible**	**Possible**
Use with confidential data	**No**			**Possible**	**Possible**	**Possible**
Use with professional secrets	**No**				**Possible** *Requires enterprise data protection agreements*	**Possible** *Enterprise data retention and security controls*
Use for provider's own purposes (e.g., training, service improvement)	**Yes—training can be disabled** *Training on by default; opt out in Settings*			**No** *Business terms prohibit training on customer data*		**No** *API data not used for training*
Use within a company	**Possible with restrictions** *No personal data, no confidential data, training must be disabled*			**Possible** *Designed for team collaboration*	**Possible** *Full enterprise controls*	**Possible** *Full commercial protections*

Notes

Free, Plus, and Pro tiers use for personal/individual tasks only. Training is on by default but can be disabled in Settings.

ChatGPT Team and Enterprise have a Data Processing Addendum available, but it must be concluded separately with OpenAI.

OpenAI's Business Terms prohibit training on customer data for Team, Enterprise, and API customers.

Microsoft Copilot

Microsoft's consumer Copilot, Microsoft 365 Copilot (business), and Azure OpenAI Service

	CONSUMER		BUSINESS/M365		AZURE/API
	Microsoft Copilot Bing.com—consumer	**Copilot in M365 for Home and Copilot Pro** Consumer add-on	**Microsoft 365 Copilot Chat** Included in M365 (business)	**Microsoft 365 Copilot** Add-on subscription (business)	**Azure OpenAI Service** API service for companies
Notes	**Consumer/personal use**		**Included in Microsoft 365 for companies**	**Additional subscription for companies**	**Enterprise API service**
Terms of Use	**Microsoft Services Agreement & Copilot AI Experiences Terms**		**Microsoft Customer Agreement (MCA) & Microsoft Product Terms**		**Microsoft Customer Agreement & Microsoft Product Terms**
Data Processing Agreement (DPA)	**Not available**		**Microsoft Products and Services DPA** *Included*		**Microsoft Products and Services DPA** *Included*
Use with personal data	**No**		**Possible** *If web search is disabled**	**Possible**	**Possible**
Use with confidential data	**No**		**Possible** *If web search is disabled**	**Possible** *If necessary amendments in place and web search is disabled**	**Possible**

	CONSUMER		BUSINESS/M365		AZURE/API
	Microsoft Copilot Bing.com—consumer	**Copilot in M365 for Home and Copilot Pro** Consumer add-on	**Microsoft 365 Copilot Chat** Included in M365 (business)	**Microsoft 365 Copilot** Add-on subscription (business)	**Azure OpenAI Service** API service for companies
Use with professional secrets	**No**		**Possible** *If necessary amendments in place and web search is disabled**	**Possible** *If necessary amendments in place and abuse monitoring is disabled*	**Possible**
Use for provider's own purposes (e.g., training, service improvement)	**Ambiguous** *Info page: No. Copilot AI Experiences Terms (Section 5): Possible*		**Possible with active web search***	**No**	**No**
Use within a company	**Not recommended**		**Possible** *If web access is disabled. Restricted if web search is active (no personal data, no confidential data)*	**Possible**	**Possible**

Notes

For web search, the Microsoft Customer Agreement (MCA) and Data Protection Addendum (DPA) do not apply; the Microsoft Services Agreement for private customers applies instead.

According to the Microsoft Copilot AI Experiences Terms (Section 5), provider use of data for training may be "Possible" for consumer tiers, though the information page states "No."

EU/EFTA/UK tenants: When Anthropic's Claude models are used as a subprocessor in M365 Copilot, they are currently excluded from Microsoft's EU Data Boundary. EU tenants should conduct a DPIA before enabling this integration.

Google Gemini

Google's Gemini consumer apps, AI Studio developer tiers, Google Workspace, and Vertex AI

	CONSUMER		AI STUDIO/DEVELOPER		BUSINESS/CLOUD	
	Google Gemini Apps AI service for private users	**Google Gemini Advanced** AI service for private users	**Gemini API in AI Studio (Unpaid)** API for hobby users/developers	**Gemini API in AI Studio (Paid)** API for developers	**Gemini for Google Workspace** Included in Workspace (business)	**Gemini API in Vertex AI** API service for companies
Notes	**Consumer/personal use**		**API for hobby users, students, and developers**		**Included in Google Workspace for companies**	**API service for companies**
Terms of Use	**Terms of Service & Gemini Apps Privacy Hub**		**Google API's Terms of Service & Gemini API Additional Terms of Service**		**Google Workspace Terms of Service & Service Specific Terms**	**Google Cloud Platform Terms of Service & Service Specific Terms**
Data Processing Agreement (DPA)	**Not available**		**Not available** *Google Controller: Controller Data Protection terms apply*	**Google Data Processing Addendum** *For products where Google is a data processor*	**Cloud Data Processing Addendum**	**Cloud Data Processing Addendum**
Use with personal data	**No**		**No**	**No**	**Possible**	**Possible**
Use with confidential data	**No**		**No**	**No**	**Possible**	**Possible**

	CONSUMER		AI STUDIO/DEVELOPER		BUSINESS/CLOUD	
	Google Gemini Apps AI service for private users	**Google Gemini Advanced** AI service for private users	**Gemini API in AI Studio (Unpaid)** API for hobby users/developers	**Gemini API in AI Studio (Paid)** API for developers	**Gemini for Google Workspace** Included in Workspace (business)	**Gemini API in Vertex AI** API service for companies
Use with professional secrets	**No**				**Possible** *If necessary amendments in place and abuse review is disabled*	**Possible** *If necessary amendments in place and abuse review is disabled*
Use for provider's own purposes (e.g., training, service improvement)	**Yes—training can be disabled** *Use for training can be disabled*		**Yes** *Used for training*	**Possible with Search Grounding (web search)***	**No**	**No**
Use within a company	**Limited possibility** *No personal data, no confidential data, training must be disabled*		**Not recommended**	**Possible with restrictions** *If Search Grounding is disabled (no confidential data)*	**Possible**	**Possible**

Notes

For users in the European Economic Area, Switzerland, or the United Kingdom, the same terms regarding Google's use of data apply to the Unpaid Service of Google AI Studio as to the Paid Service.

Search Grounding (web search) in AI Studio Paid routes data through Google's search infrastructure, which may be subject to different data handling terms.

Professional secrets use via Vertex AI requires careful review of the Cloud Data Processing Addendum and may require additional contractual amendments depending on applicable professional ethics rules.

Anthropic Claude

Anthropic's Claude consumer plans, Claude for Work (Team/Enterprise), Anthropic API, AWS Bedrock, and Google Vertex AI

	CONSUMER PLANS			CLAUDE FOR WORK		API	CLOUD PLATFORMS	
	Claude Free Consumer	**Claude Pro** Consumer	**Claude Max** Consumer	**Claude Team** Claude for Work	**Claude Enterprise** Claude for Work	**Anthropic API** Direct/ Commercial	**Claude on AWS Bedrock** Via Amazon	**Claude on Google Vertex AI** Via Google Cloud
Notes	**Consumer plans—not intended for business use with sensitive data**			**Team collaboration plan for businesses**	**Full enterprise plan with advanced controls, SSO, admin policies**	**Developer & Business API—Commercial Terms apply**	**Via Amazon Web Services**	**Via Google Cloud Platform**
Terms of Use	**Consumer Terms of Service & Privacy Policy**			**Commercial Terms of Service**		**Commercial Terms of Service & API Services Agreement**	**AWS Customer Agreement & Anthropic terms (via Bedrock)**	**Google Cloud Terms & Anthropic terms (via Vertex AI)**
Data Processing Agreement (DPA)	**Not available** *Consumer accounts have no DPA*			**Possible** *DPA with SCCs automatically incorporated in Commercial Terms*		**Included** *DPA + SCCs in Commercial Terms; Zero-Data-Retention (ZDR) addendum available*	**AWS DPA applies** *AWS Data Processing Addendum; Anthropic as subprocessor*	**Google Cloud DPA** *Cloud Data Processing Addendum; Anthropic as subprocessor*

	CONSUMER PLANS			CLAUDE FOR WORK		API	CLOUD PLATFORMS	
	Claude Free Consumer	**Claude Pro** Consumer	**Claude Max** Consumer	**Claude Team** Claude for Work	**Claude Enterprise** Claude for Work	**Anthropic API** Direct/ Commercial	**Claude on AWS Bedrock** Via Amazon	**Claude on Google Vertex AI** Via Google Cloud
Use with personal data	**No** *No DPA; training on by default unless opted out*			**Possible**	**Possible**	**Possible**	**Possible**	**Possible**
Use with confidential data	**No** *No DPA; data may be used for training by default*			**Possible** *No training on commercial data*		**Possible** *No training; ZDR addendum available*	**Possible**	**Possible**
Use with professional secrets	**No**			**Possible with restrictions** *Requires appropriate config; human review possible for policy violations*	**Possible with restrictions** *Stronger admin controls; review abuse monitoring policy*	**Possible with restrictions** *Possible if ZDR addendum in place—ensures maximum isolation*	**Possible with restrictions** *AWS infrastructure controls; Anthropic subprocessor limits apply*	**Possible with restrictions** *Google Cloud infrastructure; Anthropic subprocessor limits apply*
Use for provider's own purposes (e.g., training, service improvement)	**Yes—training ON by default** *Training ON by default (since Sept. 28, 2025). Opt out in Settings → Privacy. Opted in: five-year retention. Opted out: 30-day retention.*			**No** *Commercial Terms explicitly prohibit training on customer data*		**No** *API data never used for training. Seven-day log retention (from Sept. 2025).*	**No** *Claude never uses Bedrock customer data for training*	**No** *Claude never uses Vertex AI customer data for training*

	CONSUMER PLANS			CLAUDE FOR WORK		API	CLOUD PLATFORMS	
	Claude Free Consumer	**Claude Pro** Consumer	**Claude Max** Consumer	**Claude Team** Claude for Work	**Claude Enterprise** Claude for Work	**Anthropic API** Direct/ Commercial	**Claude on AWS Bedrock** Via Amazon	**Claude on Google Vertex AI** Via Google Cloud
Use within a company	**Not recommended** *No DPA; training on by default; employees may inadvertently bind the company; no professional secrets protection*			**Possible** *Designed for teams; admin controls; no training on data*	**Possible** *Full enterprise controls; SSO; admin policy management; audit logs*	**Possible** *Full commercial protections; configure via DPA; ZDR available*	**Possible** *Enterprise AWS governance; configurable retention; no training*	**Possible** *Google Cloud governance; configurable controls; no training*

Notes

As of September 28, 2025, Anthropic updated its Consumer Terms. Claude Free, Pro, and Max users are opted IN to model training by default. Opt out via Settings → Privacy → toggle off "Help improve Claude." Opted in = five-year retention; opted out = 30-day retention.

The Zero-Data-Retention (ZDR) addendum is available to API customers. It ensures prompts and outputs are not logged beyond abuse-check purposes and are deleted immediately after each call.

A Business Associate Agreement (BAA) for HIPAA compliance is available to Enterprise and certain commercial API customers on request.

Claude never uses customer data from Bedrock or Vertex AI for model training, regardless of the hosting environment.

Rule 1.7—Conflicts of Interest: Current Clients

Rule 1.7 prohibits representation if there is a significant risk that a lawyer's responsibilities to another client, a third party, or the lawyer's own interests will materially limit the representation—unless informed consent is obtained, where permitted. Generative AI introduces new categories of conflict that lawyers must recognize and address.

One emerging issue is reliance on AI tools whose outputs are shaped by data from many users, including other clients or third parties. If an AI tool retains or learns from one client's confidential information and reuses it in work for another, this may create a material limitation conflict: the lawyer cannot safely rely on the tool without risking disclosure. Even when vendors state that client data is segregated, the lawyer must understand how the system trains, stores, and compartmentalizes information.

Finally, AI-assisted workflows may create conflicts within multi-client representations. If two clients use the same AI-assisted intake or document-generation process, the lawyer must verify that prompts, templates, or stored data are not cross-contaminated.

Hypotheticals:

- A law firm uses an AI deposition tool that retains transcripts to improve its model. The tool begins surfacing themes from one client's deposition in work for a second client. The lawyer must stop using the tool for both matters and evaluate whether a material limitation conflict requires withdrawal.
- A firm receives discounted access to a new AI drafting system but learns the product lacks adequate confidentiality protections. Rule 1.7 prohibits the lawyer from using it if doing so places the firm's financial benefit above the client's interest in data security.

Rule 1.15—Safekeeping Property

Rule 1.15 governs the safeguarding of client property—primarily funds, documents, and other items entrusted to the lawyer. While generative AI does not change the core duty, it introduces new categories of "property" and new risks in how client materials are stored, transmitted, and handled inside AI systems.

Client property now often includes digital items such as evidence files, scanned records, proprietary business documents, confidential data sets, and client-generated narratives uploaded for analysis. When lawyers place these materials into an AI tool, they must ensure that the system preserves confidentiality, maintains the integrity of the data, and prevents unauthorized access or use. Rule 1.15 requires lawyers to treat these uploaded materials with the same care as client funds—meaning secure storage, controlled access, and clear documentation of where materials go and who can view them.

Many AI tools store uploaded files temporarily or allow drafts to be saved in cloud-based histories. Lawyers must confirm whether data persists, whether it can be deleted, and whether the vendor contractually restricts its use. If a system's retention practices conflict with a lawyer's obligations to safeguard client property, the lawyer cannot use the tool for that purpose.

AI-based organization tools that manage client folders, generate indexes, or classify documents must also be supervised. If a tool misfiles documents or merges materials across matters, the lawyer must correct errors promptly and ensure no client suffers harm.

Hypotheticals:

- A lawyer uploads a client's financial records to an AI tool to generate a summary. The vendor's default settings store all uploads indefinitely. Rule 1.15 requires the lawyer to either change the settings, obtain proper assurances, or avoid the tool entirely; indefinite retention risks exposing client property.
- An AI system used for intake mistakenly merges documents from two different clients with similar names. The lawyer must immediately segregate the files, notify affected clients if required, and evaluate whether continued use of the tool is consistent with Rule 1.15.

Rule 1.18—Duties to Prospective Clients

Rule 1.18 applies when someone consults with a lawyer about the possibility of forming an attorney-client relationship. Even if no engagement follows, the lawyer must protect the person's confidential information and avoid taking on future matters where that information could be materially adverse. Generative AI makes these obligations more complex because initial consultations—once conducted privately—are now often mediated by AI-powered intake tools, chatbots, or automated screening systems.

When prospective clients submit information through AI-driven forms or chat interfaces, the lawyer is responsible for ensuring that the technology preserves confidentiality and does not store, reuse, or share sensitive details. If the system's design permits data to be used for training or cross-matter analysis, the lawyer risks creating an imputed conflict before the representation even begins. Rule 1.18 requires firms to understand how AI systems handle intake information and to adopt configurations that prevent disclosure outside the firm.

AI-based tools that provide preliminary assessments or generate automated "eligibility" responses must also be monitored to avoid unintentionally creating obligations. If the tool gives inaccurate or overly specific analysis, a prospective client may reasonably believe the lawyer has already offered legal advice. Clear disclaimers and appropriate design guardrails are critical.

Finally, information obtained through AI-assisted intake may later restrict the lawyer from accepting a representation adverse to the prospective client if the information could be significantly harmful.

Hypotheticals:

- A firm uses an AI-powered intake chatbot that stores all prospect messages on the vendor's servers for "model improvement." A prospective client discloses damaging facts related to a potential lawsuit. Because the lawyer cannot ensure confidentiality, the firm risks creating a conflict under Rule 1.18 and cannot accept the adverse party as a client later.
- An AI intake tool automatically generates an analysis telling a prospective client they "likely qualify" for a specific visa. If the client reasonably interprets this as legal advice, the firm may have unintentionally created duties that exceed a routine inquiry.

Rule 3.3—Candor Toward the Tribunal

Rule 3.3 prohibits lawyers from knowingly making false statements to a court, submitting documents containing falsehoods, or failing to correct inaccuracies that arise during a proceeding. Generative AI heightens these risks because LLMs can fabricate citations, misstate legal standards, invent facts, or exaggerate evidentiary support with great confidence and fluency. Even when the lawyer does not intend to mislead, relying on unverified AI output can quickly lead to violations.

Under Rule 3.3, a lawyer must independently verify all authority, facts, and arguments derived from an AI tool before submitting them to a tribunal. The duty is proactive: a lawyer cannot claim that a model's hallucinations were "unexpected" or that the tool "seemed trustworthy." Courts around the country have already sanctioned lawyers for filing AI-generated briefs containing nonexistent cases.

The rule also applies after a filing. If a lawyer later discovers that an AI-generated statement or citation included in a submitted document is inaccurate or misleading, Rule 3.3 requires remedial steps—often including notifying the tribunal and opposing counsel. Generative AI does not reduce this obligation or excuse delayed correction.

AI tools used to summarize transcripts, generate factual narratives, or produce issue spotting must be supervised carefully. If an AI-generated summary distorts key testimony or omits harmful facts, the lawyer must correct the record and cannot rely on the flawed summary to shape arguments.

Hypotheticals:

- A lawyer uses AI to draft a motion and fails to check the citations. Two cited "cases" do not exist. Filing the motion violates Rule 3.3(a)(1), and upon discovery, the lawyer must disclose the error to the court rather than silently replace the brief.
- An AI tool incorrectly summarizes deposition testimony, omitting the deponent's admission harmful to the client. If the lawyer relies on that summary in court, the omission constitutes a failure of candor under Rule 3.3(a)(3), even if the mistake originated with the AI.

Rule 5.1—Responsibilities of Partners, Managers, and Supervisory Lawyers

Rule 5.1 requires partners and supervising lawyers to ensure that the firm has measures in place to provide reasonable assurance that all lawyers comply with the Rules of Professional Conduct. Generative AI significantly expands what "reasonable" supervision must include. Leaders must understand how AI tools are selected, how they function, how data is handled, and how the tools are monitored to avoid ethical failures.

Supervisory lawyers must ensure that attorneys using AI systems do so competently and with proper verification procedures. This includes policies requiring lawyers to check all AI-generated citations, confirm legal standards, review drafts before use, and avoid delegating strategy or judgment to the tool. Firms adopting AI without training or guidance risk systematic rule violations, which may trigger supervisory liability under Rule 5.1.

Infrastructure also matters. Rule 5.1 obligates leaders to implement safeguards around confidentiality, data retention, and access controls for AI-enabled workflows. If a lawyer in the firm inadvertently exposes client information to an AI vendor or relies on flawed output because the firm lacked basic AI training or protocols, supervising lawyers may bear responsibility.

The rule also applies when firms deploy internal AI tools—such as automated drafting, intake, or conflict-checking systems. Leaders must ensure these tools are accurate, transparent, properly updated, and integrated into quality control processes.

Hypotheticals:

- A firm allows lawyers to use public LLMs without training. A junior associate files a brief containing hallucinated cases. Because firm leadership failed to establish verification protocols or provide training, the partner supervising the matter may be responsible under Rules 5.1(a) and (b).
- A firm's internally built AI tool automatically drafts client letters. It begins producing responses that omit required disclosures. Partners who failed to test, monitor, or implement review procedures may be liable for inadequate supervision.

Rule 5.2—Responsibilities of Subordinate Lawyers

Rule 5.2 makes clear that subordinate lawyers remain personally responsible for complying with the Rules of Professional Conduct—even when acting at the direction of a supervising lawyer. In the context of generative AI, this means junior lawyers cannot rely on a superior's instructions or a firm's technology practices as a shield when AI-related misconduct occurs. Each lawyer must exercise independent judgment in evaluating AI outputs, verifying accuracy, and ensuring compliance.

A subordinate lawyer cannot assume that an AI-generated draft is accurate simply because a partner recommended the tool. Under Rule 5.2, the lawyer must check citations, ensure factual accuracy, and confirm that the draft reflects appropriate legal standards. If something appears incorrect or fabricated, the lawyer must not adopt it without investigation. The rule also requires subordinate lawyers to understand the basic risks of using AI—such as hallucinations, confidentiality issues, and bias—and to raise concerns when an AI workflow appears unreliable or ethically questionable.

Rule 5.2(b) recognizes a narrow provision under which a subordinate lawyer may rely on a supervisor's "reasonable resolution of an arguable question of professional duty." This does not apply to mechanical failures such as AI hallucinations. A subordinate lawyer cannot defer to a supervisor's instruction to "just file it" when an AI-generated document contains unverified or dubious content.

Hypotheticals:

- A partner instructs an associate to file an AI-drafted brief without further review because "the tool is reliable." The associate

notices unusual citations, but files the document anyway. When the citations prove fictitious, the associate has violated Rule 5.2(a) for failing to exercise independent judgment.
- An AI intake tool appears to save prospect data in a way that may violate confidentiality. A subordinate lawyer who identifies the problem must alert a supervisor, not assume compliance simply because the firm selected the tool.

Rule 5.3—Responsibilities Regarding Nonlawyer Assistants

Rule 5.3 requires lawyers to ensure that nonlawyer assistants—whether human staff or technology tools—act in a manner consistent with the lawyer's ethical obligations. In the generative AI context, the Model Rules treat AI systems as nonlawyer assistants whose work must be supervised, validated, and integrated into firm processes with appropriate safeguards.

A lawyer using an AI tool for drafting, research, summarization, intake, or document processing must ensure the tool does not introduce inaccuracies, confidentiality breaches, or other ethical violations. The lawyer cannot rely on vendor assurances alone; Rule 5.3 requires reasonable efforts to understand how the system works, how data is handled, and what risks the tool presents. This includes verifying whether client information is stored, used for training, or made accessible outside the firm.

The rule also requires lawyers to supervise the actual output. AI-generated documents must be reviewed carefully, legal citations must be checked, and factual narratives must be compared against the record. Failing to supervise AI's work is equivalent to failing to supervise a human employee.

Firms must adopt policies, training, and quality controls to ensure responsible use of AI across all lawyers and staff. If the firm deploys internal AI tools—such as automated client communications or document assembly systems—lawyers must ensure that the tools perform reliably and that errors are corrected promptly.

Hypotheticals:

- A firm uses an AI transcription tool that misidentifies speaker statements, inserting incorrect answers into a deposition summary. If a lawyer relies on that summary without checking the transcript, the lawyer violates Rule 5.3 because the AI tool was inadequately supervised.
- An AI-powered intake system automatically classifies matters and assigns urgency levels. It mistakenly routes a time-sensitive

case to a nonurgent queue. Lawyers who failed to monitor the system or implement review procedures may be responsible for resulting harm.

Rule 5.4—Professional Independence of a Lawyer

Rule 5.4 protects a lawyer's professional independence by prohibiting nonlawyers from directing or regulating the lawyer's professional judgment. While generative AI tools lack legal agency, lawyers must ensure that AI vendors, proprietary algorithms, or automated workflows do not dictate legal outcomes in a manner that compromises independent judgment.

AI systems can recommend strategies, evaluate risks, or suggest settlement positions. These outputs are assistive data points, but they cannot replace a lawyer's granular analysis. A lawyer abdicates their role under Rule 5.4 if they "rubber-stamp" an AI recommendation without independent verification. The lawyer—not the software—remains the fiduciary responsible for all strategic decisions.

Rule 5.4 also governs the relationship with AI providers. Lawyers must ensure that End User License Agreements (EULAs) do not grant vendors contractual rights that interfere with a lawyer's ability to act in the client's best interest. The lawyer's primary duty is to the client, never to the optimization metrics of a technology provider.

Hypotheticals:

- A firm uses an AI platform to rank litigation strategies. The lawyer adopts the top-ranked "aggressive" strategy because the AI's "success probability" is high, without reviewing the jurisdictional nuances or the client's specific risk tolerance. Rule 5.4 requires the lawyer to exercise independent judgment rather than outsourcing conclusions to a "black box" system.
- A legal tech vendor offers a discount on its AI platform, provided the lawyer agrees to use the vendor's automated mediation service for all qualifying disputes. This arrangement may violate Rule 5.4 if it limits the lawyer's independence in determining the best dispute resolution path for a specific client.

Rule 5.5—Unauthorized Practice of Law (UPL) and Multijurisdictional Practice

Rule 5.5 prohibits lawyers from practicing in jurisdictions where they are not licensed and from assisting others—including nonlawyers—in the unauthorized practice of law. Generative AI intensifies these concerns because AI tools can produce legal analysis, offer jurisdiction-specific guidance, and interact with users in ways that resemble legal advice.

Lawyers must ensure they do not allow AI systems to provide individualized legal advice directly to clients without appropriate supervision. If an AI tool interprets statutes, recommends legal strategies, or applies law to a user's facts, the lawyer must retain control over the final output and ensure the client understands the advice comes from the lawyer, not the tool. The lawyer also cannot deploy an unsupervised AI system that effectively acts as a standalone legal adviser.

Multijurisdictional practice issues arise when AI delivers guidance for jurisdictions where the lawyer is not admitted. If the lawyer uses AI-generated analysis to counsel a client on the law of a state where the lawyer is not licensed—without complying with exceptions such as temporary practice rules—the lawyer risks violating Rule 5.5.

Similarly, firms must be cautious when AI tools automatically generate client-facing materials for multiple jurisdictions. The lawyer must review jurisdiction-specific content before it is sent, and firms must avoid giving clients the impression that the technology itself is authorized to practice law.

Hypotheticals:

- A firm deploys an AI chatbot on its website that answers user questions such as "Do I have a viable wage-and-hour claim under California law?" without lawyer review. Because the AI applies law to facts and presents conclusions, the firm risks facilitating UPL under Rule 5.5(a).
- A Tennessee lawyer uses an AI tool to draft an immigration compliance memo for a New York employer. The AI includes analysis of New York employment law. If the lawyer adopts and delivers that content without meeting multijurisdictional practice exceptions, Rule 5.5 is implicated.

Rule 7.1—Communications Concerning a Lawyer's Services

Rule 7.1 prohibits lawyers from making false or misleading statements about their services. Generative AI introduces new risks because lawyers increasingly use AI tools to create website content, blog posts, profiles, marketing materials, videos, and automated responses. If AI produces exaggerated claims, inaccurate descriptions, or unsupported statements—and the lawyer publishes them—the lawyer is responsible for the resulting Rule 7.1 violation.

AI tools are prone to confidently generating statements the lawyer never made, cases the lawyer never handled, or achievements that are inaccurate or overstated. Lawyers must review all AI-generated marketing content carefully to ensure it does not imply guaranteed outcomes, inaccurately describe experience, or suggest endorsements or comparative claims without support. Because Rule 7.1 applies even when the lawyer did not intend to mislead, failing to supervise AI-generated marketing materials can result in an ethics violation.

Lawyers must also take care with auto-generated content such as AI-written social posts, newsletters, video scripts, and bios. If AI misstates success rates, fabricates awards, or implies specialties the lawyer does not have, Rule 7.1 is implicated regardless of whether the tool or the lawyer wrote the words.

This rule also extends to AI avatar videos, chatbots, and automated messaging. These tools cannot promise results, create unjustified expectations, or misrepresent the lawyer's role.

Hypotheticals:

- A lawyer uses AI to refresh their website bio. The AI-generated draft claims the lawyer has "won more asylum cases in the region than any competitor." The lawyer posts it without correction. Because the claim is unverifiable and potentially misleading, the lawyer violates Rule 7.1.
- An AI chatbot responding to client inquiries states, "Your case has a very high chance of approval based on our firm's past success." If this falsely implies guaranteed results or suggests the lawyer has reviewed the matter, Rule 7.1 is implicated.

Rules 7.2 and 7.3—Advertising, Referrals, and Solicitation

Rules 7.2 and 7.3 govern how lawyers may advertise their services and how they may solicit prospective clients. Generative AI affects both areas by automating outreach, creating marketing content at scale, and generating personalized messages that may cross the line into solicitation if not carefully supervised.

Under Rule 7.2, lawyers may advertise, but advertisements must comply with all ethical rules, including accuracy, transparency, and proper identification of the lawyer responsible for the content. When lawyers use AI to create ads, social posts, newsletters, landing pages, or video scripts, they must review the content to ensure it does not imply specialization without certification, make unsupported comparisons, or include misleading claims. AI's tendency to embellish credentials or invent affiliations can easily trigger violations if published unchecked.

Rule 7.3 regulates direct solicitation—particularly targeted outreach to individuals known to need legal services. AI systems that generate personalized messages, analyze online behavior, or send automated follow ups may convert permissible marketing into prohibited solicitation. Lawyers must monitor AI-powered CRM tools, automated email sequences, and chatbots to ensure communications do not exert undue pressure, promise results, or target vulnerable individuals in ways the rule restricts.

The lawyer is responsible for the content, timing, and tone of any AI-generated communication. Vendors and algorithms cannot be allowed to initiate client contact in ways that violate solicitation rules.

Hypotheticals:

- A lawyer uses an AI marketing platform that automatically sends personalized LinkedIn messages to people who post about being sued. Because the tool targets individuals known to need legal services and urges them to contact the firm, the lawyer risks violating Rule 7.3's restrictions on real-time solicitation.
- An AI system creates a promotional video claiming the firm is "the top immigration firm for O-1 visas in the United States." If the lawyer publishes the video without verifying the claim, Rule 7.2 is implicated.

Rule 8.4—Misconduct

Rule 8.4 identifies categories of professional misconduct, including dishonesty, fraud, deceit, misrepresentation, conduct prejudicial to the administration of justice, and discriminatory or harassing behavior. Generative AI intersects with these prohibitions in multiple ways because AI tools can produce inaccurate content, mask the lawyer's own involvement, or generate outputs that betray bias or mislead others if used without adequate supervision.

Rule 8.4(c) prohibits conduct involving dishonesty, fraud, deceit, or misrepresentation. A lawyer who knowingly uses AI-generated content that includes fabricated citations, misleading statements, or manipulated evidence risks violating this rule. Even unintentional misuse can become a violation if the lawyer fails to take corrective steps after discovering inaccuracies. Relying on AI to "clean up" documents or transcripts without checking whether the tool has rewritten factual content can also lead to misrepresentation.

Rule 8.4(d) prohibits conduct prejudicial to the administration of justice. Submitting AI-generated filings without verification, allowing AI tools to distort evidentiary materials, or using AI to create delay or confusion can fall into this category.

Additionally, AI tools may contain or reproduce biased outputs. If a lawyer knowingly uses AI-generated language that reflects discriminatory assumptions—or permits automated systems to interact with clients in ways that treat individuals differently based on protected characteristics—the lawyer may violate Rule 8.4(g) or state analogs.

Hypotheticals:

- A lawyer uses AI to rewrite a client's affidavit. The tool smooths the narrative, but invents small factual details to improve coherence. If the lawyer submits the affidavit without correcting the fabricated content, the conduct may constitute dishonesty under Rule 8.4(c).
- An AI chatbot on a law firm's website gives harsher responses or dissuades potential clients from certain backgrounds based on biased training data. If the lawyer knew or should have known the system was producing discriminatory outputs, Rule 8.4(g) may be implicated.

16.3 Privilege

In 2026, a federal court decision highlighted a privilege problem that lawyers can no longer ignore: what happens when a client uses a consumer generative AI tool to analyze legal materials?

In *United States v. Heppner*,[6] a financial services CEO facing securities fraud charges uploaded legal documents from his law firm into the free consumer version of Anthropic's Claude and asked it to analyze his case. When prosecutors sought the AI-generated materials, the court ordered them produced. The court rejected both attorney-client privilege and work-product protection.

The court focused on three key facts: Claude was not a lawyer. Anthropic's consumer terms did not promise confidentiality. And the AI materials were not created at the direction of counsel. That combination proved fatal to the privilege claim.

Importantly, the court did not say that all AI-assisted legal work is unprotected. It left open the possibility that the result might have been

6. No. 25 Cr. 503 (S.D.N.Y. Feb. 17, 2026).

different if the lawyer had directed the client to use an enterprise AI platform with appropriate confidentiality protections.

That is the real lesson of *Heppner*. The privilege issue is not simply whether AI was used. It is how AI was used, who directed the use, what platform was used, and what the platform's terms said about confidentiality, data retention, training, and disclosure.

For lawyers, the case underscores the need to give clients clear instructions about AI use. Clients should not be uploading pleadings, legal memos, discovery, attorney emails, or other sensitive materials into consumer AI tools. Lawyers should review the terms of any AI platform used for legal work, distinguish consumer tools from enterprise tools, and confirm that confidential information is protected. They should also consider updating engagement letters, protective orders, litigation holds, and discovery protocols to address AI-generated materials and AI interactions as potential electronically stored information.

Heppner is likely to become an early warning case. It shows that careless AI use can create real privilege and confidentiality risks. But it also suggests that those risks can be managed when lawyers control the process, use appropriate platforms, and treat AI use as part of the client's overall information governance strategy.

■ APPENDIX

Generative AI Ethics Regulatory Chart

Compiled by Greg Siskind (GSiskind@visalaw.com)

Jurisdiction	**Ethics Opinions and Official Guidance/Reports**
American Bar Association	Title: Generative Artificial Intelligence Tools—ABA Formal Opinion 512 Date: July 29, 2024 URL: https://www.americanbar.org/content/dam/aba/administrative/professional_responsibility/ethics-opinions/aba-formal-opinion-512.pdf — Title: House of Delegates Resolution 604 Date: February 2023 URL: https://www.americanbar.org/content/dam/aba/administrative/news/2023/mym-res/604.pdf
Arizona	Administrative Order 2024-33 created the Arizona Steering Committee on Artificial Intelligence and the Courts. While the Committee is still active, all existing Ethical Rules apply to an attorney's use of generative AI. Go to https://bit.ly/4f4axax to read the Committee's Nov. 14, 2024 ethical best practices for use of generative AI. More information about the Committee and its work can be found at: URL: https://www.azcourts.gov/cscommittees/Arizona-Steering-Committee-on-Artificial-Intelligence-and-the-Courts — Title: Guidance for the Use of Generative Artificial Intelligence in the Practice of Law in Arizona Date: Undated Practitioner-oriented "best practices" framework for responsible GenAI use in the Arizona legal profession. URL: https://www.azbar.org/for-legal-professionals/practice-tools-management/practice-2-0/choosing-and-using-technology/best-practices-for-using-artificial-intelligence/

Jurisdiction	Ethics Opinions and Official Guidance/Reports
Arkansas	Arkansas Supreme Court administrative orders on AI: https://acrobat.adobe.com/id/urn:aaid:sc:va6c2:9dc2ac08-4b2d-4eff-98db-78fc69ab05b3
California	Title: Practical Guidance for the Use of Generative Artificial Intelligence in the Practice of Law Date: November 16, 2023 URL: https://www.calbar.ca.gov/Portals/0/documents/ethics/Generative-AI-Practical-Guidance.pdf
District of Columbia	Title: DC Bar Ethics Opinion: Ethics Opinion 388 Date: April 2024 URL: https://www.dcbar.org/For-Lawyers/Legal-Ethics/Ethics-Opinions-210-Present/Ethics-Opinion-388
Florida	Title: Florida Bar Ethics Opinion 24-1 Date: January 19, 2024 URL: https://www.floridabar.org/etopinions/opinion-24-1/ — Title: Florida Supreme Court Opinion No. SC2024-0032—*Amendments to Bar Rules (Generative AI)* Date: August 2024 URL: https://supremecourt.flcourts.gov/content/download/2439771/opinion/Opinion_SC2024-0032.pdf
Illinois	Title: Report to President Shawn Kasserman Date: September 27, 2023 URL: https://www.americanbar.org/content/dam/aba/administrative/center-for-innovation/ai-task-force/skm-c360i23100414470.pdf — Title: The Illinois Attorney's Guide to Implementing AI (from the Attorney Registration and Disciplinary Commission) Date: October 1, 2025 URL: https://iardc.org/Files/Implementing-AI-Guide/?page=1
Kentucky	Title: Kentucky Bar Association Ethics Opinion KBA E-457 Date: March 15, 2024 URL: https://nationalcenterforstatecourts.app.box.com/s/0f5iqlvcgyaumn7wvl10sku8mon3q41f

Jurisdiction	Ethics Opinions and Official Guidance/Reports
Massachusetts	Title: The Wild West of Artificial Intelligence: Ethical Considerations for the Use of A.I. in the Practice of Law by Afton Pavletic, Assistant Bar Counsel, Massachusetts Board of Bar Overseers Date: Undated URL: https://bbopublic.massbbo.org/web/f/The_Wild_West_of_Artificial_Intelligence.pdf
Michigan	Title: Judicial officers must maintain competence with advancing technology, including but not limited to artificial intelligence. JI-155 Date: October 27, 2023 URL: https://www.michbar.org/opinions/ethics/numbered_opinions/JI-155 — Title: Artificial Intelligence for Attorneys—Frequently Asked Questions (State Bar of Michigan) Date: May 2024 URL: https://www.michbar.org/opinions/ethics/AIFAQs
Minnesota	Title: Minnesota State Bar Report: Implications of Large Language Models (LLMs) on the Unauthorized Practice of Law (UPL) and Access to Justice Date: June 20, 2024 URL: https://mnbars.org/docDownload/2460104
Missouri	Title: Office of Legal Ethics Counsel & Advisory Committee of the Supreme Court of Missouri: Informal Opinion Number 2024-11 Date: April 25, 2024 URL: https://mo-legal-ethics.org/informal-opinion/2024-11/
New Jersey	Title: Legal Practice: Preliminary Guidelines on the Use of Artificial Intelligence by New Jersey Lawyers Date: January 24, 2024 URL: https://www.njcourts.gov/sites/default/files/notices/2024/01/n240125a.pdf — Title: Task Force on Artificial Intelligence (AI) and the Law: Report, Requests, Recommendations, and Findings Date: May 2024 https://njsba.com/wp-content/uploads/2024/05/NJSBA-TASK-FORCE-ON-AI-AND-THE-LAW-REPORT-final.pdf

Jurisdiction	Ethics Opinions and Official Guidance/Reports
New Mexico	Title: STATE BAR OF NEW MEXICO ETHICS ADVISORY COMMITTEE FORMAL ETHICS ADVISORY OPINION FORMAL OPINION: 2024-004 TOPIC: Using Generative Artificial Intelligence in the Practice of Law URL: https://www.sbnm.org/Portals/NMBAR/GenAI%20Formal%20Opinion%20-%20Sept_2024_FINAL.pdf?ver=5uRiJtLGRjm0qR_niws94Q%3d%3d
New York	Title: Report and Recommendations of the New York State Bar Association Task Force on Artificial Intelligence Date: April 2024 URL: https://nysba.org/wp-content/uploads/2022/03/2024-April-Report-and-Recommendations-of-the-Task-Force-on-Artificial-Intelligence.pdf?srsltid=AfmBOoog0xON8fH_8YMOHE1zcIlw6Yz-84LL7inlok3CjZ3ik13xuaTx — Title: Formal Opinion 2024-5: Ethical Obligations of Lawyers and Law Firms Relating to the Use of Generative Artificial Intelligence in the Practice of Law Date: 2024 URL: https://www.nycbar.org/wp-content/uploads/2024/08/20221329_GenerativeAILawPractice.pdf
North Carolina	Title: Proposed 2024 Formal Ethics Opinion 1 Use of Artificial Intelligence in a Law Practice Date: July 18, 2024 URL: https://www.ncbar.gov/for-lawyers/ethics-and-governing-rules/ethics-opinions/opinions/2024-formal-ethics-opinion-1/ — Title: Modernizing unauthorized practice of law regulations to embrace technology, improve access to justice URL: https://www.ncsc.org/resources-courts/modernizing-unauthorized-practice-law-regulations-embrace-technology-improve
Oregon	Title: OSB Formal Opinion 2025-205 Date: February 2025 Comprehensive opinion on competence, confidentiality, supervision, candor, and nonhourly/value billing where appropriate. URL: https://www.osbar.org/_docs/ethics/2025-205.pdf

Jurisdiction	**Ethics Opinions and Official Guidance/Reports**
Pennsylvania	Title Ethical Issues Regarding the Use of Artificial Intelligence (Pennsylvania Bar Association Committee on Legal Ethics & Professional Responsibility and Philadelphia Bar Association Professional Guidance Committee Joint Formal Opinion 2024-200). Date: May 22, 2024 URL: https://www.pabar.org/Members/catalogs/Ethics%20 Opinions/Formal/Joint%20Formal%20Opinion%202024-200.pdf
Texas	Title: State Bar of Texas Taskforce for Responsible AI in the Law: Interim Report to the State Bar of Texas Board of Directors Date: July 18, 2024 URL: https://www.texasbar.com/AM/Template.cfm?Section =Immediate_Past_President&Template=/CM/ContentDisplay .cfm&ContentID=63475 — Title: Proposed Opinion 2024-6 (proposed November 2024) URL: https://www.texasbar.com/AM/pec/vendor/drafts /PO_2024_6.pdf#:~:text=In%20prior%20Opinions%2C%20 this%20Committee,obligation%20extends%20to%20a%20 lawyer%E2%80%99s — Title: Texas Opinion 705: The Professional Ethics Committee for the State Bar of Texas Date: February 2025 URL: https://www.legalethicstexas.com/resources/opinions /opinion-705/
Virginia	Title: Proposed Legal Ethics Opinion 1901 on Reasonable Fees and the Use of Generative AI URL: https://www.vsb.org/common/Uploaded%20files/docs /032725-prop-leo-1901.pdf
West Virginia	Title: WV Legal Ethics Opinion 24-01 Date: June 14, 2024 URL: https://storage.googleapis.com/msgsndr/Rgd68xOkcVdte TsBkf6O/media/667ac9c219bb7a1f7a4df4c2.pdf — Title: JIC Advisory Opinion 2023-22 Date: October 13, 2022 URL: https://www.courtswv.gov/sites/default/pubfilesmnt /2023-11/JIC%20Advisory%20Opinion%202023-22_Redacted .pdf

Jurisdiction	Ethics Opinions and Official Guidance/Reports
Federal Judicial Conference	From the Advisory Committee on Evidence Rules URL: https://www.uscourts.gov/sites/default/files/2024-11_evidence_rules_committee_meeting_agenda_book_final_10-24.pdf — Committee on Rules of Practice and Procedure URL: https://www.uscourts.gov/sites/default/files/2024-12/2025-01_standing_committee_agenda_book_final_12-19.pdf

Disclosure of the Use of Generative AI in Legal Services (Sample Engagement Letter Language)

We are committed to providing you with the highest level of legal service, utilizing the latest advancements in technology to enhance our efficiency and effectiveness.

Use of Generative AI

As part of our commitment to innovation and excellence, we utilize generative artificial intelligence (AI) in various aspects of our legal services. Generative AI helps us streamline processes, conduct thorough legal research, draft documents, and perform comprehensive data analysis, among other tasks. This technology allows us to deliver faster, more accurate, and cost-effective services to our clients.

Why We Use Generative AI

1. *Efficiency*: Generative AI can reduce the time required to complete complex tasks, enabling us to work more efficiently, prepare your case more quickly, and respond to your needs promptly.
2. *Accuracy*: AI-driven tools enhance our ability to quickly and accurately conduct answers to legal questions.
3. *Cost Effectiveness*: By automating routine tasks, we can reduce operational costs, which allows us to offset inflationary pressures and still provide the level of service our clients expect.
4. *Innovation*: Staying at the forefront of technological advancements allows us to provide you with cutting-edge legal solutions.

Confidentiality and Security

Please rest assured that all AI tools used by our firm comply with stringent confidentiality and data security protocols. In addition to not allowing your data to be seen by parties outside our law firm, note that none of your data will be used to train our software, and none of your data will be aggregated with other client data as part of any software development, including AI tools. Your personal information and case details remain protected under our security measures, ensuring compliance with all applicable privacy laws and regulations.

Opt-Out Procedure

We understand that the use of AI in legal services is a relatively new development, and we are committed to transparency regarding its use. You have the right to opt out of the use of generative AI in your case. If you prefer that we do not use generative AI in handling your legal matters, please inform us by sending a written notice to [email address] or by mailing it to our office at [office address]. We will ensure that your case is managed without the use of AI tools.

CHAPTER 17

Why Implementation Matters

Artificial intelligence will not replace lawyers—but lawyers who successfully implement and govern AI will replace those who do not.

This chapter proceeds from a single point of focus: if you've done the work of reading this entire book, it is all practically meaningless unless you are able to successfully implement these AI capabilities at your firm. The most advanced language model will underperform if lawyers do not trust it, cannot explain it, or lack clarity on when to use it. Conversely, a modest, narrowly-scoped tool can generate outsized returns when embedded in a disciplined rollout. Some AI capabilities are native, and will really only require internal approval from a security and privacy standpoint. But other, more sophisticated tools, especially those that are industry specific, will require more extensive training and perhaps even some internal process changes.

The pages that follow do not prescribe a one-size-fits-all blueprint, because every firm reading this book is likely different. Instead, the chapter offers a menu of interlocking practices—strategy, policy, training, change management, and client transparency—from which any organization can assemble a program suited to its context.

17.1 What Makes AI Implementation Challenging?

Three components stand out. First, professional responsibility rules impose nonnegotiables as it relates to duties of competence and confidentiality. A lawyer may consult an algorithm, but the signature on a pleading vouches for the result. Second, legal work can be very collaborative at times, but also can operate in silos in other instances; for example, a drafting AI assistant that works well for corporate associates may worry the litigation group that fears waiver of work product protection. Third, law remains a relationship business. Some clients may demand the use of AI while others strongly urge against it.

Because firms vary widely, each section of this chapter begins with some first principles, then presents practical tools that can be scaled as needed:

- **Section 17.2** explains how to articulate a vision, choose success metrics, inventory AI-ready tasks, and secure leadership sponsorship.
- **Section 17.3** translates those strategic aims into a firm-wide AI use policy that extends existing confidentiality, cybersecurity, and professional conduct rules.
- **Section 17.4** offers a tiered training framework—from bite-sized primers for technophobic partners to hands-on labs for early adopters—so every professional can use AI safely and productively.
- **Section 17.5** addresses change management: how to pilot for early wins, reward adoption, and channel feedback to refine the program.
- **Section 17.6** tackles client communication and transparency, showing when and how to disclose AI assistance without eroding trust.

Throughout, the emphasis remains practical. Checklists and real-world examples will show how firms are to move from experimentation to internalizing the change.

17.2 Developing an AI Strategy

A successful AI program is less about buying the right software and more about identifying areas of need and internal alignment on execution. The following chart contains five questions that can help keep stakeholders at your firm moving in the right direction; each question corresponds to a planning element in the table.

Element	Key Questions	Practical Tips
Vision	What business problem(s) do we need to solve?	Define 2-3 measurable outcomes—e.g., **25 percent reduction** in first-draft time, **15 percent increase** in client satisfaction scores, etc.
AI Task Inventory	Where can AI automate my or my team's work?	List repeatable tasks (research memos, contract review, intake triage, knowledge-base searches). Prioritize by time spent. Favor tasks that have fewer implications if error occurs.

Element	Key Questions	Practical Tips
Roadmap and Sequencing	In what order should we implement?	Start with low-risk, high-volume use cases (summaries, transcript analysis). Gradually implement more advanced tools, like customized agents connected to your DMS.
Stakeholder Alignment	Who owns what?	Identify a key stakeholder sponsor (managing partner, COO, or GC). Form a cross-functional AI Steering Committee (IT, KM, Risk, LPM, associates, and at least one skeptical partner).
Budget and Resourcing	How will we pay for and staff this?	Use early pilot programs to generate internal buy-in; document ROI and reinvest in proven solutions. Depending on firm resources, invest in training and resources for the COO or hire an AI engineer.

(1) Define the Vision (Pain Points) + (2) Build a Task List

Identify the specific challenges in your firm you want AI to solve. Sometimes the problem is not always clear. One way of identifying potential focus areas for an AI solution is to build a high-level task list. In the task list, look for repeatable or high-volume tasks. Then prioritize the tasks that require the largest amount of time to complete. Oftentimes, AI may not be the right initial solution. Perhaps a better foundation procedure or process is needed, then AI or additional software can be brought in to improve further. Lastly, favor tasks that have fewer implications if error occurs.

(3) Plan a Reasonable Rollout

Pilot AI in a sandbox environment with test data before connecting to any internal systems or client data. If you do not have good example documents, you can have your team use AI to generate example ones. Also, take existing documents and de-sensitize them. Make sure to give pilot users at your firm plenty of time to explore the capabilities and validate the outputs as expected. Check for accuracy and consistency. By consistency, we mean you get a similar response nine out of ten times when asking the same query. Also, work with your team to define clear success criteria for the pilot, including accuracy expectations, review of responsibilities, and the specific conditions that must be met before expanding the rollout.

(4) Establish Project Ownership

Clear ownership will define the success of any AI implementation. Those involved can span from IT, legal team members assisting on prompts, and early adopters pioneering the capabilities and training other team members.

(5) Budget Considerations

Many firms have not updated technology budgets to the existing landscape we have today. Track hours saved and errors reduced, then reinvest that value into software or roles (e.g., an AI solutions engineer) or an internal AI Center of Excellence. When the value of early implementations is realized, further investment approvals become a formality.

Your lawyers are already experimenting with AI—blocking it would be as futile as forbidding Google Search. The focus should be on harnessing these tools safely and strategically.

Recap: Start by defining what success looks like. Never launch an AI initiative to solve a problem that doesn't exist. Listen carefully to vendor claims, document use cases, and then validate them through pilots and peer references.

17.3 Designing a Firm-Wide AI Use Policy

An AI policy is what allows a firm to connect AI ambitions to real tasks that are carried out in daily practice. Most firms already have client confidentiality guidelines, cybersecurity standards, and professional responsibility policies; an AI policy extends those same principles to machine-generated work products. The immigration boutique law firm Siskind Susser, for example, requires training at the point of onboarding and biannually on approved AI tools. The policy also establishes that uploading or providing client data to any unapproved LLM or AI product is not allowed. Next we have outlined nine important components of an effective AI policy.

Scope and Purpose

State that the policy governs every lawyer, paralegal, staff member, intern, and outside vendor who accesses firm systems, whether on firm-issued or personal devices. Anchor the purpose in professional duties: the goal is to reap speed and accuracy gains without compromising competence or confidentiality.

Approval Process

No software should touch client data until it has been properly vetted. Require vendors to document encryption at rest and in transit, and disclose how prompts and outputs are stored or discarded, data retention policies with the LLM provider, and accuracy benchmark data that may be available. Once the product has successfully made it through security vetting, an initial pilot occurs. If the pilot is successful and the firm wants to move forward, the software can be added to the approved AI vendor list with version numbers and renewal dates.

Permitted and Prohibited Uses

Spell out which tasks are acceptable to use with AI solutions—drafting internal memos, summarizing discovery, brainstorming arguments—and which remain off limits, such as generating client advice that bypasses attorney review, uploading privileged documents to public models, or fabricating citations. Treat AI output as a junior associate draft that always requires review before it is filed, emailed, or otherwise relied upon.

Permitted (with human review)	Strictly Prohibited
Drafting first-pass summaries, memos, or correspondence	Generating client advice that bypasses attorney review
Extracting clauses for contract comparison	Creating deepfakes or impersonations
Translating or summarizing deposition transcripts	Uploading privileged or identifying client data into public models
Brainstorming arguments or outlining workflows	Producing false or misleading factual assertions

Documentation and Disclosure

Require users to save prompts, model settings, and redline history in the document management system for at least as long as the underlying matter file, so the firm can defend its work if challenged. Engagement letters should include language authorizing "secure, attorney-supervised AI technologies," and highly sensitive matters should trigger separate client consent. Where courts demand transparency, file the prescribed certificate or footnote noting that authorities have been manually verified.

Version Control and Data Governance

If the firm is able to choose between different LLMs, set up a process to test new models as they are made available to confirm comparable outputs. Route sensitive data only through vendors that contractually have zero-retention policies or model training. Store prompt-answer pairs in the DMS as work products and publish suggested prompts internally so teams produce consistent outputs and citations.

Training and Competency

Make a short list of essential training materials for the approved vendors. Look for more general AI training courses that are CLE-eligible. Cover all of the key capabilities, limitations, and prompt-writing basics. Refresh the content whenever a major feature ships or the policy changes.

Monitoring, Auditing, and Enforcement (Where Possible)

Log outputs and create admin alerts for disallowed file types where possible. An example of auditing would be a quarterly audit that samples 5 percent of AI-assisted outputs for accuracy and policy compliance. Provide consequences similar to other internal policies when employees do not follow it.

Additional Note on Monitoring Tools

The firm's IT or technical team should be able to assist law firms in setting up solutions that help monitor the use of generative AI internally. IT can block or quarantine uploads that breach policy, or set up data-loss prevention so a partner can explore ChatGPT while the system strips client names or PDF exhibits before they leave the firm's network.

Liability and Professional Responsibility

The policy must underscore that AI never shifts accountability away from the attorney. Lawyers remain responsible for accuracy, citation integrity, and ethical compliance, and should seek a second set of human eyes whenever doubt arises.

Updates and Sunset Clauses

Technology evolves too quickly for a static procedure. Commit to a formal review every six months, or sooner when necessary. Continuous iteration keeps documents relevant and underscores to regulators that the firm takes governance seriously.

In practice, these nine elements turn a policy from a checklist into a living governance framework. The goal is to manage risk and signal to clients that the firm is committed to innovation and data privacy.

17.4 Training Programs

For solo and small firms, consider identifying key internal team members who are early adopters and evangelists for the technology and give them the resources required to test use cases and become ambassadors for internal adoption.

Larger organizations may want to consider dedicated resources focused entirely on R&D and training functions. This can be a facet of the IT or legal operations team. Below is a high-level outline for initial employee training and implementation at the firm:

- Core Curriculum for All Employees
  - What AI is and isn't
  - Ethics and confidentiality
  - Prompt engineering basics
- Role-Specific Training
  - For litigators: drafting motions, analyzing depositions
  - For paralegals: intake and document prep
  - For admins: billing/timekeeping automation
- Live Demos and Hands-On Sessions
  - Scenario-based training: "Use AI to summarize a complaint"
  - Provide office hours or internal standup call to troubleshoot live

17.5 Change Management and Adoption Tactics

As mentioned previously, firms should begin by deploying AI in low-risk, high-reward areas—such as generating first-pass summaries, calendaring deadlines from court notices, or drafting internal memos. These early wins demonstrate some time savings without touching the most sensitive legal work, all while building confidence. Once attorneys and staff see value in their day-to-day work, adoption tends to accelerate naturally.

Incentives also matter. Make annual reviews and some aspects of compensation tied to successful adoption of new AI tools, as well participation in things like contributing to internal prompt libraries or providing a certain amount of product feedback during pilot programs. Of course, not everyone will embrace change immediately. Some lawyers worry that AI might replace their role or diminish the craft of lawyering. These concerns should be met head-on with education and reassurance. AI is a tool, not a substitute for judgment, strategy, or advocacy. By framing adoption as a way to elevate the profession rather than replace it, firms can reduce resistance.

Finally, firms should build structured feedback loops. Encourage users to report what works, where the tools fall short, and what features would make the AI more useful. A dedicated channel creates a culture of continued learning; this could look like a monthly roundtable, an internal survey, or even a committee of early testers.

17.6 Client Transparency

It is important to communicate the use of AI with clients, often placed directly in the engagement letter. A clear messaging strategy might emphasize that AI allows the firm to deliver faster turnaround, reduce costs, and dedicate more attorney hours to high-value work. In this way, AI becomes a competitive advantage.

As a rule of thumb, firms should disclose AI use when it materially affects client work or could raise questions of ethics or accuracy. For example, if a draft filing relies heavily on AI-assisted drafting, it is wise to be transparent with both the client and, when appropriate, the court. However, disclosing that AI generated a first draft of an internal memo or meeting summary may be unnecessary and even confusing. The guiding principle should be: disclose where it matters, avoid overexplaining where it does not.

There is also a marketing upside. Many clients, especially business clients, want to see their legal partners innovating. By highlighting AI capabilities in business development materials, pitches, or client seminars, firms can position themselves as forward thinking.

Sample Messaging Templates for Clients

1. Engagement Letter Disclosure

"Our firm uses advanced technology, including secure artificial intelligence (AI) tools, to improve efficiency and deliver high-quality legal services. These tools may assist with tasks such as summarizing documents, generating first drafts, or managing case deadlines. Every AI-assisted output is reviewed by an attorney before it is finalized. By leveraging these tools, we are able to focus more of our time on strategy and advocacy while reducing overall costs to our clients."

2. Court Filing or External Disclosure (Where Appropriate)

"This document was prepared with the assistance of AI drafting tools, under the supervision of counsel. The filing has been carefully reviewed and edited to ensure its accuracy and compliance with all applicable rules and professional obligations."

3. Marketing/Business Development Material

"Our firm integrates artificial intelligence responsibly into our case management system. This allows us to summarize complex records, monitor deadlines, and generate drafts with greater efficiency. The result: lower costs, faster turnaround, and more attorney time dedicated to strategy and advocacy. We see AI not as a replacement for lawyers, but as a powerful tool to enhance the quality of our service."

PART V

The Road Ahead

CHAPTER 18

The Future of AI and Legal Work

As the authors of this book, we are obviously big users and advocates for artificial intelligence and more broadly for the advancement of the practice of law. An underappreciated part of the legal profession is the camaraderie, mentorship, and frequent selflessness of one practitioner giving to another their expertise or learned tips on how to accomplish or improve their practice. Most of us were fortunate to have great mentors who taught us how to practice law, draft a brief, market our services, and build and protect our reputations. Nearly all of us have been to a CLE where a speaker shared some great tip that changed the way we approached a certain topic. The strategic and clever adoption of AI is another great opportunity for lawyers to lift one another and help raise the entire practice. Law firms are not software companies, and our clients do not want us to act like them. Our goal is not to add as many users as possible, no matter the costs or losses, in order to pump up our firm's valuation. We are trying to advocate for our clients and help them through often difficult and anxious times. To that end, we can help each other learn what is and is not working with the implementation of AI in our law practices. Which AI prompts or products are yielding results? Where have we wasted time or resources that could have been better spent? Where is AI helpful, and where is it overpromising? Where are the ethical pitfalls that may or may not be obvious?

18.1 Lawyering Through the Early Days of Adoption

It certainly feels that we are in a real AI boom as every company tries to figure out how to add AI to whatever they are doing. It is almost hard for a day to go by without something coming across our screens exclaiming "AI is taking jobs" or disrupting industries. While there may be levels of truth to those arguments, this is not the first time industry has been shaken by technology, the legal industry included. Years ago, one of us asked his CPA and tax lawyer whether TurboTax was hurting his business. Shockingly, he said he loved TurboTax. He said that the low-hanging fruit of simple personal returns was never where he made his living, and people were putting so much garbage into TurboTax and getting so much garbage out that he had replaced all of the simple work with more substantive work fixing people's returns that they thought they could DIY. It was like asking a chiropractor what they thought about CrossFit. We do not want anyone creating legal troubles for themselves, but the point is that TurboTax did not get rid of tax lawyers—it just changed the work they found themselves doing. TurboTax has been around for years now, and we have not met many tax lawyers who do not have work.

Whether it was fax, email, the internet, case management, cloud computing, or AI (and we could increase this list for pages), these technologies caused the practice of law to evolve, but have not and will not bring it to extinction. The practice of law remains a human process. People trust TurboTax when they think their situation is simple, but they want a referral from someone they trust when the IRS is knocking on the door. Over the next decade we expect AI to have a profound impact on the way we work through daily tasks in our law firms, and we are bullish on the impact that AI will have, but we do not expect the client-attorney relationship to end or even to become less human. If anything, we think AI could actually free us up for more human-to-human client interaction.

As discussed throughout this book, generative AI is very good at certain things, like generating content—especially when it does not have to be 100 percent accurate. So there are a lot of tasks in the law firm ripe for AI and automation over the next several years. Some of these processes involve the business of running a law firm, such as creating engagement letters, creating training materials, creating marketing plans, or creating blog posts and website copy or other marketing materials. There are other processes that are inherently legal tasks that are also already being done by AI and have great promise for the next several years, such as summarization and translation of legal documents, legal research, and creating first drafts of briefs and memos. Ultimately there is never going to be a point where the AI is so good that the lawyer is not obligated to treat the output as a first draft or double check the citations that come in the legal research. But these tools are still in their infancy and already quite good, so it is reasonable to expect them to improve and become standard tools like email and internet research over the next decade.

We believe that more domain-specific legal AI products will hit the market and they will leverage the power of RAG (Retrieval-Augmented Generation) systems by combining curated and domain-specific legal libraries with the power of the big Large Language Models, like the latest versions of ChatGPT or Claude. Just as in legal publishing and in the earlier days of case management software, attorneys are likely to trust the focused products that are putting an emphasis on their specialty. So tax lawyers may rely on an AI research tool with a specifically curated tax library, and product liabilities attorneys may look to their own product with the right library for them. Over the next several years, the accuracy of the LLMs in their outputs is only going to improve. So while the early days of citation-generated legal research have not been perfect, we are confident it is going to continue to improve with increasing strengths of LLMs, fine-tuning, and search enhancements.

The lawyer-specific and practice area-specific products are also more likely to invest in and focus on the features that lawyers will come to require. For example, lawyers are always going to need a product that is not jeopardizing their client's data, which means the big players in the LLM world, like OpenAI and Anthropic, will probably not be the main legal drafting tool for law firms—though they will likely be used for lots of other nonconfidential tasks, like marketing content. Legal-specific products that focus on the features lawyers need, like security, will most likely rise to the top for lawyers. Usually through a boom there is some mass adoption as well, and certain products will become the trusted name in their respective niche.

Important decisions will have to be made to determine what the appropriate standard operating procedures for using AI for different workflows are in your firm. Unfortunately, some of this will probably come as we learn from bad experiences and the misuse of AI. For example, we see more and more lawyers being sanctioned for citing hallucinated case law (cases made up by generative AI), and now attorneys are becoming more aware of having to have a human in the loop during AI legal research to actually read and confirm whether the cases exist and if they are in fact saying what the AI generates in its response. Human-in-the-loop standard procedures will also need to be thought out for AI drafting and AI translations. We have hopefully hammered home throughout the book that AI outputs are essentially first drafts. So as your firm begins to use AI drafting tools or increases its use of AI drafting tools, it will be critical to build best practices for human review of the outputs. There are probably tasks your firm trusts paralegals or law clerks to prepare a first draft of, and similarly the firm may soon trust those or other drafting assignments to AI. Perhaps your firm will have paralegals and law clerks using AI for these tasks and then have a senior attorney review—similar to if they were drafting them from old templates as in days past. Attorneys have always had an ethical duty to oversee the work their staff is creating, and that ethical duty will extend to the work created by AI as well. Processes like creating first drafts will be much quicker using AI, but the processes of attorney review and supervision will not be.

Additionally, as more domain-specific tools become available, we believe that AI drafting will become much more reliable. For example, a product that is focused on drafting wills that is built with expert estate lawyers involved, and that leverages a curated estate law library, will be quite capable of creating high-level first drafts. Some of these tools are already able to use your templates or samples to draft in your style, or reuse certain arguments or preferences you have drafted in the past. The ability of generative AI tools to refine and improve these drafting outputs is only going to improve. In the early days of generative AI legal tools, we have also seen some tools with great outputs but subpar user experience, and other tools with very pretty software but no substance. The products that survive this AI spring and make it to the next season will strike a balance between both user experience and expert output.

Outside of domain-specific RAG systems, we will also be watching for interesting advancements among legal-specific LLMs. The big players in the LLM world are not focused on the needs of lawyers, as they are trying to build products that can do everything for everyone—not an easy task. Some legal tech companies are taking a different approach, working on their own LLMs that are for legal use only. The difference is that these models are only trained on the law, the primary and secondary legal materials the creators of the LLM think are relevant, and they are trained and fine-tuned only to produce legal outputs. The cons to this approach for now have been that they are less powerful, and there are fewer of these options available. The long-term pros, though, may be they are much cheaper to maintain than the ChatGPTs of the world, and may ultimately be much more accurate at providing legal research outputs and citations since they are being trained to focus on very specific legal outputs, and they are not combing through as large of a dataset (i.e., most of the internet). Eventually, we could see companies building their own practice area-specific LLMs, in the way that we are already seeing practice area-specific RAG products (e.g., an immigration tool using GPT to search an immigration dataset). These products would be trained and fine-tuned specifically for your area of law, and that could be a game changer if the more focused LLM led to high accuracy in results and fewer hallucinations. It also remains to be seen whether this could lead to greater domain-specific fact analysis and strategy. Lawyers are increasingly more specialized, and our AI may turn out to be that way, too.

18.2 AI as an Additive and Not a Replacement or Window Dressing

An important area that we expect to improve over the next decade is what we consider "knowledge management." This would be the integration of AI in the knowledge bank and materials your firm already has sitting on servers, in the cloud, and in your case management or document management systems—AI more seamlessly integrated with your years of samples and templates, and the way you like things prepared. Often in law firms, there is a knowledge-management gap between the senior partners and the junior attorneys. The junior attorneys do not know the tricks or winning arguments the senior partner includes in his or her briefs, or more importantly, does not know the "special sauce" those lawyers have been using to win cases for years. We expect AI to become more integrated into our firm's document management, templates, and firm document history, and become more seamless in leveraging the years of successful materials sitting on our firm's systems.

We expect AI drafting tools, for example, to become sophisticated enough that the outputs at one IP firm are not the same as the outputs at another. This is not just because they are using different prompts, but because the AI is using the firm's materials, and each firm has a different output that includes their "special sauce," tricks, or arguments that they have created and relied on for years. Improving AI for knowledge management would also look like better AI searching within your firm as well—not just in a law library. So if your firm is currently doing keyword searches in a document management system to find documents, that will become a dated approach as systems begin leveraging natural language in that process. For example, in your current system, when you are searching for samples within your firm, a lawyer may keyword search "summary judgment, noncompete clauses." In an AI system that is leveraging your firm's materials, you may be able to simply say "show me examples of motions for summary judgment in cases involving noncompete clauses in Colorado they were written by attorney John Doe." Hopefully that leads to an example in your firm's system that you like, and then with better AI systems, you would be able to prompt that template to become a draft based on the facts of the case you are working on.

Basically, we are talking about more interconnected systems that are all leveraging AI, as opposed to a tool for legal research, a tool for legal drafting, a tool for legal translations, and so on. The future of AI should include more intelligent workflows and not just single tasks, whether that be through agents or integrations. Advocates of AI agents, as discussed in

Chapter 15, are currently making big promises. With AI agents, we expect big breakthroughs in workflow automations, but we are skeptical as well, and anticipate even greater supervisory roles needed for attorneys reviewing the work. The more we delegate to AI, the more there is also to verify. This should still offer major time savings if, for example, an AI agent is researching something, applying the relevant fact patterns, and creating the first draft in minutes, as opposed to the days it may take a person. Integration and making all our systems work well together is often easier said than done. There is a reason you do not currently have all of your legal tech stack in one software, because it is hard for one company to build a product that is good at doing everything you need. Sometimes it is even harder than we expect to make a bunch of products that are decent at what they do talk to one another in useful ways. But we hope that over the next decade, AI leads to greater integration of both your software and your firm's content. That means AI systems working through complex workflows without moving from software to software, but it also means workflows utilizing your firm's materials and not just the materials in the AI. For example, the tool is researching a problem that you have, applying the results of that research to the facts of a case you are providing, drafting an initial email or memo on the case, and structuring that memo in the way you like your memos structured, based on the templates in your firm's library.

Most AI products are currently focused on big legal tasks and legal markets like research, contract review, e-discovery, and drafting motions and briefs. There is reason to believe that AI, especially through the development of AI agents, will eventually work its way into other parts of the law firm. We covered AI receptionists and developments in the intake process. But again, looking at bigger workflows, we will hopefully see intelligent systems that go from prospective lead to converted client, to onboarded client, and so on. Fuller integration would look like systems that work through consultation, engagement letter, invoicing, intake, review, research, draft, and assemble. We are not suggesting AI will be doing all of this autonomously, but that AI will help make all of this more efficient and cohesive, so you are hopefully not switching from one software system to another, cancelling out some those efficiencies. And of course, through these vertical integrations, there will be many human-in-the-loop reviews and human review of the outputs as well. AI agents are also expected to play a role in invoicing, timekeeping, billing, and other operational parts of the law office as well. For example, the software you use for tracking your time intelligently converts that information into invoices in your billing system, sends those invoices, tracks payments, and sends reminders to clients and updates to your accounting team.

18.3 Being Honest About AI's Weaknesses

We are already used to AI promises galore, but there are some areas of the practice of law that will not be right for AI in the next decade. These include the deeply human parts of our jobs and the technical parts of the job that AI is just not very good at. As discussed at the beginning of the book, AI is not good at some technical functions, like making predictions. There are data science tools and machine-learning models that can be created for predictive purposes, but generative AI tools will probably not be a good tool for these assignments. So reliably predicting case outcomes or predicting future performance will probably need to be left to other tools. AI is also probably not going to be great at other technical topics, like pricing your services, which has a lot of quantitative and qualitative factors to consider, including things that would be hard to explain in words—like your reputation, your years of experience, your clientele, and so on. It may be helpful in conducting research to include in that conversation, but maybe less so in trying to find technical answers. AI can summarize and list points of risk, but it is not able to quantify risk to a client in a meaningful way.

It is also well documented that AI is often filled with biases based on the way the models are trained, who they are trained by, and the materials they are trained with. Even if we are bullish on AI, we cannot argue that it will become a fair and effective tool for determining staffing needs or handling other human resources functions that have more human elements. AI is probably not going to become great at understanding varying cultures, picking up on nuance, or knowing when to be empathetic. These human parts of law practice and law practice management are just not going to get replaced by AI.

Clients do not just want a brief. They want to be heard, they want to be able to reach their attorney, they want communication with the humans working on their case, they want to be reassured, they want to be explained nuances that are causing delays or different outcomes, they want a person with experience who has seen similar situations in the past to tell them what the concerns are and what the chances of success are. Getting to a brief or a legal citation quicker is a great advancement for lawyers, but that alone does not change the client experience. Ultimately, if your client has an amazing experience working with you, then it will not make a difference whether the first draft of the work product you prepared in their case was completed using AI or not—they are not drafting the brief either way. The bigger questions will be did they trust you, did they have a good experience working with you, and would they recommend you to the people in their lives they care about? AI will not change the rapport and trust between the lawyer and the client. Often, clients are coming to a lawyer because they are in a stressful or scary situation. Having someone experienced that they trust and can feel supported by may be more important to the client then whether it takes 20 human hours or 20 AI minutes to draft a first version of a response. Sure, clients will appreciate cases moving faster; some clients appreciate that their attorneys are keeping up with the times and using the latest tech available, and the clients will also appreciate lower legal costs where these increases in efficiency drive down hourly billing. But it is not a one-for-one exchange, and the deeply human parts of the attorney-client relationship are not going away.

In fact, as you and your competitors implement similar AI systems over the next decade, the human element will likely rise even higher on the list of client priorities. We believe AI will be better at knowledge management and so everyone will not be putting out the same work product, but the point remains that human skills will outweigh some technical skills. Empathy, the ability to clearly articulate how you are going to help, and a calm and confident ability to convey strategy and expectations to the client will likely be a much bigger differentiator between two lawyers than a brief. Lawyers who succeed at talking to their clients have always had a competitive advantage, because ultimately the lawyer is selling themselves, their firm, their approach, and their services, but these human skills will be even more important as some of our technical skills become more automated.

Legal fees should be impacted by artificial intelligence over the next decade, especially for those working on an hourly model. ABA Model Rule 1.5 says that an attorney "shall not make an agreement for, charge, or collect an unreasonable fee or an unreasonable amount for expenses." The model rules point to several factors that should be considered for what is a reasonable fee, and those factors do include things like "the experience, reputation, and ability of the lawyer or lawyers performing the services." However, the rules also point to the "time and labor required, the novelty and difficulty of the questions involved, and the skill requisite to perform the legal service properly." So yes, an attorney with a distinguished reputation may be able to charge more than a new lawyer, but there is supposed to be some correlation between the time and labor required to complete the case. If the brief that previously took two weeks is now taking two hours, there should be some market correction on pricing. Obviously, attorneys might not like that, but if AI is really creating those types of time savings, then there should be greater bandwidth to take a higher volume of work—a problem many attorneys struggle with, because we are only human and can only handle so many time-consuming cases at a time.

18.4 The Evolving Roles in an AI-Enabled Firm

Lastly, with the widespread adoption of AI by law firms over the next decade, there will inherently be some shifting of traditional jobs or roles within the law firm. We believe that AI will give us more time to dedicate to clients and client communications, more time for the human elements of the job, and less time for research and preliminary drafting.

Paralegals are often included on lists of jobs that AI will replace. We do not believe that. We believe that AI will automate parts of the paralegals' job and allow them more time to offer client services. At least, we believe law firms will be able to do this if they choose. A decade ago, paralegals at our law firm spent more than half of their day doing data entry. We used to send our intake questionnaires to clients as a Word doc or a PDF. Clients would either print it out, handwrite the answers, and email it back to us, or use Word or Adobe to edit the doc and email it back. Either way, there was no connection between the intake and our case management system that we used for completing the government forms that accompanied our clients' applications. So, the paralegal would sit there and do manual data entry, typing the client's name from the intake onto the forms, and their date of birth, and their place of birth, and so on. This easily took up half of their day. Eventually, case management systems began offering intake questionnaires and auto-populating the forms. The client would receive the intake through our platform, complete the intake, and then the data they put on the intake was pushed through to the government forms at the push of one button. The fields on the intake were mapped to the fields on the forms, and the paralegal could populate the forms instantly. Half of their day's work was now gone. Yet we employ more paralegals now than we did then. Technology automated half of their role, and we need more of them.

The reason that we needed more paralegals after these breakthroughs is because once paralegals were freed up from hours of data entry each day, it turned out there was higher-level work for them to be doing. All of our paralegals are college graduates, and many of them speak multiple languages. Data entry was never a good use of their time and did not maximize their potential. They were too smart to be doing that work; it just had to be done, so they were doing it. Once data entry was off their plates, they started helping with first drafts of cover letters and taking on more substantive parts of the process. This had a domino effect up the org chart as well, where paralegals could take on some work of law clerks, who could help junior associates, who could help senior associates, who could help the partners.

We believe that the implementation of AI will be something like the automation around data entry. What we think should happen is that paralegals will find themselves spending less time entering data and moving exhibits around, which means they will have more time for clients. Our vision is that paralegals will use their newfound time for more concierge-style service. We have all been guilty of taking on a new client and then not hearing from them and saying when they are ready to move forward, to contact us. But our clients are busy too, and they might not have an assistant to get you the materials you need or set reminders to check in about their case. If the paralegals have more time, then they can be your clients' assistant, too. They can proactively contact the client, ask how they can help get materials from the client, help organize them, and be their real partner in the process by providing a higher level of service—again, emphasizing that the human element and the client experience will be the greatest differentiator in future legal services.

Junior lawyers and law clerks are often tasked with the preliminary work that generative AI is already good at, but we expect it to become great at. These are tasks like preliminary legal research and preliminary first drafts. Senior attorneys and partners often give these younger reports assignments to research something, do a first review of documents, create a summary, create an outline, or use a sample motion and try a first draft on the case. In all these examples, AI can handle these tasks today. This means that the people in these positions will have to become proficient at using AI to do these things, while still learning how or why they are being done. This is like the classic childhood example of using a calculator to solve your math homework, but still having to write it out so that you actually learn why the calculator reached the answer. One could argue that junior lawyers and clerks could be more disrupted than paralegals, since paralegals can pivot to the front lines of client-facing concierge services. Clerks and associates who want to succeed will need to put in the effort to both learn the technical skills of being proficient with AI tools for legal research and legal drafting, as well as learn the theory of the law being found or being implemented. Young lawyers and clerks should embrace AI, because prospective employers will probably be looking for hires with these technical skills. This is especially true where managing partners are older and see the writing on the wall with AI, but feel they may be nearing the ends of their careers already, or are too old to learn new tricks and instead want the next generation of the firm to keep them competitive with AI. These will be skills that eventually become standard, but in the next decade should be highly desirable for law firm managers making hiring decisions when they look at résumés and talk to the potential junior lawyers they interview.

Partners and senior attorneys may have more time available to them with the greater implementation of AI and automation. However, the buck will stop with them, and ultimately the widespread implementation of AI in your law firm means major ethical responsibilities, quality control responsibilities, and oversight duties. Partners are going to be responsible more than ever for the citations and briefs coming out of their offices. We are seeing case after case of attorneys using hallucinated results and being sanctioned or reprimanded. It seems likely that the patience for this from courts, clients, and state bars will only become thinner than it already is, with how widespread and covered the issue has become. With the power of AI will come the responsibility of AI, and that responsibility will fall on the partners.

Partners should see huge increases in efficiencies with less time needed for initial document review, discovery, legal research, and drafting. Some of this time will have to be reallocated to quality control and human review of drafts. If AI can do the case in half the time, that does not mean you can take double the cases, because that does not factor in the time for human review, so maybe it's actually a 20 or 30 percent time savings after a senior attorney or partner reviews the work. Whatever the breakdown, the point remains that human oversight and involved law firm management are going to be integral to the law firm of the future.

Partners will need to choose the right processes at their firm for AI, and then the right AI for those processes. Then partners will need to implement standard operating procedures that include human review so that AI is always being treated as a first draft and product is never being submitted without human review. In addition, partners will need to implement firm-wide AI policies and train their staff on how to ethically use AI, and use AI in the way that aligns with their firm's approach toward AI. Really, your law firm should already be doing this now, if it has not already begun. Searching on ChatGPT is becoming as commonplace as searching on Google. And you should assume your staff searches ChatGPT the way they do the Google. If you do not clearly define how your employees should be using AI, how they should not be using AI, and what products they are allowed to use for work, then it is only human nature that the employees will use the free tools available to make their jobs easier. This is how you end up with employees putting client information into ChatGPT or getting made-up case citations from one of the general LLM products out there. By not making very strict policies, employees may take matters into their own hands and use what is available for free. Partners will be better off selecting AI products that they trust and that are secure for their client data, and then train their staff on how and when to use these tools; otherwise they are burying their heads in the sand and ignoring the potential risk. We cannot express how important staff training will become. That does not just mean lawyer training—that means every person working at your company that is using a computer, so everyone. Just as law firms have had to train people on phishing emails, they must be trained on how to ethically use AI in accordance with your law firm's practices.

Assuming partners are proactive in implementing ethical AI practices, standard operating procedures, human oversight, and the proper checks and balances on the technology, then the results could be fantastic and should allow partners to also have more time for the human parts of their job. Client relationship building, meeting with clients, taking on projects to generate new business—the list could go on and on. Over the next decade, we should see better AI tracking tools as well as more sophisticated AI legal tools become. Dashboards, KPIs, and other metrics that have made their way into case management and practice management tools will make their way into AI platforms as well, giving firm leadership a better bird's-eye view of the AI being used. We are already seeing a lot of tools hit the market that can detect the use of AI, and those tools will become commonplace, like the plagiarism and grammar-check tools of years past.

Over the next decade, the entire law firm will face some changes from the adoption of AI, not just the lawyers. Accounting departments may see agentic AI tools, or at least more sophisticated AI integrations, as previously discussed. The marketing team is likely already benefiting from the efficiency of AI for drafting marketing and website content. HR tools are already commonplace. The IT department or outside IT providers will be critical in vetting the security of AI tools, both from a technical standpoint and legal ethics standpoint. We may also see new roles created by the use of AI. Could more law firms add positions in data science or AI engineering? Or could we see law firms start offering services that they didn't previously offer because it was outside their bandwidth? Could law firms start creating first drafts of materials that clients are normally expected to create, and start new product offerings? For example, we often send entrepreneurial clients to professional writers to write business plans to include in applications about their new businesses. A law firm may create a Custom GPT for writing business plans and start having a business-minded person or MBA-type working on business plans instead of outsourcing that part of the process.

Law firms will continue with widespread adoption of AI over the next decade. Our hypothesis is that this will automate some parts of the practice, giving us more time to focus on the human parts of being a lawyer. Additionally, roles like the paralegal, which have been associated with doomsday predictions, could find their roles evolving into more white-glove concierge service focused on client experience instead of file assembly. Partners and law firm managers will bear great responsibilities with these changes, but they also have the most to gain. Firm leaders that implement AI with a plan, with proper staff training, with appropriate senior oversight, and with an informed sense of skepticism will benefit the most. At the end of the day, the human elements of the practice of law will be the biggest differentiators in the client experience over the next decade, just as they have been in past. No matter the advancements in AI, clients will want trust, empathy, and easy communications with the lawyers they hire in their most stressful times. AI will be able to change the way we work, but it will not change the way clients feel, so the goal of implementing AI should be to give us more time to enhance that human experience.

PART VI

The Lawyer's AI Shopping Guide

CHAPTER 19

Choosing the Right Tools for the Job

Every law firm is going to have to determine what parts of their workflows they want to bring AI into, and then which AI is the right tool for that job and that firm. The most obvious starting point is legal research and drafting, where we are seeing the biggest splashes from the big players in legal tech. Many of the legal research tools include a suite of other AI tools anyway. For example, Westlaw users may use their product CoCounsel (which Thomson Reuters acquired) in order to do things like document analysis, summarization, or drafting. So, you may choose to be a Westlaw user because you love their legal research tool, and then since you are already in that system, you may choose to use CoCounsel for your document analysis and legal drafting.

In the world of AI legal research and drafting, there are basically three categories of products:

1. **General AI tools** like ChatGPT, Claude, Copilot, Gemini, or Perplexity.
2. **Legal tools that are not practice-area specific,** like Westlaw, Lexis, Harvey, or vLex/Fastcase (vLex and Fastcase were separate companies that merged and then were acquired by Clio).
3. **Practice area-specific AI tools** like Visalaw.ai (immigration), Ironclad (contracts), Supio (personal injury), Everlaw (e-discovery), or Eve (labor and employment).

19.1 General AI Tools

General AI tools like ChatGPT, Claude, Copilot, Gemini, and Perplexity have a lot to offer lawyers. These products have the most powerful, well-funded, and robust Large Language Models in the world. With that power comes amazing outputs. That is also the reason why many of the products in groups two and three (legal-specific products and practice area-specific products) are built as RAG systems, using OpenAI or Claude's LLMs to search their company's dataset.

The main challenge with these products is that they are not using specific legal libraries and are not being trained to perform legal tasks. So, when you ask ChatGPT a question of law, you may get an answer from somewhere on the internet that you would not normally trust for legal advice, like a Reddit thread. As a lawyer, that broad search with limited guardrails is unhelpful. Additionally, the general AI tools are not going to provide proper citations to the results they found. If you prompt them to provide citations, they may very well "hallucinate" the citations, or, in layman's terms, make them up. This is why we are constantly seeing lawyers getting disciplined or sanctioned for submitting work product with made-up cases. The problem with these powerful AI tools is that they are always going to give you an answer. It may not be the right answer, or the answer you want, but they are trained to generate responses, so they are going to give you something. Again, these can be scary and unhelpful tool when it comes to legal research, where you are looking for factually accurate responses to important legal questions and you need citations that you can then go read and verify that they are correct.

While these tools are not good for legal research, they can be great at other things, where accuracy is less important than legal research. For example, general AI tools are amazing at generating or drafting content. The newer versions of ChatGPT and Perplexity almost beg the user to let them generate more content. You will give the bot a prompt and get a result, and it is quickly asking if you want it to expand that, put it in a table, write an email, make it longer, and so on. When one of us uses ChatGPT for outlining, it often generates the outline and then says something like, "Would you like me to next expand this outline into a full-prose draft (10–15 pages), or add a detailed table comparing the exhibits?" Usually, we actually do not want ChatGPT to take that next step for us, because while we trust it with simple outlining, we do not trust it with drafting beyond that.

There are a lot of practice management tasks discussed in this book, though, that these general AI tools are perfect for: creating marketing content, creating website copy, writing training plans, creating some policies, helping turn your CLE materials into PowerPoint presentations, and so on. These are all great uses of the power of general AI products. Ultimately, you are just trying to save some time and get a first draft, but you are not looking for legal analysis, citations, or even real accuracy. This is low-risk use of AI, and high-powered LLMs can handle these tasks in seconds.

So, for nonlegal tasks that are appropriate for using general AI products, how do you choose which of these is the right one for you? Some of us may like certain tools for some things and other tools for other tasks, and may not be completely dedicated to any of them. Heavy Microsoft users may want to use Copilot as a starting point, since the integrations into Outlook, Teams, and the rest of the Microsoft suite make for really nice use cases, especially since most lawyers spend the bulk of their time in their email and other communications tools like Teams. Heavy Google users may lean at least initially toward Gemini for the same reason.

With ChatGPT, Claude, or Perplexity, you are probably moving into a system that you would not be otherwise using, but the value is so high with some of these tools that the lack of integration may be easier to digest. Plus, with the way the top generative AI tools can easily convert an output into a Word document, PowerPoint slides, or Excel spreadsheet, it is easier to be agnostic about your AI. This is good because ultimately, we find that ChatGPT and Claude are better tools for complex reasoning and are better suited for large, complex prompts that you want to run. As you become more sophisticated at creating prompts for your workflows, you really must factor in the right system's bandwidth when picking which system to use to run your prompts. Also, if you're creating larger documents like training plans or articles, you need to take into consideration the allowable size for the output.

The latest version of Claude Cowork was released after the initial writing of this text. While still in its infancy, Cowork is proving (to us) the most robust experience yet for users, as it integrates directly into many of our workspaces (including a web browser) and has a native application on the desktop. Cowork allows the user to set up agents and assign them multistep tasks or processes like summarizing documents, reviewing materials, and drafting responses or emails, and more. Interestingly, even Claude itself will remind the attorney user, based on its support materials, that Anthropic recommends attorneys not include sensitive data.

As an overview, here are some pros and cons of each of the general tools discussed for lawyers.

OpenAI's ChatGPT

- Pros: Feels like the greatest bandwidth for inputs and outputs, such as creating custom law prompts or workflows and getting really large and strongly reasoned outputs.

- Cons: While there are integrations, they are not directly in the Microsoft or Google workspaces where lawyers most often find themselves.

Anthropic's Claude

- Pros: Does well with drafting, and some studies show that it offers a lower hallucination rate. The latest version of Claude Cowork is available in web or desktop versions, which allows Claude to work with you on your materials, as opposed to moving things in and out of the web like most people are used to doing in ChatGPT. The new version allows for the most robust task assignment and the easiest creation of AI agents we have yet seen.
- Cons: The latest version of Claude Cowork integrates across common workplaces for attorneys and can give the user the feeling that what they are doing is secure, when in fact they are still using a general LLM and must not be feeding client or confidential data to the AI. Claude itself, when prompted, will remind lawyers not to allow sensitive data to be used, which can be harder to manage once Claude is integrated in your workspace.

Microsoft's Copilot

- Pros: Built right into the native Microsoft workspace, which means it is fully integrated into Outlook, Word, Excel, Teams, and PowerPoint—the systems most of us use for a lot of our work. Also, it is easy to feel confident that the use cases within the Microsoft systems and workflows will continue to evolve in meaningful ways, just as a bet on Microsoft.
- Cons: What it is best at—working within Microsoft processes—is also what makes it the most limiting. It is not as robust for custom prompts or workflows, and its inputs and outputs can be limiting.

Google Gemini

- Pros: Similar to the Copilot review, except relevant for Google users. The built-in uses in Gmail, Docs, Sheets, and so on are really meaningful for people who find themselves in the Google workspace full time.
- Cons: Less adoption by the legal community also means less innovation or discussion among practitioners (so far) of Gemini among legal users. Also, like Copilot, it lacks some of the robust outputs

and tools you would like to see outside of Google-specific platforms, but most likely Google will close any gaps pretty quickly.

Perplexity

- Pros: Strong output and really good at drafting. Can offer some citation capabilities that the other systems struggle with—though we would not trust legal research or citations to any of these general AI products.
- Cons: Perplexity feels like a tool you would use alongside several other tools, so it is probably separate from your Microsoft/Google use cases, and being used next to your legal-specific research tool. But you may only assign it certain drafting projects because it does not offer the type of security needed to put your client data in it, so you probably still need a legal-specific drafting tool for actual case work.

All of these tools are excellent in their own right, and they each have things that they are better or worse at than the others, so a lot of this comes down to your preference for certain native systems like Microsoft and Google, or what tasks you plan to assign the general AI product that you are using, since you should not be using it for legal research or anything involving client data. We are of the belief that none of these systems, even their enterprise offerings, are appropriate for use with client data or any confidential materials.

19.2 Legal Tools that Are Not Practice Area-Specific

Westlaw, Lexis, and vLex/Fastcase are all examples of lawyer-specific AI products, but are not practice area-specific. So, if your firm offers services in multiple areas of law, this could be a huge selling point. Additionally, some are already in the Westlaw or Lexis universe and have strong AI capabilities within the systems they have long used for legal research. With Westlaw, Lexis, and vLex/Fastcase, we are talking about RAG systems that leverage the LLMs of the big players in generative AI (discussed in the preceding section, like ChatGPT or Claude) and use those powerful LLMs for searching the massive law libraries that have made these companies such powerful legal research tools.

Most importantly, these systems are built for lawyers and offer the types of security that a lawyer needs. Client data can be put into most of these systems, and can be used in the actual case analysis and drafting of legal briefs based on your clients' materials.

Thomson Reuters Westlaw

Westlaw is one of the biggest names in the world for legal research. It operates in more than 60 countries and offers one of the largest legal libraries in the world. Many law firms have been Westlaw loyalists for years, long before AI offerings were a factor. In the AI department, Westlaw has not been shy. It acquired the product CoCounsel from Casetext, Inc. for $650 million in August 2023. CoCounsel was a revolutionary AI legal assistant that really paved the way for what we are now seeing in AI legal tech across the board, offering chat-based research, clickable citations, document analysis, drafting, summarization, and much more. Westlaw also offers a deep research tool, Westlaw Advantage, which is at the forefront of agentic AI research.

The list of pros for using Westlaw's AI tools include:

- The AI tools are built on top of the massive Westlaw library.
- If you already work in the Westlaw universe, then using its AI tools is probably a no-brainer, especially if you do not work in a practice area with a high-level tool built directly for your specialty.
- It offers a lot of options, including the CoCounsel product for legal drafting, document review, summarizing, and generally just working with your clients' materials in a secure AI environment.
- It has deep research capabilities now offered through Westlaw Advantage that allow for multistep (or agentic) assignments.
- Westlaw states that it does not use your inputs/outputs and client materials to train underlying models, which is usually the first thing a lawyer will want to see.
- It meets most law firm security tests and holds SOC 2 and the other generally accepted security standards.

The cons for Westlaw as your AI tool of choice include:

- A pretty damning Stanford study in 2024 found that Westlaw's research results were hallucinated in nearly 33 percent of outputs and that the responses were only accurate 42 percent of the time. This study has been challenged regarding some flaws in the research, and revised results still showed that Westlaw did better than general tools like OpenAI's GPT4, but the results are still nothing to brag about.
- It is really expensive; prohibitively expensive for some practitioners and firm sizes.
- The high costs do not even necessarily include all of the AI functionality you would want, and some of those tools have additional charges beyond the already high costs of Westlaw.

- If you are not already in Westlaw, then that means there is probably a more cost-effective option out there. It feels like it would not be common to just sign up for Westlaw for its AI tools—most people who love their AI offerings already used the product or wanted to be in the product, and this was the final selling point.

LexisNexis

The Westlaw and Lexis discussion in legal AI feels similar to the Microsoft Copilot and Google Gemini discussions in the previous section on general AI products. If you are already in the Westlaw or Lexis universe, then it makes sense to take advantage of the AI offerings these legal tech giants have made available, and it is also easy to believe that they will only continue to get better given the size of the companies, budgets, and law libraries at Lexis and Westlaw. So if you already find yourself devoted to Lexis, then you may love Lexis + AI and Protégé.

Lexis + AI is the company's main AI product, which offers legal research and drafting. Lexis + AI nicely includes Shepard's© Citations, which, just like in non-AI legal research, is a wonderful tool for seeing the status of a source that is being cited in your response. Also, with a RAG system built on one of the world's largest legal libraries, it is right there with Westlaw as a world leader in legal research. The company's other AI product, Protégé, is a competitor to Westlaw's CoCounsel product. Protégé is a "legal assistant" or chat bot that can perform AI tasks securely with your clients' materials and your work product. Protégé offers similar tools like drafting, document review, and summarization.

The pros to Lexis + AI and Protégé include:

- Similar to Westlaw, if you are already in the Lexis system, then it makes sense to try and use their neatly integrated tools.
- By using Lexis tools, you benefit from one of the largest law libraries in the world.
- While the Stanford study referenced in the Westlaw discussion was not glowing for Lexis or Westlaw, it did conclude that Lexis + AI was correct in 65 percent of questions (as opposed to 42 percent by Westlaw), and that Lexis + AI hallucinated half as often as Westlaw (approximately 17 percent of results). Again, this study has been challenged and should not be considered conclusive.
- Shepard's© Citations is a big advantage for those using systems without it—especially the smaller legal research products that cannot compete with that functionality.

- The Protégé product offers most of the tools you would come to expect from an AI assistant, like drafting, document review, and summarization.
- Lexis also ensures that you and your clients' data is not being used to train its models.
- Lexis also offers all the security guarantees you would expect from a leader in legal tech, including SOC 2 Type 2, third-party audits, and data segregation.

The cons to Lexis + AI and Protégé include:

- Similar to Westlaw, the costs can be prohibitive, and you probably would not choose Lexis simply because of its AI tools.
- Similar to Westlaw, all of the AI capabilities are not included in every subscription, so this could add more costs to an already expensive subscription.
- Most people using it were probably already loyal to Lexis, and are now glad to have strong AI capabilities native in their primary legal research platform that they had already relied upon.
- The agentic and multistep workflows are still finding their way, though this is true for most of the world of agentic AI.

vLex/Fastcase

Fastcase and vLex were separate legal research companies that merged in 2023, becoming what has been described as the world's largest subscriber base of lawyers and law firms. The company also boasts more than 1 billion legal documents from more than 100 countries. vLex was really known for its international clientele, serving lawyers all over the world, but is probably less of a household name in the United States compared to Westlaw and Lexis. Fastcase, meanwhile, grew in the United States through its partnerships with local and state bar associations, where membership in the bar would often come with access to the Fastcase research library. Fast forward to 2025, and vLex/Fastcase were acquired by Clio for $1 billion, in the world's largest legal tech acquisition to date, which sent shockwaves through the legal tech world.

vLex's main AI offering is Vincent AI, which similar to the other companies' tools that can handle legal research with reviewable citations in their massive law library, case and document summary, and analysis and legal drafting. Vincent is also building agentic tools like the others.

According to Clio, Vincent AI and the vLex product will integrate through what they call an "Intelligent Legal Work Platform," the idea being that your AI legal research and drafting tool will be a native part of your case management system, if you are a Clio user, that is. This acquisition and integration are really the first example of this approach, and Clio is leading the way toward a totally integrated system for lawyers, where everything from client intake to case management to CRM to legal research, brief drafting, billing, and case assembly are all happening in one system. The massive pool of companies that already integrate with Clio is a big advantage, as well.

Pros for Clio's vLex/Fastcase system include:

- It has maybe the most robust system for international practices with the vLex background, adding AI capabilities to a massive multijurisdictional research library.
- Clearly, if you are already in Clio, then this makes a ton of sense because you may be able to give up your expensive legal research subscription and stop moving back and forth between your clients' materials in Clio and your legal research and drafting in one of the other tools. For Clio users, this level of integration is a greater offering than just adding AI capabilities to your favorite research tools, as you may actually be able to ditch another (expensive) tool in your tech stack.
- Vincent AI offers the AI tools you would expect from any legal AI assistant.
- It is built for lawyers and offers the level of security needed, just like Westlaw and Lexis.

Cons for Clio's vLex/Fastcase system include:

- If you are not already in Clio, then this may be an even greater leap than going to Westlaw and Lexis, because you are probably not just signing up for its AI capabilities but migrating to the entire "Intelligent Legal Work Platform"—meaning this is becoming your case management system, CRM system, legal research tool, drafting tool, and more. If you are just looking for AI tools and are otherwise very happy with your case management system, then this might not make sense.
- Pricing is still unclear, since Vincent AI is on par with the other AI tools before you start factoring in the full bill of working within the Clio platform—though it could be competitive to what people are paying for Lexis or Westlaw, combined with their case management.

Harvey AI

Harvey has gotten a lot of attention in the legal tech world, especially based on its venture capital raised and company valuations. Unfortunately, we were denied trial accounts to test for this book, but we felt like, given its reputation, we still needed to include what we could gather about it. Harvey claims it is now being used by 74,000 lawyers at 700 firms worldwide.

Based on its publicly available marketing materials, Harvey operates as a chatbot interface in desktop and mobile form and also integrates directly into some Microsoft applications. It has the functionality you would expect of legal analysis, research, and drafting tools—similar to the AI offerings of the other big legal tech companies listed previously. Based on videos reviewed, it offers some "knowledge management," as we refer to it—meaning it taps into your firm's resources and integrates those into responses in Microsoft (or through integrations it has with document management software like NetDocuments).

Harvey has a "strategic alliance" with Lexis. The Lexis press release from June 2025 explained it this way: "LexisNexis© Legal & Professional and Harvey today announced a strategic alliance to integrate LexisNexis generative AI technology, primary law content, and Shepard's© Citations within the Harvey platform and jointly develop advanced legal workflows. The alliance combines LexisNexis AI technology and industry-leading content for high-quality and verifiable legal answers, with the AI transformation users expect in Harvey, unlocking a powerful new experience for Harvey customers."[1]

From a security standpoint, Harvey claims that it does not train models using your data and lists the security certifications you would come to expect, like SOC 2 Type 2, ISO 27001, and GDPR.

19.3 Practice Area-Specific AI Tools

The last of our three groups is growing in number and specialty. We are seeing more and more legal tech AI startups devoting themselves to specific practice areas. Ultimately, a lot of lawyers are specialized, their research is usually specific to their area of practice, and (especially) solo

1. *LexisNexis and Harvey Announce Strategic Alliance to Integrate Trusted, High-Quality AI Technology and Legal Content and Develop Advanced Workflows*, LexisNexis, June 18, 2025, https://www.lexisnexis.com/community/pressroom/b/news/posts/lexisnexis-and-harvey-announce-strategic-alliance-to-integrate-trusted-high-quality-ai-technology-and-legal-content-and-develop-advanced-workflows.

and small firms need tech that does not completely break the bank, so they do not want to pay for a library and feature set that is never going to apply to them.

A lot of the tools that you find in the "AI assistants" category, like CoCounsel, Protégé, and Vincent, are becoming pretty commonplace, and small legal tech startups can offer similar tools for legal analysis, summarization, translations, and the like. That is also why most of those tools have pretty much the same features. So, the big differentiators lie more in curation and specialization in features like legal research, legal drafting, knowledge management, and integrations.

With the big legal tech giants, you get massive general law libraries that people have come to know from Westlaw, Lexis, and vLex. This shows why even a company like Harvey ultimately needed to tap into one of the big general law libraries. But practice area-specific tools are going the other way and just trying to master one niche. These tools are trying to perfect certain visa cover letters to USCIS for immigration lawyers, or EEOC charges to the Equal Employment Opportunity Commission. Most of these products offer the same general AI tools, but then offer hyper-focused research libraries only covering that specific area of law, and expert drafting capabilities built for very specific legal documents.

We believe that the benefit to these products is that they are usually created by experts in a specific practice area or in close coordination with lawyers in that space. These AI tools use very curated datasets, so the AI can be even more accurate in its searches since it is only searching a specialized library, compared to a Lexis, Westlaw, or vLex. If you are a labor and employment lawyer, do you really want your legal citations to be mixed up with real estate or something completely unrelated? Of course not. Additionally, by being hyper-focused, the drafting tools can be very specific and refined. So instead of training models to try and analyze documents and do everything under the sun, these tools are made with singular purpose.

There are a lot of tools out there in this category, and we are seeing a lot more pop up at conferences and elsewhere. Since we do not practice every area of law, it is impractical for us to review them all with a high level of domain expertise. There are a few that have come up a lot, which include:

- Ironclad for contracts law
- Supio for personal injury attorneys
- Everlaw for e-discovery
- Eve for labor and employment lawyers
- Sixfifty for HR compliance

A more substantive list of legal tech products is included as an Appendix.

To illustrate this final topic, we are going to describe how our software at Visalaw.ai was built and works. Our software is dedicated to immigration professionals, and most readers of this book will probably not practice immigration law, but it can serve as an example of the pros and cons of practice area-specific tools.

Visalaw.ai is a RAG-based AI system built on the world's largest immigration law library that we have curated. Our law library consists of all the available U.S. immigration primary laws, like statutes and regulations, and includes massive amount of agency materials, like agency guidance, form information, stakeholders' minutes, government announcements, and more. We have relevant case law and immigration-specific decisions from groups like the Board of Immigration Appeals (BIA), the Administrative Appeals Office (AAO), and the Board of Alien Labor Certification Appeals (BALCA). We also have several publishers of immigration law books and articles that provide us with their content to include in the library.

We have humans curating the library full time, adding new materials every day and taking out old materials that need to be removed. We also have web scrapers working to gather updated materials from USCIS, the Department of State, CBP, ICE, the Department of Labor, and other relevant agencies and websites. At the time of this writing, the library has about 215,000 immigration-specific documents. If users want, they can access separate libraries with full case law search and ethics opinions separated by state, but the primary focus remains on the main library of immigration law, and that is the default database being searched when a user logs in for legal research.

Just like any of the other AI tools discussed, a user can ask a question in natural language to a chatbot, and the Visalaw.ai bot is powered by GPT to search the immigration law library and generate a response. With the response comes in-line citations that can be clicked, so the lawyer is taken directly to the citation to read the materials for themselves. The bot also prompts follow-up questions and can be prompted to use the materials to create other outputs, like turning the response into a letter to a client or an email. Because this tool is built entirely for one type of lawyer, we are also able to set up research filters for even more focused research, where you can ask your question to the part of the library that only deals with I-9 compliance, or the part that only deals with physician immigration.

Aside from highly focused and curated legal research, there are other domain-specific advantages. Within Visalaw.ai, we offer the summarization and document analysis tools you see in all these AI legal tech products. The difference in the practice area-specific tools is that a lot of common tools can be standardized. So in Visalaw.ai, there is a library of prompts that we have already created for immigration lawyers, so they do not have to become prompt engineers. Immigration lawyers can upload their documents to their own private library and run a preset prompt to analyze a Request For Evidence from USCIS, or one to summarize a Freedom of Information Act request, or another to analyze a Notice to Appear (NTA) from the Department of Homeland Security—all common workflows for an immigration lawyer. Since immigration lawyers often deal with documents from all over the world, there are also built-in translation tools that offer both free AI translations or paid certified translations, where the documents are actually pushed to a human-in-the-loop translation service for review and certification.

Lastly, the Visalaw.ai tool offers drafting capabilities, helping immigration lawyers draft complex briefs and memos. These cover employment-based topics, like the Extraordinary Ability visas, which often have 20- to 30+-page memos, or simpler things like H-1Bs, which usually only need a few pages of explanation by the attorney. They also cover family-based immigration and humanitarian cases, like Cancellation of Removal and Asylum. The key is that because it was built by immigration lawyers for immigration lawyers, we have thousands of sample documents to build the drafting system on, and we know what good and bad outputs look like.

The complex drafting system is built on a system of prompts that operate in the background while the user answers questions and uploads their clients' documents. Users can drag and drop hundreds of supporting documents, and they will be sorted for the specific visa drafting process. The user is then fed small steps with prompts happening in the background, and then at the end, the system generates one large draft for the user—so they experience it as one document creation. Once the brief is generated as a Word document, the user can go in and start working on what is already a nice first draft. The generated brief will cite the clients' uploaded materials and even quote the exhibits.

The system is built to be secure for lawyers, like all the others in this chapter except for the general AI tools. We even include a "private GPT" function for people who want to use GPT for other purposes without training OpenAI's model. Our system does not train models with the users' materials, and the entire system is SOC 2 Type 2 certified and GDPR compliant, as you would come to expect.

The Visalaw.ai drafting tool has hundreds of hours of immigration-specific development put into it and countless hours just on certain types of cover letters, so this is a far cry from a do-it-all tool, but that cuts both ways for people who are looking for tools that are more generalized. This is an example of what a very focused product is like, and products like this and the ones listed earlier are available or becoming available in countless fields of law.

The pros to this practice area-specific approach are:

- Highly specialized drafting tools are usually built by or in coordination with actual practitioners in the area, since someone is providing all the examples and templates.
- There is a curated library that is focused on the practice area, which leads to greater search results and less hallucinations.
- It has the ability to preset common prompts or complex workflows for people who are doing similar work, so the user does not have to figure these things out.
- There are other convenient plug-ins and tools that are common for the specific area, thought of by people who are doing this specific work (like translation tools for immigration lawyers).
- These tools should offer the security needed and are created with lawyers in mind—though each one needs to be vetted.

The cons to the practice area-specific tools include:

- A smaller law library then you would get from Westlaw, Lexis, or vLex.
- If you are in a multipractice firm, then these tools may only be beneficial to some practitioners at the firm and not be worth the cost to others.
- In many cases, these companies are smaller than the big legal tech giants, so they have fewer resources.
- These companies are usually slower to integrations.

Shopping for AI tools really comes down to choosing the right tool for the right job. General AI giants like ChatGPT, Claude, Copilot, Gemini, or Perplexity offer unbelievable power, and some offer major integrations into your daily workspace, like your inbox, chat, and other tools lawyers spend a lot of their days working in. The tradeoff, though, is these tools are not ever appropriate for sensitive information or client data. You cannot put your clients' information in these tools, so they are best used for other tasks like practice management and times when you do not need security or legal accuracy. The big legal tech tools that are not practice area-specific offer amazing research libraries, and have all acquired or built advanced AI assistants that sit on top of their general law libraries. These tools are secure for lawyers to use, and are created with lawyers in mind. The tradeoff is the outputs are generalized as well, since they are trying to be great at everything, and there are high costs, which make these tools completely unapproachable for some attorneys and law firms. Lastly, practice area-specific tools are the up and comers. They are hyper-focused on their research libraries, drafting tools, and other features like custom prompts and workflows. The tradeoff is that these products are mostly from startups, and are so focused that they are mostly just attractive to attorneys who are equally specialized.

■ APPENDIX 1

AI Legal Software Directory

About This Directory

This appendix catalogs AI-powered legal technology products available as of 2025. The legal AI market has grown rapidly, with solutions ranging from general purpose assistants to highly specialized tools for specific practice areas.

The directory organizes products by their scope—or the breadth of legal tasks each addresses:

- **Wide Scope** (37 products): General AI capabilities applicable across multiple practice areas, including legal research, document drafting, and broad query handling.
- **Medium Scope** (61 products): Focused on specific workflows such as contract lifecycle management, litigation support, e-discovery, or in-house legal operations.
- **Narrow Scope** (23 products): Targeting specific practice areas or highly specialized tasks such as immigration, personal injury, estate planning, or patent analysis.

For each product, we provide a brief description, country of origin, founding year, company size, target practice areas (where applicable), notable software integrations (where applicable), and website. This information was current at the time of compilation, but the legal technology market evolves rapidly; readers should verify details directly with vendors.

Finally, the authors owe a special thank you to Ethan Landau, who created this directory for this book.

Wide-Scope AI Legal Tools

General purpose AI assistants applicable across multiple practice areas.

A1: The Legal Workbench (Sarvam.ai)

General AI legal tool built on India-specific LLM from Sarvam

India • Founded 2023 • 51–200 employees

Focus: Indian Law

www.sarvam.ai

Aila

AI assistant for in-house legal teams to handle internal legal queries and basic tasks

UK • Founded 2024 • 0–1 employees

Focus: In-House

www.trustaila.com

AI Lawyer

General legal AI for lawyers and basic legal document drafting for nonlawyers

Poland • Founded 2024 • 2–10 employees

ailawyer.pro

AI Legal Assistant

Legal AI specific to Australian law, for small firms and in-house contract review

Australia • Founded 2023 • 11–50 employees

Focus: Small Firms, In-House

Integrations: Clio, ActionStep, Smokeball

legalassistant.au

Atlas Fuse (ClearPeople)

AI assistant to query company's Office 365 content and for basic drafting—not legal-use only

UK • Founded 2003 • 11–50 employees

Integrations: Office 365

www.clearpeople.com/products/atlas/atlasfuse

Caseflood AI

AI voice agent for client intake for high inbound call volume practice areas

USA • Founded 2025 • 11–50 employees

Focus: High-Volume Consumer Practices

caseflood.ai

ClausePilot

Contract drafting and RAG legal research focused on European boutique firms

Austria • Founded 2025 • 2–10 employees

Focus: Euro Law Firms, Euro In-House

Integrations: MS Word

clausepilot.com

ClioDuo (Clio)

Clio's suite of AI tools, now including Vincent from vLex acquisition

Canada • Founded 2008 • 1,000–5,000 employees

Integrations: Clio

www.clio.com/features/legal-ai-software

CoCounsel (Thomson Reuters)

AI legal research and drafting, from Thomson Reuters' 2023 acquisition of Casetext

USA • Founded 2013 • 10,000+ employees

Integrations: WestLaw

training.thomsonreuters.com/legal-cocounsel-drafting

CORTO

AI chat + Word add-in that queries case matters from Dropbox and OneDrive

Australia • Founded 2023 • 11–50 employees

Focus: Small Firms

Integrations: Word, OneDrive, Dropbox

www.docorto.ai

David AI (2nd Chair)

AI for searching uploaded case files

USA • Founded 2023 • 2–10 employees

Focus: Small Firms

www.2ndchair.ai

ELTEMATE CRAIG (Hoven Lovells)

Array of AI tools for enterprise law firms and large in-house legal departments

Netherlands • Founded 2023 • 51–200 employees

Focus: In-House, AmLaw200

eltemate.com

EyeLevel Legal AI (EyeLevel)

Legal-focused Retrieval-Augmented Generation, enabling LLMs to query specific content libraries

USA • Founded 2018 • 11–50 employees

www.eyelevel.ai/legal

FirstRead

Word add-in for initial document review; drafting assistance based on firm templates

USA • Founded 2022 • 2–10 employees

first-read.com

Fledger

AI trained on firms' own documents

Netherlands • Founded 2020 • 2–10 employees

www.fledger.ai

Genie AI

Large template library for in-house drafting; additional features beyond legal use

UK • Founded 2017 • 11–50 employees

Focus: In-House

Integrations: MS Word

www.genieai.co

Jylo

AI assistant for document review and basic workflows

UK • Founded 2024 • 11–50 employees

jylo.ai

KAILA (Karnov Group)
AI legal research based on Karnov Group's (a legal publisher) content from across Europe
Denmark • Founded 1924 • 1,000–5,000 employees
www.karnovgroup.com/en

Lawdie
AI for legal research and document templates
USA • Founded 2024 • 2–10 employees
Focus: Small Firms
www.lawdie.co

Lexi
AI legal assistant
Singapore • Founded 2025 • 2–10 employees
www.getlexi.io

LexisNexis AI tools (LexisNexis)
Variety of AI tools within LexisNexis ecosystem
USA • Founded 1973 • 10,000+ employees
www.lexisnexis.com/en-us/products/lexis-create-plus.page

ndMAX (NetDocuments)
AI suite native to NetDocuments ecosystem
USA • Founded 1998 • 201–500 employees
www.netdocuments.com/solutions/legal-ai

Newcode.ai
Document summarization
Norway • Founded 2021 • 11–50 employees
newcode.ai

Noxtua

AI legal research in partnership with C. H. Beck, a leading German legal publisher

Germany • Founded 2017 • 11–50 employees

www.noxtua.com

Omnilex

Swiss-focused legal AI trained on Swiss laws

Switzerland • Founded 2023 • 11–50 employees

omnilex.ai/en

Oratio Technologies

German-focused AI legal chatbot

Germany • Founded 2024 • 2–10 employees

www.oratiotechnologies.com

Redwood (Talking Tree)

Basic document drafting for startup lawyers and in-house tasks

USA • Founded 2024 • 2–10 employees

Focus: In-House, Startups

talkingtree.app/redwood

Relaw

AI notetaker for client intake and subsequent workflows

USA • Founded 2024 • 2–10 employees

www.relaw.ai

Ruli

AI assistant for contract review

USA • Founded 2024 • 2–10 employees

Focus: In-House, Transaction

www.ruli.ai

Saga

European-focused AI legal assistant

Netherlands • Founded 2024 • 11–50 employees

Focus: Large Law (Europe)

sagalegal.io

Sana Agents (Sana)

AI agent platform by Sana Labs—enterprise AI that can be configured for legal ops

Sweden • Founded 2016 • 201–500 employees

Focus: AmLaw200, In-House

sana.ai/agents

Spellbook Associate (Spellbook)

Word add-in for AI contract review and drafting

Canada • Founded 2018 • 51–200 employees

Focus: In-House, Contract Law

www.spellbook.legal/associate

SquadBox (HalfSerious)

Software allowing firms to create their own AI tools

Canada • Founded 2011 • 51–200 employees

www.squadbox.ai

Trellis AI (Trellis)

AI-enhanced legal research and analytics platform focusing on state trial court data

USA • Founded 2018 • 51–200 employees

Focus: Litigation

trellis.law

Uncover (Opus 2)

Dutch company acquired by Opus 2 in UK: case analysis, basic drafting for litigation

UK • Founded 2022 • 201–500 employees

Focus: Litigation

www.uncoverlegal.com

Unplex

Office add-in for contract review and case summarization

Switzerland • Founded 2024 • 2–10 employees

Focus: In-House

www.unplex.ai

Zeno

Dutch-focused document analysis and legal research

Netherlands • Founded 2024 • 2–10 employees

zeno.law

Medium-Scope AI Legal Tools

Products focused on specific legal workflows such as contracts, litigation, or e-discovery.

Ace4 AI

AI document and deposition summary and analysis

USA • Founded 2024 • 2–10 employees

Focus: Litigation, In-House

ace4.ai

Agiloft AI (Agiloft)

AI features within established contract lifecycle management software suite

USA • Founded 1992 • 201–500 employees

Focus: In-House

Integrations: Salesforce, Office 365, DocuSign, SAP, NetSuite, and more

www.agiloft.com

AI Agent Studio (Onit)

AI tool within Onit's existing enterprise legal management, handling invoices for outside counsel, contract management, etc.

USA • Founded 2011 • 501–1,000 employees

Focus: In-House

Integrations: Onit ELM

www.onit.com

Alexi

AI suite running on privately hosted LLM

Canada • Founded 2017 • 11–50 employees

Focus: Litigation, AmLaw200

Integrations: iManage, Azure, Filevine, NetDocuments

www.alexi.com

Aloi

AI for contract review and drafting based on firms' internal documents

Sweden • Founded 2025 • 11–50 employees

Focus: Transactional, AmLaw200

www.aloi.law

Anytime AI

Plaintiff-side AI for intake, medical record review, timelines, demand letter drafting, deposition summary, legal research

USA • Founded 2023 • 11–50 employees

Focus: Personal Injury, Medical Malpractice

www.anytimeai.ai

AtlasAI

AI suite running on Azure-hosted LLM with strong integrations

USA • Founded 2024 • 11–50 employees

Focus: AmLaw200, In-House

Integrations: Azure, iManage, NetDocuments, SharePoint

atlas-ai.io

August

Contract review with AI trained on firms' documents

USA • Founded 2023 • 11–50 employees

Focus: Midsize, In-House

www.august.law

BEAMON AI (Bryter)

German-focused AI with workflows for contract handling and review

Germany • Founded 2018 • 201–500 employees

Focus: Midsize, In-House

Integrations: MS Word

bryter.com/beamon

Brightflag (Wolters Kluwer)

AI features within existing enterprise legal management

USA • Founded 2014 • 51–200 employees

Focus: In-House

Integrations: Oracle, SAP, Workday, NetSuite

brightflag.com

Callidus (StrongSuit)

AI assistant for document review

USA • Founded 2023 • 11–50 employees

Focus: Litigation, Family Law

callidusai.com

CaseMark

Litigation AI for summarizing depositions, evidence, and creating court materials

USA • Founded 2023 • 2–10 employees

Focus: Personal Injury, Litigation

Integrations: Smokeball, Clio

www.casemark.com

Casepal

European-focused AI tool

Belgium • Founded 2024 • 2–10 employees

Focus: In-House

Integrations: SharePoint

www.casepal.co

Casey

Product for allowing lawyers to build their own AI tools

UK • Founded 2024 • 2–10 employees

Focus: In-House, Large Law Firms

casey.legal

Cecilia AI (Disco)

Litigation AI for summarizing depositions, evidence, and creating court materials

USA • Founded 2013 • 501–1,000 employees

Focus: In-House, AmLaw200

csdisco.com/offerings/cecilia

Cicero (Automatise)

Litigation-focused AI product running on private LLM

Australia • Founded 2022 • 11–50 employees

Focus: Litigation

Integrations: Relativity, iManage

www.cicero.com.ai

ContractKen

AI contract review via Word add-in

USA • Founded 2021 • 2–10 employees

Focus: In-House

www.contractken.com

Copilot (LawDroid)

AI assistant for automating specific legal workflows

Canada • Founded 2016 • 2–10 employees

lawdroid.com/copilot

Ctrl AI

Agentic AI for handling data for large volumes of disputes

UK • Founded 2024 • 11–50 employees

Focus: In-House, AmLaw200

www.ctrl-ai.co.uk

DecoverAI

Unclear what it does beyond AI e-discovery

USA • Founded in 2024 • 11–50 employees

Focus: Personal Injury, Medical Malpractice, Construction Litigation

www.decover.ai

Definely Enhance (Definely)

Word add-in for AI contract review

UK • Founded 2017 • 51–200 employees

Focus: AmLaw200, In-House

Integrations: MS Word

www.definely.com

Dioptra

Word add-in for AI contract review

USA • Founded 2021 • 2–10 employees

Focus: In-House

Integrations: MS Word

www.dioptra.ai

Dodonai

Litigation AI for summarizing depositions, evidence, and creating court materials

USA • Founded 2022 • 2–10 employees

Focus: Personal Injury, Medical Malpractice

www.dodon.ai

DraftPilot

Word add-in for AI contract review

UK • Founded 2024 • 11–50 employees

Focus: In-House

Integrations: MS Word

draftpilot.ai

Eskwai (Kwame AI)

Ghana- and Africa-focused legal research and drafting

Ghana • Founded 2022 • 2–10 employees

eskwai.kwame.ai

Eve

AI client intake and e-discovery

USA • Founded 2020 • 11–50 employees

Focus: Personal Injury, Employment Law

www.eve.legal

Everlaw AI Assistant (Everlaw)

AI features within established e-discovery company for mid/large litigation firms and large in-house

USA • Founded 2011 • 201–500 employees

Focus: Litigation

Integrations: iManage, NetDocuments

www.everlaw.com/product/everlaw-ai-assistant

Flank
AI chatbot for handling legal department requests at large enterprise
Germany • Founded 2023 • 51–200 employees
Focus: In-House
www.flank.ai

Gavel Exec (Gavel)
Word add-in for transactional attorneys; draft, redline, and analyze contracts
USA • Founded 2020 • 11–50 employees
Focus: AmLaw200
Integrations: MS Word
www.gavel.io/exec

GC AI
Word add-in for AI contract review and editing
USA • Founded 2023 • 11–50 employees
Focus: In-House
Integrations: MS Word
gc.ai

Habeas
Australian-focused AI legal research with large Australian content library
Australia • Founded 2023 • 2–10 employees
www.habeas.ai

Harvey
Customization heavy AI tool for large law firms
USA • Founded 2022 • 501–1,000 employees
Focus: AmLaw200, In-House
Integrations: NetDocuments, iManage, Office 365
harvey.ai

Ivo
Word add-in for contract review
USA • Founded 2021 • 51–200 employees
Focus: In-House
www.ivo.ai

JUNE
CMS for enterprise teams with AI workflows
Germany • Founded 2020 • 51–200 employees
Focus: In-House
www.june.tech

Junior Assistant
AI emailbot for contract review
USA • Founded 2024 • 2–10 employees
usejunior.com

Jurist (Ironclad)
AI Word add-In within Ironclad CLM software
USA • Founded 2014 • 501–1,000 employees
Focus: In-House
Integrations: MS Word
ironcladapp.com/product/ai-assistant/legal

Leah (ContractPodAI)
Contract lifecycle management for in-house legal teams
UK • Founded 2014 • 201–500 employees
Focus: In-House
contractpodai.com

LEGALFLY
AI contract review and analysis
Belgium • Founded 2023 • 51–200 employees
Focus: In-House
legalfly.com

LegalOn Technologies

AI features of existing CLM software

Japan/USA • Founded 2017 • 501–1,000 employees

Focus: In-House

www.legalontech.com

Legora

Azure-hosted AI workspace for litigation and transaction document review

Sweden/USA • Founded 2023 • 201–500 employees

Focus: AmLaw200, In-House

Integrations: Office 365, NetDocuments, iManage, SharePoint

legora.com

Lexion (DocuSign)

Contract review and analysis, acquired in 2024 by DocuSign with Word add-in

USA • Founded 2018 • 51–200 employees

Focus: In-House

Integrations: Office 365, Salesforce

www.lexion.ai

Libra (Libra Technology GmbH)

German- and EU-focused AI workspace for legal research, document drafting, and contract review

Germany • Founded 2023 • 11–50 employees

Focus: AmLaw200, In-House

Integrations: MS Word, SharePoint

libratech.ai

Litera One (Litera)

AI features of existing CLM, with checklists and tools for transactions

USA • Founded 2001 • 501–1,000 employees

Focus: AmLaw200

Integrations: Office 365

www.litera.com

Lopti
CLM and management of outside law firms
Brazil • Founded 2024 • 11–50 employees
Focus: AmLaw200, In-House
lopti.ai

Lucio
India-focused document review/analysis
India • Founded 2022 • 11–50 employees
Integrations: MS Word
www.lucioai.com

Maite.ai
Spain-focused case law summaries and contract review
Spain • Founded 2023 • 2–10 employees
Focus: In-House, Spanish Law Firms
www.maite.ai

Paxton Legal AI (Paxton)
AI for legal research, contract review, summarization, and basic drafting
USA • Founded 2023 • 11–50 employees
Focus: Personal Injury, Family Law
www.paxton.ai

Pincites
AI tool for contract review, summarization, and negotiation
USA • Founded 2023 • 2–10 employees
Focus: In-House
www.pincites.com

PONS (PONS LABS)
AI legal workspace with EU focus
Norway • Founded 2022 • 2–10 employees
www.pons.io

Qanooni
AI Office 365 add-in with UAE and Gulf countries focus
UAE • Founded 2025 • 11–50 employees
qanooni.ai

Querious
AI Zoom plug-in for guiding and summarizing client intake and discussions
USA • Founded 2024 • 2–10 employees
www.querious.ai

Relativity aiR (Relativity)
AI features within established e-discovery offering
USA • Founded 2001 • 1,000–5,000 employees
Focus: Litigation, Investigations, In-House
Integrations: iManage, Clearbrief
relativity.com

Robin
AI contract review
UK • Founded 2019 • 201–500 employees
Focus: In-House
robinai.com

Servient
AI-powered e-discovery platform to analyze large document sets for litigation
USA • Founded 2003 • 51–200 employees
Focus: Litigation
www.servient.com

SuperInsight
AI medical records review and analysis
USA • Founded 2023 • 2–10 employees
Focus: SSD, VA, Personal Injury
Integrations: CASEpeer, Clio, MyCase
www.superinsight.ai

Syllo (TLATech, Inc.)

AI litigation lifecycle management

USA • Founded 2019 • 11–50 employees

Focus: Litigation

syllo.ai

Synapse (Ontra)

Contract automation; also NDA outsourcing for finance firms

USA • Founded 2014 • 201–500 employees

Focus: In-House, Finance

www.ontra.ai

UniCourt DEEP (UniCourt)

AI docket extraction from established company

USA • Founded 2014 • 51–200 employees

Focus: AmLaw200, In-House, Insurers

Integrations: Litera, Snowflake, Azure, Salesforce

unicourt.com

VeraAI (Icertis)

AI features within established CLM provider

USA • Founded 2009 • 1,000–5,000 employees

Focus: In-House

Integrations: SAP, Salesforce, Microsoft

www.icertis.com

Wilson AI

AI contract review for in-house teams

USA • Founded 2024 • 2–10 employees

Focus: In-House

www.getwilson.ai

Wordsmith AI

Contract review and compliance audits for in-house teams

Scotland • Founded 2023 • 51–200 employees

Focus: In-House

wordsmith.ai

Narrow-Scope AI Legal Tools

Specialized products targeting specific practice areas or highly focused tasks.

askLisa

Brazil-focused AI chatbot and dashboard/metrics for in-house teams to field questions and requests from other departments

Brazil • Founded 2021 • 11–50 employees

Focus: In-House

Integrations: Teams, Slack

www.asklisa.com.br

CaseBlink

End-to-end immigration case prep platform

USA • Founded 2023 • 2–10 employees

Focus: Immigration

caseblink.com

CaseChat (esumry)

AI litigation prep and deposition analysis

USA • Founded 2018 • 2–10 employees

Focus: Litigation

www.esumry.com/casechat

CounselPro

AI to analyze and organize PDF financial statements for forensic accounting

USA • Founded 2024 • 2–10 employees

Focus: Family Law, Estate, Consumer Bankruptcy

www.counselpro.ai

Deliberately.ai

AI for client intake, document management, and drafting

USA • Founded 2024 • 11–50 employees

Focus: Family Law

deliberately.ai

Disclosure Ready (Legal Ready)

Disclosure management and document organization

Australia • Founded 2024 • 11–50 employees

Focus: Family Law

Integrations: Smokeball, Actionstep, Affinity, EvolveGo, FilePro, iManage, NetDocuments

www.disclosureready.com

DocuClipper

Automated data extraction from financial statements

USA • Founded 2023 • 11–50 employees

Focus: Family Law

www.docuclipper.com

Emmi

AI conflict checks for law firms

UK • Founded 2024 • 2–10 employees

www.myemmi.ai

Fern AI

AI platform focusing on labor/employment law tasks

USA • Founded 2024 • 2–10 employees

Focus: In-House, Labor/Employment

www.fernlabs.ai

JudyAI (Gemini Legal)

Filing services + AI for medical records indexing

USA • Founded 2004 • 201–500 employees

Focus: Workers' Comp

Integrations: Clio, Filevine

gemini.legal

Jus AI (Jus Mundi)

AI research features from an existing international arbitration-focused software company

France • Founded 2019 • 51–200 employees

Focus: International Arbitration

jusmundi.com/en/jus-ai

LegalMike

Dutch-focused AI legal research

Netherlands • Founded 2023 • 11–50 employees

Focus: Litigation

legalmike.ai

Matey AI

AI e-discovery—classify documents, build timelines, summarize documents

USA • Founded 2023 • 11–50 employees

Focus: Criminal Defense

www.matey.ai

MIKE Virtual Paralegal (Scissero)

Document review for in-house teams at finance firms for M&A deals

UK • Founded 2018 • 51–200 employees

Focus: Finance, In-House

www.scissero.com/mike

Orbital Copilot (Orbital)

UK commercial real-estate law AI tool

UK • Founded 2018 • 51–200 employees

Focus: UK Commercial Real Estate

www.orbital.tech

PatSnap

AI features from an existing global patent and R&D analytics firm

Singapore • Founded 2007 • 501–1,000 employees

Focus: Patent, In-House IP

Integrations: BizInt Smart Charts

www.patsnap.com

Precedent

AI tool to submit insurance claims and draft demand letters

USA • Founded 2022 • 51–200 employees

Focus: Personal Injury

Integrations: SmartAdvocate, Clio, Litify

precedent.com

Pre/Dicta

AI judicial analytics and litigation prediction based on judge and case specifics

USA • Founded 2018 • 11–50 employees

Focus: AmLaw200, In-House

www.pre-dicta.com

Settify (InfoTrack)

AI client intake, recently acquired by InfoTrack

Australia • Founded 2016 • 11–50 employees

Focus: Family Law, Estate

Integrations: Clio, Smokeball, Actionstep, LEAP

settify.com/us

SimplyConvert

Client intake and AI case analysis

USA • Founded 2018 • 51–200 employees

Focus: Personal Injury, Mass Torts, SSD

Integrations: Filevine, Litify, SmartAdvocate, Captorra

simplyconvert.com

Supio

Medical record review, drafting for demand letters/complaints/motions, and case analysis

USA • Founded 2021 • 51–200 employees

Focus: Personal Injury

www.supio.com

Visalaw.ai

Legal content library-based AI legal research, document analysis, and petition drafting for immigration

USA • Founded 2020 • 2–10 employees

Focus: Immigration

www.visalaw.ai

Wisetax

AI platform to streamline tax law research and automate drafting of tax analysis reports

France • Founded 2019 • 2–10 employees

Focus: Tax

wisetax.fr

■ APPENDIX 2

AI Notetakers: Which Products are Appropriate for Lawyers

1. Adoption of AI Notetaking Tools in Legal Practice

Attorney-client conversations are among the most consequential moments in legal practice, yet they remain one of AI's most underutilized opportunities. Attorneys considering the adoption of AI notetaking tools in conversations encounter unique legal and ethical risks. Until recently, attorneys faced a binary choice: use general purpose AI notetakers never designed for the legal profession, or go without. A new category of tools, legal conversational intelligence, is emerging to address the unique needs of the legal industry. The following section provides a list of key considerations when attorneys are deciding whether to bring AI tools with notetaking functionality into client conversations.

2. Key Considerations of AI Notetaking Tools in Legal Practice

a. **Confidentiality, Privilege, and Work Product (ABA Model Rule 1.6, Recent Litigation)**
   i. Vendor terms of service that permit data retention, model training, and/or third-party disclosure do not reasonably create an expectation of privacy that is necessary for maintaining protection under attorney-client privilege or the work product doctrine (*United States v. Heppner*, No. 25 Cr. 503 (JSR) (S.D.N.Y. Feb. 17, 2026))
   ii. Prioritize tools with ephemeral processing, zero data retention and/or customizable data retention, contractual prohibitions on using your data to train and fine-tune AI models

b. **Wiretapping and Recording Consent (Federal and State Laws)**
   i. Fifteen (15) states require all-party consent to record or even intercept audio, including California, Florida, Illinois, Massachusetts, and Pennsylvania
   ii. Notetaking tools that record by default without prompting consent collection expose attorneys to liability in all-party states (*Brewer v. Otter.ai Inc.*, No. 5:25-cv-06911 (N.D. Cal. filed Aug. 15, 2025))

c. **Biometric Privacy (IL BIPA and State Equivalents)**
   i. Notetaking tools that involve speaker diarization (i.e., ability to distinguish between speakers and assign identities) may generate voiceprints under biometric privacy laws (*Illinois Biometric Information Privacy Act (BIPA)*, (*Cruz v. Fireflies.AI Corp.*, No. 3:25-cv-03399 (C.D. Ill. filed Dec. 18, 2025), Basich v. Microsoft Corp., No. 2:26-cv-00422 (W.D. Wash. filed Feb. 5, 2026))
   ii. BIPA requires written notice, informed consent, and a publicly available retention/destruction policy before collection
   iii. BIPA has a private right of action and statutory damages run $1,000–$5,000 per violation, plus reasonable attorney's fees and costs

d. **Client Disclosure and Consent (ABA Model Rule 1.4, ABA Ethics Opinion 512)**
   i. Clients must be notified and should give consent before their audio is accessed, especially if the tool is self-learning (*ABA Ethics Opinion 512*)
   ii. Engagement letters provide an early opportunity to notify clients about AI tools and obtain consent to use them in representation
   iii. Prioritize technology that supports providing notice that the attorney is using the AI tool and collecting consent to such use in representation, including from nonclients who may participate in a conversation

e. **Competence (ABA Model Rule 1.1)**
   i. Attorneys must understand how the tool works, its limitations, and review all AI outputs before relying on them

f. **Supervision (ABA Model Rules 5.1 and 5.3)**

i. Supervising attorneys are responsible for ensuring staff use AI tools in compliance with firm policy and applicable ethics rules

g. **Vendor Due Diligence**

i. Marketing claims about privacy often diverge from what the actual terms of service permit, so attorneys should review the contractual obligations carefully, not just the website and marketing materials

3. Comparison of General AI Notetaking Tools and Legal Conversational Intelligence Tools Purpose-Built for the Legal Practice

The following is a side-by-side comparison of the relative features, architecture, privacy, security, and ethical considerations of general purpose AI notetakers and a new category of purpose-built legal conversational intelligence tools. The analysis is based on publicly available Terms of Service for each tool. Specific terms are shaded by relative risk: Significant Risk, Moderate Risk, Low Risk. Terms change frequently and may vary by payment tier. The version used for the analysis is reflected in the chart.

Category	Otter.ai Terms of Service (Sept. 19, 2025)[1]	Fireflies.ai Terms of Service (Mar. 6, 2026)[2]	Fathom Terms of Service (Mar. 4, 2026)[3]	Plaud Terms of Service (as of Mar. 28, 2026)[4]	Zoom Transcription Terms of Service (Aug. 11, 2023)[5]	Querious Terms of Service (Mar. 23, 2026)[6]
Functionality	Automated meeting transcription, real-time captions, AI-generated summaries, action items, and keyword search. Integrates with Zoom, Teams, and Google Meet. **(Section 1)**	Automated meeting recording, transcription, AI summaries, action items, sentiment analysis, virtual meeting platform integrations, and CRM integrations. **(Section 10)**	Automated meeting recording, transcription, AI summaries, action items, and highlights. Users can "clip" moments during meetings. Integrates with Zoom, Teams, and Google Meet. **(Section 1)**	Hardware-based AI recording device capturing in-person and phone conversations using AI-powered transcription services based on a block of time. **(Paragraph 2)**	Native Zoom feature providing automated meeting transcription, closed captions, and AI-generated summaries via Zoom AI Companion. Integrated directly into Zoom meetings without a third-party bot.	Ephemeral processing of audio without creating full audio or transcript file of the conversation by default. Processing supports legal issue spotting, suggested questions, and relevant content during meetings. Post-meeting summary emails, detailed notes, and draft billing entries. Integrates with Teams, Zoom, Google Meet, Clio, and Smokeball. **(Section 3.1)**

1. *Terms of Service*, OTTER.AI, https://otter.ai/terms-of-service (last visited Mar. 28, 2026).
2. *Terms of Service*, FIREFLIES.AI, https://fireflies.ai/terms-of-service (last visited Mar. 28, 2026).
3. *Terms of Service*, FATHOM.AI, https://www.fathom.ai/terms (last visited Mar. 28, 2026).
4. *Terms of Service*, PLAUD.AI, https://partner.plaud.ai/pages/terms-of-service (last visited Mar. 28, 2026).
5. *Zoom Terms of Service*, ZOOM.AI, https://www.zoom.com/en/trust/terms/ (last visited Mar. 28, 2026).
6. *Terms of Service*, QUERIOUS.AI, https://app.querious.ai/terms-of-service (last visited Mar. 28, 2026).

Category	Otter.ai Terms of Service (Sept. 19, 2025)[1]	Fireflies.ai Terms of Service (Mar. 6, 2026)[2]	Fathom Terms of Service (Mar. 4, 2026)[3]	Plaud Terms of Service (as of Mar. 28, 2026)[4]	Zoom Transcription Terms of Service (Aug. 11, 2023)[5]	Querious Terms of Service (Mar. 23, 2026)[6]
Architecture and Data Retention	Stores full audio recordings and verbatim transcripts on Otter's cloud servers indefinitely unless manually deleted. **(Appendix 2, Section B; Appendix 5, Section 4)** Deleted content may persist in trash before permanent removal. **(Section 9.3)**	Creates and retains full audio recordings and verbatim transcripts on Fireflies' cloud infrastructure. Named defendant in BIPA class action alleging voiceprint creation without consent. (*Cruz v. Fireflies.AI Corp.*, Dec. 18, 2025)	Creates full audio recordings and verbatim transcripts. Uses third-party sub-processors and user data may be transmitted through or stored on such systems. **(Section 4)**	Audio recorded to physical device and uploaded to Plaud's cloud servers.	Transcripts and recordings stored on Zoom's cloud infrastructure or locally if configured. Retention periods configurable by account administrators. Full recordings and transcripts retained until deleted.	Ephemeral streaming architecture. **(Section 3.1)** No full audio recordings or verbatim transcripts by default (optional transcript retention available). AI-generated summaries retained 60 days by default (configurable). **(Section 3.4)** All processing within secure Microsoft Azure environment. **(Section 6.1)**

Category	Otter.ai Terms of Service (Sept. 19, 2025)[1]	Fireflies.ai Terms of Service (Mar. 6, 2026)[2]	Fathom Terms of Service (Mar. 4, 2026)[3]	Plaud Terms of Service (as of Mar. 28, 2026)[4]	Zoom Transcription Terms of Service (Aug. 11, 2023)[5]	Querious Terms of Service (Mar. 23, 2026)[6]
AI Training on Conversation Data	Reserves the rights to use data to improve services. De-identified or aggregated data may be used for machine learning purposes. **(Section 18.4)** Active federal class-action lawsuit regarding consent and data use. (*Brewer v. Otter.ai*, Aug. 2025)	States that vendor will not use "User Content" to train, retrain, fine-tune, or otherwise improve any generative AI models. However, vendor can derive usage, statistical, or other data from user content to analyze and improve services. **(Section 5(c)(ii))**	Rights to use and create de-identified data to improve services and AI features. No explanation of de-identification process. **(Section 4)** States that vendor does not allow *third parties* to train AI models on user data. **(Section 4)**	Silent regarding whether user data can be used to train or fine-tune AI models.	Explicitly states vendor does not use audio, video, or transcripts to train AI models. **(Section 10.2)**	Absolute contractual prohibition on use of client communications or AI-generated outputs for training, fine-tuning, or evaluating any AI model. Enforced through physical and logical network-level separation of production and training pipelines. Third-party providers contractually prohibited from training on Querious customer data. **(Section 3.2)**

Category	Otter.ai Terms of Service (Sept. 19, 2025)[1]	Fireflies.ai Terms of Service (Mar. 6, 2026)[2]	Fathom Terms of Service (Mar. 4, 2026)[3]	Plaud Terms of Service (as of Mar. 28, 2026)[4]	Zoom Transcription Terms of Service (Aug. 11, 2023)[5]	Querious Terms of Service (Mar. 23, 2026)[6]
Wiretapping/ Consent Compliance Support	Records by default. Compliance with recording consent for wiretapping laws is the user's responsibility. **(Section 9.2)**	Records by default. Compliance with state wiretapping laws is the user's responsibility. **(Section 5(d))**	Options to record by default or start recording manually via the settings.[7] Compliance with state wiretapping laws remains the user's responsibility.	No notification or consent capture due to ambient recording capability.	Zoom displays a recording notification banner to all participants when recording is initiated, satisfying notice requirements in many jurisdictions. Does not constitute affirmative all-party consent as required in some states.	Bot joins as a visible participant with a disclosure and reminder to collect consent. Similar default chat message posted to all participants upon joining. "Instant Meeting" feature requires attorney to affirmatively confirm all-party consent before audio analysis begins. Attorneys can customize bot image and disclaimer language.

7. *Navigating the Settings Page*, Fathom, https://help.fathom.video/en/articles/3239617#:~:text=you%20can%20configure.-,Auto%2DRecord%20Settings,recordings%20must%20be%20initiated%20manually (last visited Mar. 28, 2026).

Category	Otter.ai Terms of Service (Sept. 19, 2025)[1]	Fireflies.ai Terms of Service (Mar. 6, 2026)[2]	Fathom Terms of Service (Mar. 4, 2026)[3]	Plaud Terms of Service (as of Mar. 28, 2026)[4]	Zoom Transcription Terms of Service (Aug. 11, 2023)[5]	Querious Terms of Service (Mar. 23, 2026)[6]
Biometric Privacy (BIPA) Compliance Support	Speaker identification features may generate voiceprint data. No publicly available IL BIPA retention and destruction policy. No documented written consent or notice workflow for biometric data. **(Appendix 2, Section B; Appendix 6)**	Jurisdiction-specific information (IL BIPA) section incorporated into the Privacy Policy.	No publicly available BIPA retention and destruction policy. No documented written consent workflow specific to biometric data.	Transcription and speaker identification features may generate voiceprint data. No BIPA compliance framework. No public biometric retention policy or consent workflow.	Only reference to voiceprint in Privacy Statement. Speaker identification in transcription may implicate biometric privacy laws. No dedicated BIPA compliance framework or public biometric retention policy. No written consent workflow.	Support for IL BIPA compliance, including bot image and meeting chat message reminding user to collect consent; and publicly available Biometric Data Retention and Destruction Policy (740 ILCS 14/15(a).[8]

8. *Biometric Data Retention and Destruction Policy*, QUERIOUS.AI, https://www.querious.ai/bipa-policy (last visited Mar. 28, 2026).

Category	Otter.ai Terms of Service (Sept. 19, 2025)[1]	Fireflies.ai Terms of Service (Mar. 6, 2026)[2]	Fathom Terms of Service (Mar. 4, 2026)[3]	Plaud Terms of Service (as of Mar. 28, 2026)[4]	Zoom Transcription Terms of Service (Aug. 11, 2023)[5]	Querious Terms of Service (Mar. 23, 2026)[6]
Client Confidentiality Considerations	Security measures, physical access controls (AWS, SOC 2 Type 2), system access controls, data access controls, transmission controls, input controls (authentication), daily backups, and data segregation (by customer). **(Appendix 3)**	Security certifications for SOC 2 Type 2, GDPR, and HIPAA (through BAA—enterprise only) is available at fireflies.ai /security. Not explicitly in the Terms of Service.	Uses commercially reasonable efforts to prevent any unauthorized use or disclosure of user data including by implementing technical, administrative, and organizational security measures. **(Section 4)**	Hardware design prioritizes capture convenience over data minimization. Forbes article from September 2025 described it as "San Francisco and Shenzhen, China-based startup."[9]	Describes privacy and security in detail through whitepaper on Zoom AI Companion.[10] Documentation is not explicitly incorporated by reference into the Terms of Service.	Attorney-client privilege acknowledged via Kovel agency framework. Subpoena response protocol: 24-hour notice, privilege assertion, refusal to produce absent final court order. FRE 502(d) cooperation. SOC 2 Type 2 certified. Private AI model instances. Default PII filtering. Personnel cannot access de-crypted client communications. **(Sections 2.2, 2.3, 3, 14.8)**

9. Iain Martin, *How an AI Notetaker Became One of the Few Profitable AI Startups*, FORBES.COM, Sept. 22, 2025, https://www.forbes.com/sites/iainmartin/2025/09/02/how-an-ai-notetaker-became-one-of-the-few-profitable-ai-startups/.

10. *AI Companion Security and Privacy*, ZOOM.COM, https://www.zoom.com/en/products/ai-assistant/resources/privacy-security/ (last visited Mar. 28, 2026).

Index

D

E

R

S

T